"As a forward-thinking entrepreneur, it's clear to me that Twitter is a must-use for any smart businessperson online. Joel Comm's *Twitter Power* is the must-read guide defining how to leverage the power of this incredible tool to brand and increase sales in an increasingly competitive world."

— Joseph Sugarman, Chairman and founder, BluBlocker Sunglass Corporation and author of *The Adweek Copywriting Handbook*

"Jam-packed with clever ways to leverage the Jovian social-networking power of Twitter. The 'Twitter as Help Desk' idea alone is a fiendishly simple, revolutionary idea."

—Mark Joyner, #1 bestselling author of *Integration Marketing* www.IntegrationMarketing.com

"When Joel Comm speaks about anything to do with making money on the Internet, I listen. If you want to learn what you need to know for your business to profit from Twitter, you will find it in the pages of this excellent guide."

—Chet Holmes, Business consultant and strategist, and author of the #1 business bestseller, *The Ultimate Sales Machine*

"For months I saw and heard the buzz about Twitter, but it wasn't until Joel told me details about it that I fully understood its marketing implications. Now I can clearly see how this free site can help me further build relationships with my customers, and I am going to be 'tweeting' frequently! In fact, I have already started, thanks to Joel. So thanks for writing this book, Joel. It's going to help a lot of people grow their business!"

—Stephen Pierce, www.MakeRealMoneyOnTheInternet.com

"In the short amount of time I have had with Joel Comm, I can clearly see that this is a man who understands how to build profitable Internet businesses. *Twitter Power* is sure to set a new standard for those seeking to broaden their entrepreneurial vision to include the latest Internet technologies. I recommend you read it and begin applying it to your business right away!"

—Bill Bartmann, Billionaire Business Coach, www.billionaireu.com

"I was lucky. Joel Comm sat down with me and explained what Twitter is, how it works, and how I could and should be using it for my business. Joel knows more about using Twitter than any other human, and the proof is in his own massive success with 'tweeting.' You're even luckier; in this book, Joel will teach YOU everything you need to know about Twitter—and you don't even need to buy him lunch."

—Dan O'Day, Radio advertising guru, www.twitter/dan oday

"I'm amazed how many people are not yet using Twitter to connect with customers and associates. Once again, Joel Comm leads the way into the future by showing people how they can have increased success by taking some very simple actions. This book has inspired me to take my social media presence to the next level!"

—Christopher Howard, Wealth and personal achievement expert

"Social media has given online business the fuel to ride the next wave of the Internet for many years to come. If you want to be on the cutting edge of strategies that are being implemented by the most successful businesses, *Twitter Power* is a must-read. Joel has done a great job of demonstrating how a minor investment of time and energy can result in long-term payoffs. No wonder they call him the Social Media Expert!"

—Kristopher Jones, CEO of Pepperjam and author of *Search Engine Optimization: Your Visual Blueprint for Effective Internet Marketing*

"Joel Comm's understanding of social media and its applications for entrepreneurs and the growth of their businesses is remarkable. Beyond his knowledge, it is his ability to communicate it effectively that makes him stand apart, while his humor in delivery keeps you coming back for more."

—Jen Groover, A "One Woman Brand" and founder of Butler Bag LLC

"I've been a big fan of Joel's ability and track record to keep up and explain the importance of new web-based communication tools and trends. I consider him to be at the front edge of the Internet and a sage guide to help you grasp and understand changes in the fast-paced online world."

—Tony Rubleski, Amazon #1 bestselling author, www.MindCaptureBook.com

"Thanks, Joel, for this intriguing look at Twitter. You've proven that *Twitter Power* isn't just about making new connections to generate sales. It's about brand-building, focus groups, the exchange of ideas, and the emotion of debate. All conducted in real time via computer, cell phone, PDAs, and perhaps even TV by the time you read this. When you add in the incredibly viral nature of Twitter, the possibilities are virtually endless."

—Dan Nickerson, www.YouMetDan.com

"I've been following Joel on Twitter for a while now and I'll be frank—he annoys me. But in a good way. He always manages to grab my attention in Twitter, despite the limited words available within the microblogging platform. This clearly demonstrates that Joel understands how this new and powerful social media tool should be used. If you want to unleash the power of Twitter for your business, Joel is someone you should pay attention to."

—Yaro Starak, www.entrepreneurs-journey.com

"I'm a twittering fool. Twitter is one of the most addicting things on the net. Besides the fact you get to update everyone and talk to people you'd rarely talk to, it's a great tool for building an online buzz. Make sure you follow Joel Comm on this subject, because he's on the cutting edge of this."

—Matt Bacak, Internet multimillionaire, Atlanta, GA

twitter
power
2.0

How to Dominate Your Market
One Tweet at a Time

JOEL COMM

WILEY

John Wiley & Sons, Inc.

Published by John Wiley & Sons, Inc., Hoboken, New Jersey.
Published simultaneously in Canada.

For general information on our other products and services or for technical support, please
contact our Customer Care Department within the United States at (800) 762-2974, outside
the United States at (317) 572-3993 or fax (317) 572-4002.

Wiley also publishes its books in a variety of electronic formats. Some content that appears
in print may not be available in electronic books. For more information about Wiley
products, visit our web site at www.wiley.com.

ISBN: 978-0470-56336-6

Printed in the United States of America

10 9 8 7 6 5 4 3 2 1

Contents

Foreword

Every day 60 million emails are sent out around the world. My-Space alone has over 186 million users! Technology has given us so many ways of communicating, but are we truly connecting or just corresponding? Are we adding people into our lives who share our values or merely collecting a list of profiles? Are we deepening relationships or just maintaining them?

As much as we want to nurture every relationship, advances in technology have given us access to more relationships and less time to deepen them. And yet what most of us know, and what I have discovered working with more than 3.5 million people from over 80 countries, is that the quality of our lives is the quality of our relationships. And since life is relationships, relationships follow the rules of life—they either grow or die. Your relationships are as strong or deep as you choose to make them. If you spend quality time in your intimate relationships, if you connect with your families and your friends, those relationships will flourish. If you nurture your relationships with your clients and really meet their needs at a higher level, you build long-lasting connections. Conversely, if you don't grow your customers, you go out of business. If you don't reach your family or friends, those relationships get stripped of the substance and texture they deserve.

Ken Blanchard once described life as a game of Monopoly—no matter how many properties we buy or how many houses we build, at the end of the game "it all goes back in the box." All we have ultimately are the relationships that we nurtured, the lives that we impacted, and the ones that have touched us. All we have are the experiences that we have shared. When two people meet, a third world is created. And with today's technology, that world can grow exponentially.

Technology such as Twitter has the potential to give us more than just an opportunity to tell others what happened in our day. If we understand and appreciate what Twitter is capable of, we can use it to instantly share our lives with others, and we can use it to reach more people in a meaningful way. Imagine if you could share the magic moments in the days of your kids or family that otherwise you would have missed. Imagine if you had cost-efficient and fast marketing tools that met existing customers where they are and that also helped you acquire new customers. Imagine if you had the power to build a network of like-minded peers, a community of shared ideas and creativity.

In *Twitter Power*, Joel Comm provides us with the tools, techniques, and benefits for growing our network of resources to create even more fulfilling connections. He shows us the powerful uses of Twitter for brand expansion, building a community that ultimately enriches us personally and professionally and allows us to grow and contribute beyond ourselves.

Joel explains the effortless ways we can make a contribution by being a mentor as well as sharing in the interests and passions of others. In *Twitter Power*, Joel teaches us how we can use technology not just to correspond, but also to connect. He shows us how the Internet can give us the freedom to experience the depth of relationships, and how it can help us achieve and sustain an extraordinary quality of life—a life of meaning.

With deep respect,

Anthony Robbins
Peak performance coach
Chairman, Robbins Research International, Inc.
Author of *Unlimited Power* and *Awaken the Giant Within*

Preface

Shortly after completing the first edition of this book, the tweets started to come in. Terrorists were attacking Mumbai. Having reached India by boat from Pakistan, the terrorists split up and proceeded to kill at least 173 people in shooting and bomb attacks at hotels, a railway station, and a Jewish center.

News of the attacks, which began on November 26, 2008, and continued through November 29, 2008, spread in real time not just on cable news channels and Web sites but through short posts sent by people who were on the scene and placed for anyone to read on Twitter.

Using their mobile phones, it was everyday Mumbaikers who were telling the world what was happening in—and to—their city.

At the time, it looked like a revolution in news delivery.

Reports were being sent not by professional journalists but by regular folk. They were coming in real time, not hours after the event, once producers and editors had filtered and edited them.

But most important of all, those reports were coming in the form of a dialogue. The people who read the posts on Twitter were able to ask questions, receive answers from people on the scene, and show their support and concern for the city's residents.

It was clearly a huge moment: a tragic time for India and an incredible demonstration of the power of a system that allowed anyone to post 140-character messages that could be read anywhere around the world.

Although this is primarily a business book—a guide for entrepreneurs, managers, and business owners to making the most out of microblogging—I described the way that people had used Twitter during the Mumbai attacks in the preface to the first edition.

Little did I know then that Twitter would go on to be even more influential, helping not just to report the news but to make it.

The first signs came in April 2009. Activists in Moldova used Twitter, as well as other social media services, to organize their demonstrations against the government. But it was when the Iranian government appeared to have forged the results of that country's June 2009 elections that Twitter's power really became apparent. With mainstream reporters restricted to their offices and the government shutting down access to the Internet, Iranians used proxies and workarounds to get news of their protests to the outside world. They uploaded videos, posted pictures, and mostly they tweeted.

Dedicated hashtags allowed anyone anywhere to follow the events, draw attention to new video footage as it was uploaded, explain how to use proxies to hide Twitterers' identities from the authorities, and deliver descriptions of arrests and beatings directly to the world.

So vital did Twitter become as a channel for Iranian protestors to organize and communicate that the U.S. State Department even asked Twitter's founders to delay their server maintenance so that the demonstrators could continue their actions.

Perhaps none of this should have been surprising. Twitter's growth in the months preceding the events in Iran had been incredible. According to Nielsen Online, a ratings service, between February 2008 and February 2009, visitors to Twitter increased by an amazing 1,382 percent from 475,000 to seven million. In the following four months, it grew even further to reach more than 10 million people.

As a result Twitter's users have seen the number of their own followers leap skywards. In April 2009, Ashton Kutcher, one of Twitter's most popular celebrity Twitterers, challenged CNN to see who would be the first on the site to reach one million followers. In a widely publicized contest, Kutcher won and went on to triple the number of those followers by August 2009.

And because one of the strengths of Twitter is the ability of its users to broaden its services and reinvent the way it's used, Twitter has changed, too. Interacting with followers has been made easier with better menus and an improved interface. Search, once only provided by a third-party developer, is now an integral part of every user's timeline and is even being promoted as Twitter's main product.

And most importantly, companies have discovered all sorts of ways to turn their presence on the site into revenue.

At the end of 2008, when I put together the first edition of this book, Twitter was already showing signs that it would be a powerful player. Today, it's become that powerful player, and it's developed a strength and a presence that no one could have predicted.

What Can Twitter Do for You?

Online marketing is a fantastic way to build a business. You can do it from your own home, at your own pace, according to your own schedule, and sometimes even without start-up costs.

Providing advice and promoting products across the Web has helped me to build a successful seven-figure company. It started in my bedroom and has since taken me on speaking tours across the country and around the world.

But creating an Internet business—even a small one—does require work, and part of that work involves staying up to date with the newest tools and the latest online innovations.

That's not as easy as it sounds. Not every "next big thing" turns out be a giant. The Web is littered with links leading to services that promised a great deal, delivered little, and faded away. Part of building a successful online business means knowing which tools are likely to be useful revenue generators and which are going to be major time-wasters.

Sometimes, that's obvious. It was pretty clear when Facebook and LinkedIn came along that they were going to be both powerful and useful. The ability to renew old friendships, maintain current ones and create new connections with very little effort—and for no cost—was always going to attract large numbers of people.

And the ease with which entrepreneurs could use those sites to build networks and keep their market interested and engaged meant that an understanding of social media has become hugely important for online marketers.

The value of Twitter was far less obvious.

The system really couldn't be any simpler. It lets anyone send a message no longer than 140 characters that answers the question "What are you doing?"

You can send that message at any time from your computer or from your mobile phone, and it can be seen by anyone who has chosen to follow those messages.

That's really all there is to it.

Told you it was simple.

It doesn't sound like much, and for Internet entrepreneurs used to writing 300–500-word blog posts several times a week it also sounds painfully restrictive.

What on Earth can you put in 140 characters that could possibly be worth reading?

Surely you can't promote products, build a brand, generate interest in your company, and keep people reading with such small amounts of content?

The answers, it turns out, are "a lot" and "yes, you really can!"

Twitter has proved itself to be incredibly addictive and, for business owners, very valuable too.

Ever since I stumbled onto Twitter, I've given myself sore thumbs typing messages. I do it all the time, and I love it. It's fantastic fun, like writing a personal blog but without the effort.

The pleasure alone would be a good enough reason for me to recommend Twitter, but Twitter isn't just good fun. It's also proved to be a very important and easy way of finding new users and customers, a powerful networking tool, and an excellent way of picking up useful information.

It's helped me to build a deeper relationship with my partners, my clients, and with other entrepreneurs.

It's extended the reach of my brand, making the name of my business known to people who might never otherwise have heard of it.

It's brought me advice and suggestions from experts I couldn't have reached any other way.

It brings me a steady stream of additional web site users and provides a channel for me to alert people who have visited my sites that I've uploaded new content.

And it's brought me some fascinating reading and a bunch of wonderful new friends, too.

In this book, I'm going to explain what you can do to get the most out of Twitter and make microblogging—the sending of tiny messages—work for your business.

I'll start with a quick introduction to social media. Twitter grew out of the online networking craze that had given sites like MySpace and Facebook such giant valuations. Although Twitter can work wonders when used alone, it's at its most powerful when combined with other social media tools. This book will focus on Twitter, but I'll begin with an overview of social media sites so that you'll find it easy to connect your microblogging with other forms of online networking.

I'll then describe Twitter. I'll explain how it works, what the service can do, and reveal exactly why it's so powerful. The site might look small, but it packs a surprising punch. I'll explain the reason behind Twitter's super powers.

Then I'll start to get practical. I'll talk you through signing up to Twitter and selecting a username. Both of those are fairly straight-forward (even if it is easy to make expensive mistakes), but Twitter also lets its members create profiles to introduce themselves to other users. The profiles are pretty basic. You won't find any of the fancy bells and whistles that you can expect to see on other so-cial networking sites. But that doesn't mean you should stick to the fundamentals.

Your profile is an important marketing page. With a little thought and just a touch of creativity it can function as a useful entry point to your commercial site and help to raise the profile of your business. I'll discuss what to include, how to design it, and how to make the page pay.

I'll then talk about the most important thing you'll need to know on Twitter: how to build a following.

That's vital. Although every message—or "tweet" as they're called on Twitter—is public, if no one knows you're there, no one will know to read them.

There's a huge list of different strategies that Twitterers are using to build up followers, make new contacts, and keep in touch. Some of them are very simple. Others are a little more complex and require a bit of thought and sometimes even a little expense, too.

I'll talk you through some of the most effective ways that I've discovered to build up followers.

Finding followers isn't difficult. Much harder is keeping them. That's only going to happen if you create the sort of content that people actually want to read.

There's nothing new about that. Anyone who has ever tried to generate revenue with a web site knows that content is king. When you can write articles and posts of any length you want, upload videos, and show off your images, there are plenty of options and lots of flexibility. When you're restricted to a message of no more than 140 characters, though, creating interesting content sounds much more challenging.

It *is* more challenging, but it's also a lot more fun. You can do it quickly, without making great demands on your audience, and—once you get used to it—without a great deal of thought.

I'll explain what makes good Twitter content and talk you through some of the sorts of messages that successful Twitterers are sending.

Tweets though are just a means to an end. The goal of using Twitter is to build relationships—especially relationships that can benefit your company. In the following two chapters I look at how connecting with two different types of followers can bring those benefits.

I discuss connecting with customers on Twitter by problem-solving, winning referrals, and supplying support. I also talk about using Twitter to talk to team members, especially when they're scattered in different places.

Once you've built up your following and are enjoying using Twitter, you can start to make all of that effort pay off. There are a number of ways to do that, and I'll talk about them in detail as well.

The first is brand extension. Twitter can be a very effective branding tool for any business, and it's been used by some of the world's largest companies to drum up publicity for their products. I'll discuss how you can use your tweets and your followers to extend the power of your company's name and what the rules are for effective brand-building with Twitter.

Blog posts can also be promoted using Twitter—an important way to turn your followers not just into visitors but also into cash—and so can stores and other retail outlets. Although Twitter is not strictly a commercial area, with carefully written content it is possible to directly increase your conversions and make extra sales.

And like Facebook, Twitter has also created a network of add-ons and applications that help its users get even more out of the service. I'll introduce you to some of the most useful, and in Chapter 11, I'll explain how to add powerful solutions to the Twitter platform.

Finally, I'll provide a 30-day step-by-step plan for dominating Twitter that will take you from a Twitter Johnny-No-Friends to a powerful social networking force in just one month.

Twitter is very restrictive. It doesn't allow users to make videos, upload rich media content, or do any of the fancy things you might have become accustomed to on other sites.

Nor is it a sales arena. Although businesses are using Twitter to increase their revenues and make money, thinking of the site as a low-cost—even free—way to advertise is not going to bring results.

In fact, that's just going to cost you time that you could have spent doing something far more rewarding.

At its most basic Twitter is a communication tool. It's a channel that lets you speak to lots of people and enlighten them about your life and your work.

You can think of it as a giant virtual water cooler. It's a place where people come to chat, to get to know each other, and to network. It's a place where people come to make friends and, most importantly, to converse.

It's not a place where people come to sell, and pushing sales hard on Twitter just isn't going to work.

Success on Twitter—in fact, commercial success anywhere!—is the result of a four-step process: Know me. Like me. Trust me. Pay me.

People always prefer to do business with people they know, like, and trust. That's why conferences have always been so important. They provide an opportunity for like-minded people to get together, shoot the breeze, and build a relationship of trust.

And, having built those relationships, to build deals.

Twitter certainly isn't a replacement for a conference—nothing can compete with actually pressing the flesh and sharing a drink or a meal—but it does allow business people to get to know potential partners and customers, to show that they're likeable and approachable, to create trust, and eventually to get paid.

An Introduction to the Social Media Landscape

Once upon a time, anyone could be a media publisher. All you needed was several million dollars, a team of editors and writers, a printing press capable of shooting out a dozen copies a second, and a distribution network that would put your publication in stores across the country.

Unless, of course, you wanted to go into radio or television. In that case, things were just a little harder.

The result was that information came down. We didn't talk among ourselves; we were talked to by writers, editors, and producers who chose the subjects and told us what they thought. If we liked what we were reading, we kept tuning in and the company made money.

If we didn't like it, we stopped buying the magazine or we switched channels. Advertisers turned away, and all of the millions of dollars the publication took to create disappeared.

Today, it's all so very different. It can cost literally nothing to create content and make it available for other people to enjoy. That low cost means that it doesn't matter if it's not read by millions. You can focus on a small market—even one interested in stamp collecting in Mozambique—and still find enough people to form a community and maybe even make a profit through advertising and product sales.

It's called the "long tail," and it's something that the Internet has made fantastic use of.

But the low cost of publishing online has had another effect: We aren't being talked to by professional writers and publishers anymore; we're talking to each other.

Average folk like you and me—the kind of people who didn't study journalism at university, who never spent years as a cub reporter covering local court cases, and who were never even very good at Scrabble let alone putting together articles—are writing about the topics they love and sharing their views.

And they're hearing back, too. The conversation is flowing in both directions.

Anyone now can launch a web site, write articles, or even create videos and put them live. And anyone can comment on that content, affecting both its nature and the direction of the publication.

That's social media, and it's a publishing revolution.

So What Exactly Is Social Media?

Social media can be all sorts of different things, and it can be produced in all sorts of different ways. Perhaps the best definition of social media, though, is content that has been created by its audience.

Facebook, for example, is not a publishing company. It doesn't create any of its own content. It doesn't write articles or posts, and it doesn't upload films or images for people to view and enjoy.

It allows its users to do all of that on its behalf.

It's as though Fox were to fire all its actors, producers, news anchors, and scriptwriters, throw open its doors, and tell the world that anyone is welcome to come in and shoot their own programs.

And then let them broadcast those programs on its networks for nothing, too.

Of course, if that were to happen, you'd still have to tell people what channel you were on and when they could see your program. You'd still have to produce content that other people might actually enjoy. And inevitably, the people who took the most professional approach, put time and effort into what they were doing, and connected with their audiences would be the most successful.

But even that wouldn't allow viewers to take part in the program, something which forms an important part of social media.

Create a group on a site like Facebook and you won't be expected to supply all of the text and all of the images. You'll be expecting other group members to add their stories and photographs, too.

Even bloggers, when they write a post, expect their readers to join the discussion by leaving comments at the bottom of the post that take the argument in new directions and add new information.

This is the "social" part of social media, and it means that publishing is now about participation.

Someone who uses social media successfully doesn't just create content; he or she creates conversations.

And those conversations create communities.

That's the real beauty of social media, and while it may or may not be the goal—depending on the site—the result of social media can always be firm connections between the people who participate.

When those connections are formed around businesses, the results can be the sort of brand loyalty and commitment that sales professionals have been dreaming about since the first days of direct marketing.

The definition of social media then is a vague thing. At its broadest, it describes a form of publishing in which stories are swapped rather than published and the exchange of content happens within a community, rather like a chat in a restaurant.

At its narrowest, it describes one way in which publishers and marketers can put their messages in front of thousands of people and encourage them to build strong connections and firm loyalty.

However it's defined, though, social media has proved incredibly popular.

Facebook now claims to have more than 250 million active members—that's *active* members, not just people who created a profile and never used it. It's averaged 250,000 new registrations every day since the beginning of 2007, roughly doubling the number of active users every six months. Almost half of those users return every day, and together they share more than 1 *billion* pieces of content, including blog posts, notes, photos, and news stories each week.

MySpace, which went live shortly before Facebook, is a little cagier with its figures but is believed to be at least as popular. One in four Americans is said to be on MySpace, and in the United Kingdom, as many people own a MySpace account as own a dog.

At one stage, the site was generating around 14 billion user comments, 10 billion friend relationships and saw more than 8 million images uploaded each day.

Twitter, which was launched more than two years after MySpace—a lifetime in Internet terms—isn't quite in the same numeric league, but its growth has still been phenomenal. As a company that relies on venture capital, it can also be pretty secretive about its membership figures, but in March 2008 it was believed to be sending more than 3 million messages a day between over a million users, of whom 200,000 were active on a daily basis. Those users had created more than 4 million connections. By October 2008, TwitDir (www.twitdir.com), a directory of Twitter users, was reporting that it knew of 3,262,795 Twitterers.

Since then, those numbers have boomed. Helped by the appearance on the site of celebrities like Britney Spears, Ashton Kutcher, and Oprah Winfrey (who made her first tweet on her show, assisted by Twitter co-founder Evan Williams), Twitter's growth chart has changed from a gentle climb into a hockey stick. In April and March 2009 alone, Twitter quadrupled its number of visitors, and by the summer of 2009, it was believed to have more than 17 million users.

There is another fact about Twitter that's particularly interesting, though: It's massively underused.

Back in February 2008, the site's own blog was reporting that around half of all Twitterers follow and are followed by just 10 people. The top 10 percent of Twitterers had more than 80 followers and were following more than 70 people.

To join the top 10 percent of Twitter users then, you just needed to attract 80 followers!

To put that into perspective, I had almost 5,000 followers at that time and was following around 1,700 people!

You'd think that with Twitter's incredible growth those figures would have changed. They did. By the summer of 2009, the number of my followers had increased by a factor of 14. Other leading Twitterers have also seen the number of their followers reach incredible levels, with several members now boasting more than a million readers and a few celebrities tweeting to several million followers.

But while there are a small number of people with huge readerships, most people on the site are still just getting their feet wet. According to research conducted by Sysomos, a social media analytics company, 76 percent of Twitter's members have no more than 18 followers, and 99 percent have fewer than 700. About half of the profiles on Twitter have attracted no more than seven followers, says Sysomos.

Much of that is likely to down to Twitter's high bounce rate. In one particularly controversial study, Nielsen found that 60 percent of Twitter users fail to return to the site after their first month. When Twitter's users pointed out that many people quickly migrate to third-party clients like TweetDeck and HootSuite to post and read, Nielsen ran its survey again and found the same results.

But that still means that of the users who joined during Twitter's boom months, when the company was never out of the news, 40 percent have stuck around. And while only a small number of them may be posting regularly, that just means that there's plenty of opportunity for a dedicated user to stand out, and a huge potential audience to attract.

Twitter's growth has turned it into a massive marketing opportunity.

All of these figures just scratch the surface of the popularity of social media though. YouTube attracts more than 60 million unique visitors each month. They tune into the 10 hours of video footage uploaded to the site every minute.

Throw in the countless numbers of blogs (Technorati tracks over 100 million English language blogs alone) and it becomes pretty clear that social media is a massive phenomenon that's changing the way all of us create and use content—and the way that businesses use that content and their distribution channels, too.

Social Media, So What? Why Social Media Really Is a Big Deal

So we can see that social media sites can be big. Really, really big. But so what? There are lots of people in the telephone book, and that's very big, too. It doesn't make it a particularly useful market-ing tool.

Social media sites don't just list people though, and they don't just list any old people.

Each site lists a very special group of people.

At first glance, that might seem a little strange. Whether you're browsing through Facebook, MySpace, Flickr, or Twitter, you're going to see small pictures of people, small messages to and from people, and profiles in which those people say certain things about themselves, such as where they work, where they're from, and what they do in their spare time.

Look a little closer though and you'll start to notice a few differences.

Although the sites may seem very similar, in fact, each site has its own unique feel and its own unique demographic.

Because Facebook started at Harvard, for example (it had signed up half the undergraduate population within a month of going live), and because initially it was restricted to university students, it has a high percentage of well-educated members. The site boasts that it has an 85 percent market share of four-year universities and that "more than half of Facebook users are outside of college."

Clearly, that suggests many of Facebook's users are still in college—a fantastic market for companies hoping to pick up cus-tomers and start those customers in the habit of buying from them so they stay with them as their income rises.

Facebook isn't unique in having highly educated members. Twit-ter's membership might currently be smaller than that of older social media sites, but even with its sudden growth it appears to be very selective—even if it is self-selective.

Tracking Twitter's demographics isn't easy. Although some peo-ple have had fun following the frequency with which certain wealth-related terms (such as well-to-do neighborhoods) turn up (they found themselves following lots of local lawyers as a result), there's no way to easily conduct a demographic survey of the site's users. Hitwise, an Internet monitoring service, did however manage to produce some very interesting, and some very impressive, results.

Writing in *Time* magazine in August 2008, Bill Tancer, Hitwise's general manager of research and author of *Click: What Millions do*

Online and Why it Matters, noted that he had discovered that Twitter was 63 percent male and, at that time, 57 percent of its U.S. visitors (although not necessarily its members) were Californian—a statistic that likely reflects the site's large attraction to hi-tech workers. Twitter itself pointed out that 60 percent of its Web traffic was coming from outside the United States though, in particular, Japan, Spain, and the United Kingdom. It also notes that had it looked at other ways of accessing the site, such as SMS, the international breakdown would have been very different.

More interesting, according to Bill Tancer, Twitter's largest age demographic in the summer of 2008 was 35- to 44-year-olds. They made up just over a quarter of its users, a shift from its starting point among 18- to 24-year-olds.

Most fascinating of all though, Tancer also says that just over 14 percent of Twitter's visitors are what he calls "Stable Career" types—a "collection of young and ethnically diverse singles living in big-city metros like Los Angeles, Philadelphia, and Miami." Another 12 percent are "Young Cosmopolitans"—40-somethings *with household incomes of more than $250,000 per year*.

The publicity that surrounded Twitter in 2009 has changed some of those figures slightly. Sysomos was reporting in June 2009 that just over half (53 percent) of users were women. New York had the most Twitter users, followed by Los Angeles, Toronto, San Francisco, and Boston. And some 65 percent of Twitter's users were under the age of 25, it argued, although the research company also pointed out that only around 0.7 percent of Twitterers actually revealed their age and that those who did so were likely to be young.

While a number of 20-somethings might have joined Twitter out of curiosity, it is pretty clear that the site isn't just used by young people as an alternative to SMS. Twitter has a large following among older, professional audiences, and a full quarter of Twitter's users are high-earners, a valuable piece of information that makes the site a must-use for any serious marketer.

So we can see that social media sites aren't just attracting kids looking for places to chat with their friends and find out where to load up on free music downloads. They're also attracting smart, educated people with money to burn.

And they're attracting experts, too.

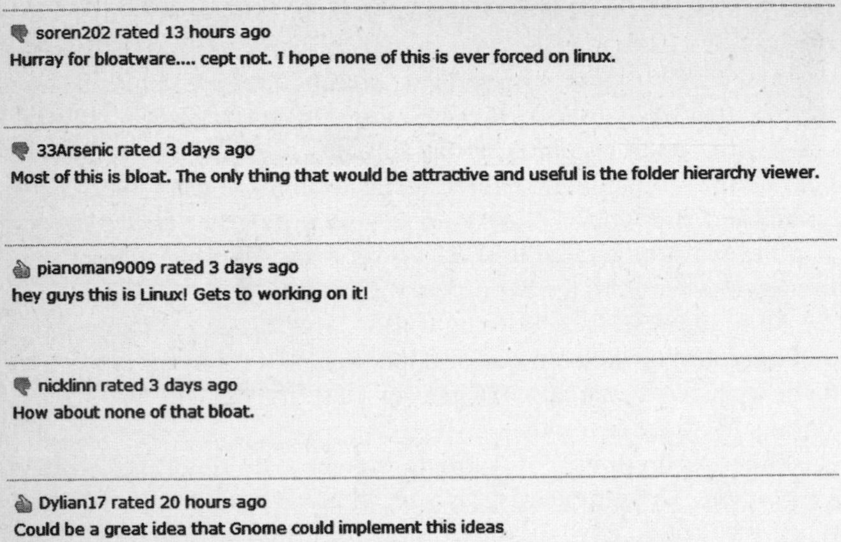

🍃 soren202 rated 13 hours ago
Hurray for bloatware.... cept not. I hope none of this is ever forced on linux.

🍃 33Arsenic rated 3 days ago
Most of this is bloat. The only thing that would be attractive and useful is the folder hierarchy viewer.

👍 pianoman9009 rated 3 days ago
hey guys this is Linux! Gets to working on it!

🍃 nicklinn rated 3 days ago
How about none of that bloat.

👍 Dylian17 rated 20 hours ago
Could be a great idea that Gnome could implement this ideas

Figure 1.1   Know what these StumbleUpon users are talking about? Me neither . . .

You can see this most clearly on specialist sites like Flickr, a photo-sharing service. Although Flickr too isn't very forthcoming about its demographic details, spend any time at all on the site you can't help but notice the number of professional photographers who use it.

Part of the site's appeal isn't just the pictures; enthusiasts also can pick up advice from experts working in their field and ready to share the benefits of their experience.

Even a social bookmarking site like StumbleUpon can generate some very expert comments in the reviews of the sites users submit. (See Figure 1.1.)

So we can see that social media sites attract absolutely huge numbers of people. We can see too that many of those people are highly educated, well paid, and experts in their fields.

You should be able to see very clearly then that social media offers a gigantic opportunity for any business-owner to promote their products to exactly the sort of market they want to reach.

Figure 1.2 My blog's home page. I write it, you read it and comment on it.

The Different Types of Social Media Sites—Content to Suit Every Market

One of the reasons that social media has proved to be so popular is that it's available in all sorts of different forms. While the networking sites with their tens of millions of members might be the most familiar, there are actually all sorts of different ways of creating and sharing social media content.

BLOGS

Yes, blogs are a form of social media, too. They're written by people on every topic you can imagine. (See Figure 1.2.) And only a tiny fraction of them are produced by professionals, even though all have the potential to generate revenue. Even my mother has a blog, which she uses to describe her travel experiences. (You can see it at TravelsWithSheila.com—tell her I said "hi.")

What really makes blogging part of social media is that it can cost nothing to use. Sure, if you want to have your own domain name and place the blog on your own server, you might have to pay a small fee—when I say "small," I mean less than $20 per month. And there are strategies you can use to bring in readers that will cost money too.

But you don't actually need to do any of that.

To become a blogger, you don't need to do any more than sign up at Blogger.com or WordPress.com any of the other free blogging services and start writing.

Within minutes, you'll be creating content and you'll form a part of the social media world.

Blogs though do take some effort. They have to be updated regularly and while you can put anything on a blog, from short posts to feature-length videos if you want, you'll have to work to keep your readers entertained, informed, and engaged. It's fun stuff, and it can be very profitable stuff, too, but it's not a sweat-free business.

Most important, while you can accept guest posts and hire writers, and although your comments will be a crucial element of your site's attraction, it will still be *you* guiding the content and setting the subjects.

Blogs *are* a form of social media, but it's a society with a clear ruler.

MEMBERSHIP SITES

That top-down feel that can be present in some social media channels is also present in membership sites. There are far fewer of these on the Web than there are blogs but there's still no shortage of them, and like any social media site, they rely on the members to produce the content that's the site's attraction.

My own membership site, for example, is toponenetwork.com. With members that number in the thousands rather than the millions, it's a long way behind Facebook, but it's not intended to be a site for the masses. It's meant to be selective and targeted only towards people who are really determined to succeed at online marketing. (See Figure 1.3.)

I use the site for coaching and to share valuable marketing information with other top marketers, but the heart of the site is the activity that takes place between them.

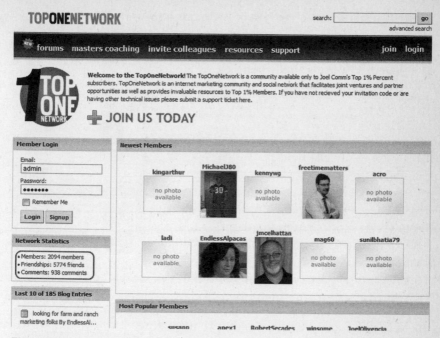

Figure 1.3 My membership site functions in much the same way as a social media site. Just check out the number of friendships and comments my members generate.

I might like to believe that it's my advice and lessons that keep everyone coming back, but a quick look at what people are discussing in the groups shows that there's a lot more to it than that.

My members have been swapping fantastic ideas and creating the sorts of connections that lead to valuable deals and joint ventures.

That wouldn't happen if the site was much more general.

If toponenetwork.com wasn't carefully targeted, it would be too difficult for marketers to find each other, network, and share the information that keeps them on the site.

But that doesn't mean membership sites can't be massive. Dating sites like Match.com are a form of social media, too. The content that people are paying to use are the profiles and pictures that the site's members have created and uploaded.

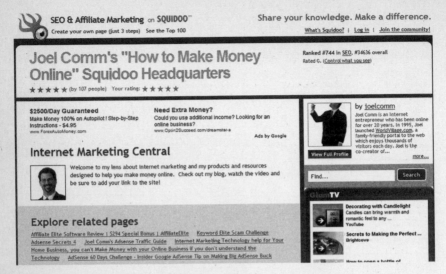

Figure 1.4   My lens on Squidoo. All my own work.

Match might have an online magazine, but no one is paying around $25 every month to read the magazine.

They're paying that price month after month to read the descriptions and look at the photos that other people have posted, and to contact those people.

It's not the site that's the attraction of social media sites; it's the society.

SQUIDOO

Squidoo doesn't look like a social media site. You don't get to make connections or build giant piles of friends in the same way that you can on other social media sites. But what you can do is create your own content and act as a hub through which people looking for the information you're supplying can pass. (See Figure 1.4.)

The site is intended to be the first stop for anyone looking for information on any topic. It's a place where experts can provide the basic information and tell people where they need to go to learn more.

I've been on Squidoo for some time now and I've found it a lot of fun and pretty rewarding, too. The site provides you with a free Web page—it calls them "lenses"—that you can construct using their modules, so it's very easy to use. All you have to do is place your own content in those modules.

You even get a share of the advertising revenue depending on the popularity of your lens.

And that's where the social aspect comes in again. Yes, Squidoo depends on its members to produce the content that users want, but it also depends on the community to identify which lenses are worth viewing. That makes networking vital.

While you can't add someone as a contact on Squidoo, as you promote your lens, you will inevitably end up making plenty of new friends.

PHOTO SITES

Squidoo relies mostly on links as the most important form of content on its lenses. Lensmasters are intended to help users find the knowledge they need somewhere else rather than supply all of that information themselves.

Squidoo only provides one page, after all.

But links certainly aren't the only form of content that can be shared—or which require active networks to make sure that they're seen.

Ever since cameras went digital, there's been a need for a low-cost—and even free—way to share those images with anyone who wants to see them online. Both Facebook and MySpace allow their users to upload their images, but neither of them is a dedicated photography site. Images are just one form of content that users are free to share on those sites, together with videos, personal histories, group discussions, and so on.

There are sites, however, that specialize in photography. They depend entirely on the photos that users upload in order to bring in other users. (See Figure 1.5.)

That broad-based content sourcing already makes sites like Flickr—one of the most popular photo-sharing sites, and now owned by Yahoo!—part of the social media phenomenon, but Flickr also has the networking power of those sites.

Like Facebook and MySpace, it's possible to create long lists of friends and join groups, where you can submit images, enter

Figure 1.5   Flickr is the big daddy of photo-sharing web sites.

competitions, and join discussions about the best way to light a child's portrait or which lens to use in which conditions. (See Figure 1.6.)

Flickr also allows its members to mark images as favorites and to place comments beneath them. Both of those activities can be valuable ways of adding new friends. Pro members, who pay a subscription fee of $24.95 per year, can even see stats that indicate how many views, faves, and comments each image has produced and even where their visitors came from.

All of that networking is vital to success on the site, and that success can have some spectacular results. In 2006, Rebekka Gudsleifdottir, an Icelandic art student whose images and networking had brought her a huge following on Flickr, was spotted by an advertising executive on the site who hired her to shoot a series of billboard ads for the Toyota Prius. Many of the images used in Windows Vista, too, were bought from photographers commissioned after they were discovered on the site.

Every day, images are licensed and prints are sold on Flickr, and it's all based on the content created by the site's users and promoted through careful networking.

That's classic social media.

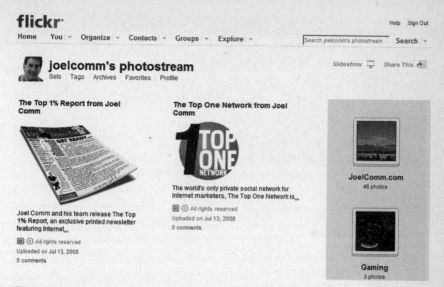

Figure 1.6 Yes, I have a Flickr stream too. You can even see my house on it.

Micro Blogs

And finally, we come to microblogging. This is a whole new thing in social media. In some ways it's the exact opposite of everything we've seen so far.

Social media sites tend to want their members to contribute as much content as possible. They may restrict that content to just photographs (or on Flickr, video now as well) and they may restrict membership to a select few (in the case of my membership site, to dedicated Internet marketers; in the case of dating sites, to dedicated singles), but on the whole they want their members to offer as much content as possible.

Microblog sites place strict limits on the content that can be uploaded, and they find that those limits encourage creativity.

A Closer Look at Microblogging

Just as there are many different kinds of social media sites, so there are many different ways to microblog. One of the most popular now actually takes place within the larger social media sites.

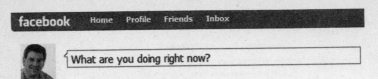

Figure 1.7   Facebook catches up with microblogging.

When Facebook realized that many of its members loved the idea of being able to update their contacts in real time, they added their own microblogging system. (See Figure 1.7.)

Facebook's system only works within the site though, so unlike Twitter, which can broadcast your tweets to mobile telephones as well, updates are only visible to friends who happen to be on the site at the time.

For Facebook users though, it's still very powerful, and Twitter users who want their updates to reach further can use Facebook's Twitter application. This lets them send tweets from within Facebook itself. I use it, and I think it's great. You can find it at www.facebook.com/apps/application.php?id=2231777543 or by searching the apps for Twitter.

Facebook isn't the only social media site to try to add microblogging to its list of features though. LinkedIn, a social networking site geared towards professional connections, has integrated a system that lets people share information about what they're working on. (See Figure 1.8.)

Just as important, the site also lets its users track what people are saying in those posts with a very neat application called "Company Buzz."

This is the first time that microblogging has been geared specifically to a business audience, and it's easy to understand the value this could have to a firm that wants to understand what its employees, customers, and suppliers are saying about it.

SPOINK

While Twitter's strong point is its simplicity, Spoink (www.spoink.com) allows its users to do things as complicated as posting audio content through a telephone, and it provides instant messaging across a range of different platforms and email, too. (See Figure 1.9.)

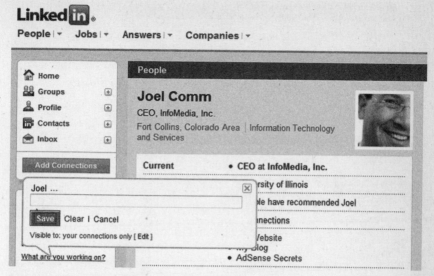

Figure 1.8   Microblogging the LinkedIn way.

For a microblogging service, it's complicated. That certainly doesn't mean it's useless though; it has a lot of different uses. But unless you have a particular challenge you need to overcome in rich media, I think it's likely to be most effective as a communication

Figure 1.9   Spoink is microblogging in rich media.

Figure 1.10   Yammer's restrictions make Twitter look like a
free-for-all.

tool to join together different platforms than a main way of keeping
lots of people informed.

YAMMER

Microblog services thrive most when they ask users to answer
a simple question and allow anyone to see the answer. Yammer
(www.yammer.com) keeps to those microblogging roots but
narrows the focus of the question—and the audience, too. (See
Figure 1.10.)

Instead of inviting people to share what they're doing (and
receiving answers that might range from saving an oil-soaked bird to
eating an avocado sandwich), like LinkedIn, it asks users to explain
what they're working on.

Figure 1.11   Plurk puts the blog back in microblogging.

But it only reveals those answers to people on the network with the same corporate email address.

That makes it a useful tool for communicating within a business, but it's not so handy for mass marketing.

PLURK

Plurk (www.plurk.com) might have a terrible name, but it does have some excellent ideas. You can think of it as MySpace to Twitter's Facebook. Instead of presenting posts (what Plurk naturally calls "plurks") vertically, the site displays them horizontally so that they appear as a timeline. (See Figure 1.11.)

In addition to seeing what people said, you get to see when they said it, and in the process, pick up a feel for their day.

Plurks can also come with qualifiers—colored tags such as <shares>, <asks>, or <says>—that mark out the nature of the content, and while they are limited to 140 characters, plurks can include images and videos. You can also restrict them to "cliques," small groups of friends with something in common, like a network.

Less useful is the "Karma" feature, which unlocks features as users are more active on the site. Although it's clearly intended to encourage people to stay active, it can also be a source of frustration for anyone who wants to get the most out of the site right away.

Blogger Chris Thomson created a side-by-side comparison of Plurk and Twitter and noted a couple of important differences between the two services. Plurk, for example, allows users to edit posts once they've been uploaded; perhaps most interesting of all,

Plurk, he says, demands your full attention. It's more conversational than Twitter, a bit like instant messaging, which means you can't always just post and run.

You might also have to deal with the responses and take part in the conversation.

Plurk has only been around since May 2008, and it will be interesting to see how it develops and how many users it picks up. It's likely that while Twitter will continue to attract well-to-do educated types who want to network professionally and mix with other experts, Plurk could become a fun microblogging forum.

That could give the site its very own marketing power.

After comparing the two services, Chris Thomson's conclusion was that he'd use both. It's possible that other potential microbloggers will choose to do the same, using one service for pleasure and the other for professional networking.

Introducing...Twitter!

And finally, we come to Twitter—the site that has really set the standard in microblogging.

The service was founded by programmers Evan Williams, Jack Dorsey, and Biz Stone in July 2006. Williams was a serial entrepreneur who had founded a company called Pyra Labs that made project management software. A note-taking feature on that software went on to become Blogger, the free blogging service later bought by Google. According to one theory, it was Williams who first used the term "blogger" to describe people who write weblogs.

In 2004, Williams left Google to form podcasting company Odeo, and two years later, he created Obvious with Biz Stone, a programmer who had joined Blogger after its acquisition by the search engine giant. The new company bought Odeo, which it later sold to a company called Sonic Mountain. It now focuses on Twitter.

The original idea for Twitter came from Dorsey, an Odeo employee. In an interview for ReadWriteTalk.com with Sean Ammirati, vice president of business development and product management at mSpoke, Stone described the moment when they first discussed the idea:

"A few of us were thinking about what are some interesting ways that maybe we can merge SMS to the Web," he said. "[Dorsey] had come up with this idea where if you just look at only the status field of an instant message application like AIM, and you just look at that as a sort of really small version of what people are already doing . . . and you just make it super simple, 'Here's what I'm doing.' . . . [W]e kind of went off in a corner and we worked for two weeks and we created a prototype. We showed the rest of the team and everyone just sort of giggled. They all kind of loved it. It was really fun. We used it over the weekend. We found it very compelling and we decided that we would keep working on it."

That was in March 2006, and initially Twitter was used by the company's employees as a fun form of internal communication. (Tech companies, it seems, might have lava lamps and space hoppers, but they never seem to have watercoolers!)

The service launched officially in October 2006, picked up a South by Southwest Web (SXSW) Award in March 2007, and by April was a separate entity headed by Dorsey.

Helped by the publicity generated by the SXSW award, boosted by references on Blogger, where the company, of course, had good connections, and most importantly making itself attractive with an open platform that let other developers extend the service, the site started to take off.

That led to some problems. In 2007, Twitter was reported to have had just 98 percent uptime—a loss of three whole days over the year—and tended to suffer particularly badly during major tech conferences (which says something about many of its users, too). (See Figure 1.12.)

It has had some very impressive successes though. Some of the world's leading personalities, corporations, and government bodies are known to use the service, including Barack Obama (@barackobama), Whole Foods Market (@wholefoods), and the British Parliament (@UKParliament).

The American Red Cross (@redcross), too, uses Twitter as a fast way to communicate information about local disasters.

Figure 1.12   Twitter's iconic "fail whale." Designed by Yiying Lu, the beluga whale supported by twittering birds is now a brand in its own right after its frequent appearance on an overstrained Twitter site.

There are two things that really distinguish Twitter though.

The first is its simplicity. Although the service now has piles of additional tools and add-ons, which extend its use, at its core, Twitter remains nothing more than a way of describing what you're doing in no more than 140 characters.

That brevity and simplicity have always been key, and they're what brought Twitter its second characteristic: critical mass.

The hardest moment for any social Web service is at the beginning. In this chapter, for example, we saw how Plurk offers some promising, fun features, but people are going to be unwilling to join in until they can see who else is there and, in particular, whether their friends are on the site.

It takes a special push to get a social media site snowballing to a size big enough for everyone to feel comfortable about climbing on board. For Facebook that was its marketing at Harvard and from there to other universities.

For Twitter it was the boost it received with its SXSW award, which had everyone talking about the service as the next big thing.

As long it has that critical mass—and with more than ten million members it certainly has that—Twitter is always going to be the microblogging service to beat.

In the next chapter, I'll explain exactly why it's likely to retain that position as the leading microblogging service.

2

What Is Twitter and Why Is It So Powerful?

So Twitter as a whole isn't unique.

Yes, it's big and that makes it unique among microblogging services (if not among social media sites).

It's got buzz that other sites just don't have.

And it's growing at the kind of phenomenal rate that's already forced the social media giants to look over their shoulders and copy it.

But it's not the only service that allows people to broadcast short messages. We've already seen that there are plenty of other sites that offer the same service in one form or another.

But Twitter is by far the most powerful microblogging service currently available, and it's the one that marketers absolutely need to be aware of.

Twitter and Its Successes

I've mentioned that at its simplest Twitter is just a means to send short updates to people who want to receive them.

The most basic way to do that is to log into your Twitter account on the Web and type your tweet into the text field. Anyone who looks at your profile can see all of your outgoing tweets. (See Figure 2.1.)

Figure 2.1   Twitter's new home page puts a big emphasis on search. Your Twitter home page will look a little different.

Followers can also see a list of tweets from everyone they follow when they log into their Twitter home pages. They'll also see tweets sent from people they follow to other people they follow, allowing them to jump into conversations between friends. (What they won't see though are tweets sent from someone they're following to someone they're *not* following. That makes it harder to spot new opportunities to make new friends, so it is worth checking out the profiles of the people you're following from time to time to see what conversations you're missing.)

Figure 2.2   What my Twitter profile looks like to one of my followers. A message goes out and is visible here . . .

joelcomm I was interviewed in Las Vegas. It's mildly amusing.
http://TwitPWR.com/nUn/
about 9 hours ago from web

problogger Reading: 15 Killer Hacks for WordPress that Are
Extremely Useful - http://is.gd/21CXd
about 9 hours ago from TwitterBar

booksquare this explains today's mood and possibly tomorrow's. i
am not sure what do when "weather" happens: http://snurl.com
/onf7c
about 10 hours ago from twhirl

Figure 2.3   ... and arrives at the home page of one of my
followers here.

Your Twitter experience then will be made up of sending your
own updates and reading tweets from others.

But that's just the start.

One of the inspirations for Twitter was the idea of combining
Web-based updates with mobile information. So Twitter makes it
possible for mobile phone users to send updates from their handsets,
and in some places to receive them on their handsets, too.

So if you had just agreed a joint venture with a marketing partner
while sitting in a bar at a conference, and you wanted to share the
news right away, you could just pull out your mobile phone and
send a quick message to Twitter. (See Figures 2.2 and 2.3.)

Yes, you'd have to pay for that SMS message. You wouldn't pay
Twitter. But you would pay your mobile phone company for one
message.

Twitter will then pass that message on to all of your followers,
including by broadcasting further SMS messages to people who have
chosen to receive their updates on their mobiles.

The benefits that can bring can be huge. I mentioned that the
Red Cross has already spotted Twitter's potential and use the site to
provide updates related to ongoing disasters.

That's a service that relies on Twitter's speed, numbers, and
mobility.

Red Cross volunteers are able to send an SMS about a new shelter
opening or the changing direction of a brushfire and have lots of
people read it at the same time. When brushfires threatened Santa
Barbara in May 2009, for example, residents were able to use the

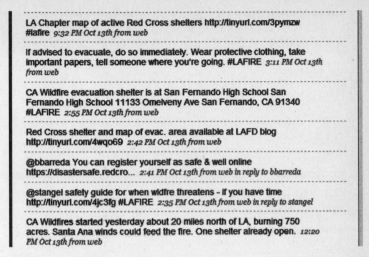

LA Chapter map of active Red Cross shelters http://tinyurl.com/3pymzw #lafire *9:32 PM Oct 13th from web*

If advised to evacuate, do so immediately. Wear protective clothing, take important papers, tell someone where you're going. #LAFIRE *3:11 PM Oct 13th from web*

CA Wildfire evacuation shelter is at San Fernando High School San Fernando High School 11133 Omelveny Ave San Fernando, CA 91340 #LAFIRE *2:55 PM Oct 13th from web*

Red Cross shelter and map of evac. area available at LAFD blog http://tinyurl.com/4wqo69 *2:42 PM Oct 13th from web*

@bbarreda You can register yourself as safe & well online https://disastersafe.redcro... *2:41 PM Oct 13th from web in reply to bbarreda*

@stangel safety guide for when widfre threatens - if you have time http://tinyurl.com/4jc3fg #LAFIRE *2:35 PM Oct 13th from web in reply to stangel*

CA Wildfires started yesterday about 20 miles north of LA, burning 750 acres. Santa Ana winds could feed the fire. One shelter already open. *12:20 PM Oct 13th from web*

Figure 2.4   The American Red Cross's tweets (@redcross) provide information and disaster-related updates.

service to learn about evacuations, closures, and rescue centers. It was a hugely important service. (See Figure 2.4.)

But Twitter also brings the benefit of immediate feedback, which can have tremendous advantages for individuals.

The Power of Twitter's Immediate Feedback

Twitter's speed means that you can send out an SMS to Twitter from wherever you are and have lots of people read it immediately. That's a service that was really meant for fun, but it's proven itself to be incredibly valuable as a way of asking for help.

In June 2008, Pastor Carlos Whittaker (@loswhit), service programming director at Buckhead Church in Atlanta, GA, found himself stuck at the Dallas airport and was told he would have to wait six hours for the next flight. Tired and not too happy at the thought of spending a night on the airport floor, he sent a tweet about his predicament.

Within just two minutes, he had received seven emails, three phone calls, and a huge number of tweets.

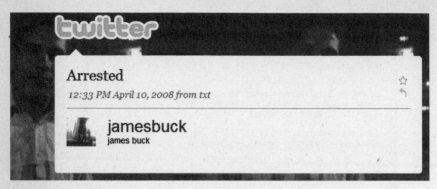

Figure 2.5 The tweet that freed journalism student, James Buck, from an Egyptian jail.

Best of all, Trevor DeVage of charity group Remedy4ThisHeart turned up and gave Carlos a key to a room at a nearby Hyatt hotel.

That was certainly a helpful response, but sometimes tweets can generate the sort of response that makes an even more important difference to people's lives.

In April 2008, for example, James Buck (@jamesbuck), a journalism student at UC Berkeley, was arrested with his interpreter, Mohammed Maree, while photographing an anti-government rally in Egypt. Sitting in the police van, he was able to use his mobile phone to send the one-word message "arrested" to his followers on Twitter. (See Figure 2.5.) They immediately alerted the U.S. embassy and his college, which quickly obtained a lawyer for him. James continued to provide updates about his arrest via Twitter and was released the following day, which he announced on Twitter with the word "free."

His interpreter was less lucky: Maree was held for 90 days, beaten and abused, and was only released after a hunger strike.

Both of those examples relied on Twitter followers taking action outside Twitter. But that's not usually where the responses take place.

One of the most enjoyable aspects of Twitter isn't updating friends and family about the small details of your life. That's fun, but it only works one way.

Twitter is a two-way communication tool, and that's very important.

It means you can ask questions and request help to very specialized problems and get the expert advice you need.

Instant Access to Smart People 24/7

Later in this book, I'm going to talk in more detail about how to use Twitter not just as a billboard for making announcements, but as way of holding conversations with people who matter.

Usually, you'll be holding those conversations with friends or customers. But because Twitter has such a well-educated and professional group of followers, it can also function as an always-open help center for just about any subject you can think of.

Look at people's Twitter pages and you'll see this time and time again. (See Figure 2.6.)

help_echo: RT @melissatucker80 -Hi I need to check some relays that make the radio system fuse to blow up. Does **anyone know**... http://bit.ly/7dhCW (expand)
2 minutes ago from *Tweetbots* · Reply · View Tweet

KPneptuness: **anyone know** who's gonna be on alexa??
2 minutes ago from *txt* · Reply · View Tweet

singedhalo: **anyone know** the name of that real estade DB that the agents use? It's a 4 letter acronym I think...
2 minutes ago from *TweetDeck* · Reply · View Tweet

dftba4life: carolyn might be coming with me on vaCA! yay! :) and i must see harry potter again preferably next time in imax **anyone know** where one is?
2 minutes ago from *web* · Reply · View Tweet

alisoncusano: I always see the same 2homeless ladies in times sq. One walks completely bent over and they have matching outfets. **Anyone know** who I'm t ...
3 minutes ago from *txt* · Reply · View Tweet

carla24: **Anyone know** any Canadian sites besides transit/Aldo to buy shoes?
3 minutes ago from *TwitterFon* · Reply · View Tweet

Figure 2.6 A random search at search.twitter.com for the keyword phrase "anyone know" suggests that a call for help—or at least a call like this—goes out on Twitter several times a minute.

Hidden among the announcements about the type of music they're listening to or the work they're doing, you'll see questions about how to fix this problem, where they can buy that gizmo, or even what they should have for supper. (Twitter users do seem to think about food a lot!)

Some of those questions are a bit silly. Some though are very technical, but Twitter can actually answer them.

The answer to singedhalo's question about the real estate database, for example, was "MLS." It took less than four minutes to come in. (And if you want to know what "MLS" stands for, don't ask me; ask someone on Twitter.)

So that's the history, and that's where Twitter came from. It's an incredibly simple tool that's already had a massive impact on people's lives. Growing out of social media sites to focus on just one tiny action, it's become hugely popular with some of the world's smartest people and highest earners. It's pulled innocents out of prison and given a lost pastor a place to sleep.

It's useful. It's important. And it can generate earnings for any Internet marketer.

But you have to know how to use it. In the rest of this book, I'm going to reveal all of the most important tips, strategies, and approaches to getting the most out of Twitter.

It's going to be hands-on, practical, comprehensive, and results-driven.

So let's start right at the beginning . . .

3

Getting Started the Right Way on Twitter

A large part of Twitter's beauty is its simplicity. Sign up to many of the other social networking sites and you'll be asked questions about your life that cover everything from where you went to school to your favorite color.

On Twitter, people are happy to let everyone know what they had for lunch (as well as breakfast, supper, brunch, afternoon snack, and what they dunked in their coffee), but that's not because Twitter asks them to.

In fact, the site keeps everything very clean and easy to use.

In this chapter, I'm going to help you get to grips with the basics of Twitter. It's not difficult to understand, but you will need to know the way the site works and how to use it. I'll explain what happens during registration, what followers and tweets are, and how to send and receive those all-important messages.

Signing Up—Does Twitter Have the Web's Most Friendly Registration Page?

At some point, every Internet entrepreneur is going to face a dilemma. They look at Google's home page with its white space and single line search box and they realize that simple is good.

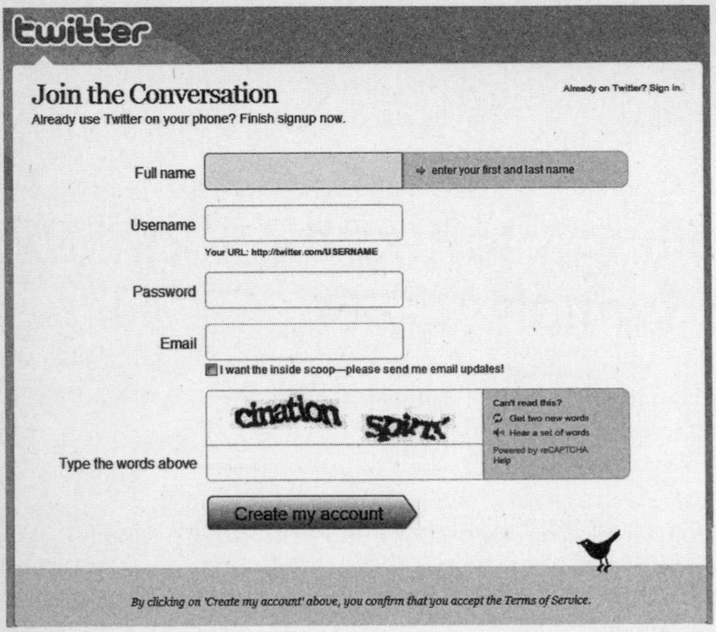

Figure 3.1 Join the conversation, but introduce yourself first.

Then they look at the list of all the features they want their site to include and they stuff their home page and their registration page—and every other page—with features and information that only a fraction of their users will want and only a few people will ever use.

It's just too tempting, and it's a mistake that gums up the works of businesses as varied as dating services and networking sites.

Twitter didn't make that mistake. Hit the big green button on their home page—it's unmissable—and you'll be taken to a sign-up page that has just four fields: name, username, password, and email address. (See Figure 3.1.)

You'll also be asked to enter a couple of words to prove that you're human.

It couldn't be simpler, could it?

Well, actually, this is where simple can be bad.

It's the first place you can make a mistake.

Twitter asks for two names because those names appear in different places and in different ways.

Your full name will appear on the right side of the page, above your mini bio. It will also be used to identify your tweets on some third-party clients such as Twitterific.

Your username, though, isn't just a phrase you're going to enter when you sign in. It will form part of your URL and will be visible whenever you promote your Twitter page.

It's like a choosing a domain name for a web site. Choose poorly and you could affect your Twitter account's ability to gather followers and build a reputation. If people who know you can't find you on Twitter because they can't figure out your username, you'll be missing opportunities.

Your username might be one of the first things you enter, but it should be an item you think about deeply.

Your full name is often a possibility, provided it hasn't been taken already and provided you can squeeze it into the space available (you've got just 15 characters), but another good option is to use your web site's domain name. That would link your site together with your Twitter account and make clear that the one is just a natural extension of the other.

Whatever you choose, just make sure that it's:

1. Closely associated with you

The formula "twitter.com/username" makes finding people on Twitter very easy. If you don't want to search around for someone, you can just pop their name after "twitter.com" and see if they're there. (Usually, when writing about Twitterers, the "twitter.com/" is replaced with "@".)

It's very simple, and it means you can have hours of (almost) endless fun. Try surfing to twitter.com/billgates, for example, or twitter.com/stevejobs. Or toss in any other celebrity you can think of and try to spot which are real Twitterers.

But people are only going to be able to use this easy URL facility to find you if your username is a phrase that's closely associated with you. (See Figures 3.2 and 3.3.)

Figures 3.2 and 3.3   This is the username that I chose for my Twitter page, and this is how it appears in the browser. Creative? Nope. Memorable and easy to find? Absolutely!

That's made even more important by Twitter's on-site search engine, which is very precise. While Facebook's search engine will return suggestions and near-misses if it can't find an exact match, Twitter will just tell you that it can't find the person you're looking for.

If you've picked a random username, you've left a valuable advantage on the table.

2. **Easy to remember**

If a username is closely associated with you, it should be easy to remember, but that isn't always the case. Opt for something long to make it stand out and you'll increase the chances that even a small typo will send potential followers the wrong way.

Tossing in numbers as a way of keeping a version of common name to yourself works fine in passwords but as a username that's going to form part of your URL, it's a strict no-no.

Keep it short, simple to remember, and closely associated with who you are and what you do.

You can change your Twitter URL, but if you're going to do that, you should do it good and early. Creating a new name after you've already created a long list of followers may confuse them. While you'll keep your followers, you'll lose the old conversations that will only be visible on your old account. It's something you should really try to avoid.

Twitter works best when the account feels personal, so in general the best bet is to *put your real full name in the first field and use either your name or the name of your business as your username.*

Who's on Twitter? Your First Followers!

Once you've entered your name, picked a username, chosen a password, and proven that you're a human being and not a robot bent on sending everyone spam, you'll begin a two-step process that will start you following people on Twitter.

None of these steps takes more than a minute or two, but the good news is you can skip them if you want to.

The even better news is that you *should* skip the first step—at least for now.

The first request Twitter will make is for you to search any online mail service that you use—such as Hotmail, Yahoo!, and Gmail—to see whether anyone with the email addresses listed in your address book has already registered an account at Twitter. (See Figure 3.4.)

Clearly, that's going to be very, very helpful.

It means that you can start following your friends and contacts right away. And it means too that you can bring in everyone you know so that they're following you.

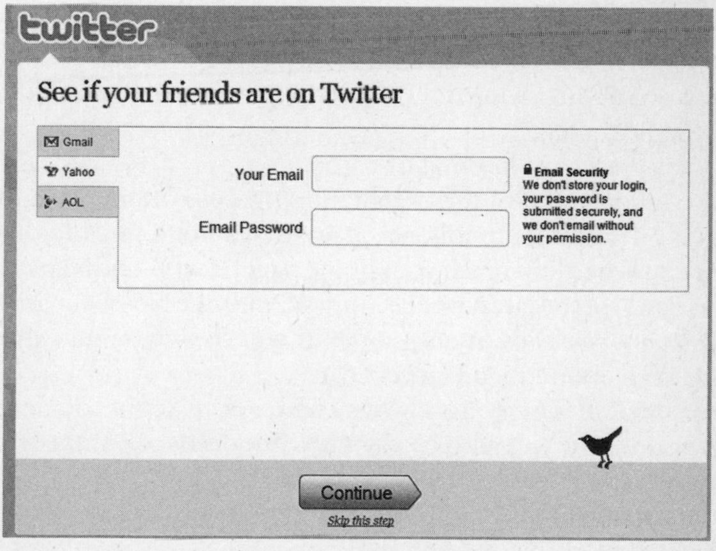

Figure 3.4 You can start searching on Twitter even before you've created your profile. But you should probably create your profile first.

So why do I think you should skip this stage when you sign up?

The most powerful way to win followers on Twitter is to follow them yourself.

If you start following people on Twitter, they'll receive a message saying that you're following them.

They'll then come to your Twitter page, and at this stage of your registration what will they see?

Nothing.

You haven't uploaded a picture yet. You haven't designed your Twitter page yet.

You haven't even issued a tweet yet!

Why would anyone choose to follow a twitterer with a profile like that?

Being able to see which of your friends and contacts are already on Twitter—and follow them all right away—is such a valuable tool that you shouldn't waste it on an empty Twitter page. Wait until your own profile is ready.

Until then, following your friends and contacts is going to be more valuable for Twitter, which will pick up referrals to everyone on your contact list, than it will be to you.

You will be able to come back to this step later when your profile is ready, so my advice would be to skip this step for now and move on to the next step.

So that you can skip that one, too.

The second step of the registration process offers you a bunch of leading Twitterers to follow. Again, that's not a terrible thing. It means that when you reach your home page, it won't be blank. You'll have a bunch of the latest tweets from people like Neil Gaiman, Paula Abdul, and all sorts of other people. It will show you quickly what Twitter is all about. (See Figure 3.5.)

But you'll be discovering what Twitter is all about soon enough anyway, and these twitterers—with hundreds of thousands of followers—are unlikely to follow you back.

Your profile will show that you're following lots of people but that no one is following you.

Ideally, you want your Twitter profile to have more followers than the numbers of people you're following. I'll explain why that's important later in this book, but for now understand that when

Figure 3.5   Ooh, look, celebrities on Twitter. But is that what you came for?

you follow many more people than are following you, you look like someone in search of a party. When more people are following you, *you* are the party.

When you start out on Twitter, you're always going to be following more people than are following you, so at this stage, it's not a huge issue. Don't follow everyone that Twitter throws at you on registration, but if you see someone who looks interesting feel free to add them.

Create an Inviting Twitter Profile

Skip past the instant searching and follow suggestions and you'll be taken right into your Twitter page. (See Figure 3.6.)

At this stage, there won't be much to see.

You'll have the default blue background. Your profile image will consist of the default brown square with the odd "o_O" logo inside.

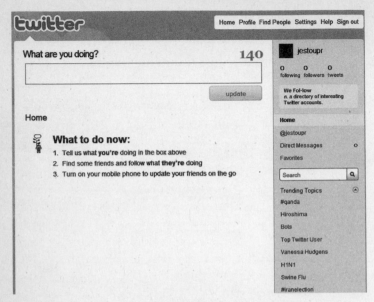

Figure 3.6   A brand new Twitter profile. Think of it as a blank canvas on which you're about to create a marketing masterpiece and start at the very top, not the bottom.

And you'll have no followers, you'll be following no one, and you'll have no updates.

This, though, isn't the page that your followers will see when they stop by to read your tweets. You can see that page by clicking the link marked "tweets" on the right. Once you're up and running on Twitter, it will show all of the tweets you've posted. Anyone can see this page by surfing to twitter.com/[your username] or by clicking on a link to your username anywhere on Twitter.

Those tweets will also be visible on this page—your Twitter home page—but they'll be surrounded by the tweets posted by the people you've chosen to follow. This is your reading page. It's the page you see when you open Twitter. Only you get to see it, and it will be unique because only you will have chosen to follow that particular mixture of Twitterers.

There are a number of links on this page that you need to be familiar with. The link marked "following" in the sidebar on the right will show you a list of the people you've chosen to follow. You'll be

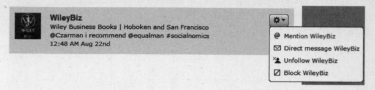

Figure 3.7   You can do four things with the people you follow, from talking to blocking.

able to choose to display them as a list of avatars, usernames and names, or in an expanded form, with bios and last tweets. You'll also be able to interact with those people in up to four different ways. (See Figure 3.7.)

"Mention" another Twitterer and you'll send a tweet that automatically includes their username. That shortens the number of remaining characters you have available, but the person you mention will be able to see that tweet very easily and write back to you. You don't have to push the link on your "following" list to do this. Pressing the reply link on one of their tweets does exactly the same thing, and so does manually writing the username into your tweet.

You can also send a direct message to someone you're following—but only if they're also following you. These land in a private inbox and can only be read by the person who receives them. Direct messages were a very useful idea once, but inboxes have now become collections of automated messages and spam requests. I've given up on them. Once you've built your Twitter account, you will too.

You can also choose to "unfollow" someone who is following you, which removes them from your list, and to "block" someone, which removes you from their list. Your tweets will no longer appear on their Twitter page, and the only way they can read what you're writing is to surf directly to your timeline. That can be useful if you're being bothered by someone, but mostly you'll find yourself using it to block the porn bots that crop up on your "follower" list every now and then.

Clicking to see your list of followers—the people who have chosen to follow your tweets—will reveal largely the same options.

Figure 3.8 Two different ways to follow the people who are following you.

You'll be able to mention a follower in your tweet, send a direct message, and block them. The list will also indicate whether or not you're already following someone following you, and if you're not following them, it will provide a way to do so—twice. (See Figure 3.8.)

Beneath the links to your followers, the list of people you're following, and your tweets, you'll be able to see a small box with a link to a featured Twitter service. These are services that have been created by companies or individuals not linked to Twitter but who have built on Twitter's platform to increase its features. Occasionally, one of those will be marked "sponsored," suggesting that Twitter is planning to use this space for advertising. At the moment, there doesn't seem to be any direct way for other companies to advertise in these spots nor, more importantly, to target their ads to keywords in tweets. It is something to keep an eye on though.

There are four links below the ad space. "Home" takes you back to your Twitter home page, but the link beneath that marked "@[username]" is very important. You should find yourself clicking it frequently—*at least once a day*.

This link shows all of the tweets that have mentioned your username. Usually those will consist of public messages deliberately aimed at you. Sometimes, they may also be tweets that talk about you. Either way, you'll want to see them and perhaps reply to them in return.

That link—and it's likely to be the one you use most on Twitter—is followed by a link to your direct messages and to your favorites, an easy way of marking tweets that you want to find later.

You'll then reach a search box. The link to tweets that mention your username won't reveal who's talking about your product or your industry, your real name, or any other keyword phrase you might want to track on Twitter. It just tracks your username. You can enter other keyword phrases in the search box and—very helpfully—you can save those searches too, making it very easy to follow what other Twitterers are saying about the topics most important to you. When Twitter rolls out its geolocation service, you'll even be able to restrict those searches to people in your area, allowing you to target a local market. Those saved searches will appear in a list below the search box.

Finally, you'll be able to see a list of "trending topics," subjects that are currently the most popular on Twitter, and another list of people you're currently following, too.

Of course, all of these lists will only start to fill when you begin tweeting and using Twitter.

That's what we're going to do now.

At the top of the page is a box in which you can make your first tweet, and beneath that is a list of things that Twitter thinks you should do next.

Those aren't the things you should do next. You certainly shouldn't start by telling "us what you're doing in the box above."

Who's "us"?

Certainly not the people at Twitter. They aren't going to read every first tweet sent by every new Twitterer.

And certainly not your followers. You don't have any! Sending a tweet at this stage won't do you any harm, but it won't do you any good either. No one will read it.

Or at least no one will read it until they've started following you. At that time, they'll be free to see the first tweet you uploaded, which, because you just did it to see what this tweeting thing is all about, might not be very interesting at all.

It's a bit like uploading a random Web page just to see what creating a Web page is like and then leaving it up for all future users to look at.

(And in case you were wondering, my first tweet back in May 2007 was: "Checking out twitter for the first time." You can see it, and lots of others, at www.myfirsttweet.com. Like I said, the first tweet is rarely interesting.)

So forget about sending tweets for now.

Don't worry about finding some friends to follow.

And you certainly don't need to concern yourself about turning on your mobile to update your friends while you're on the go.

Instead, click the "settings" link at the top of the page and give yourself a proper profile.

You'll be presented with a form that looks a lot like the sort of forms you're used to filling in on social media sites. You'll have a list of questions to answer that look simple but that actually require a little thought. (See Figure 3.9.)

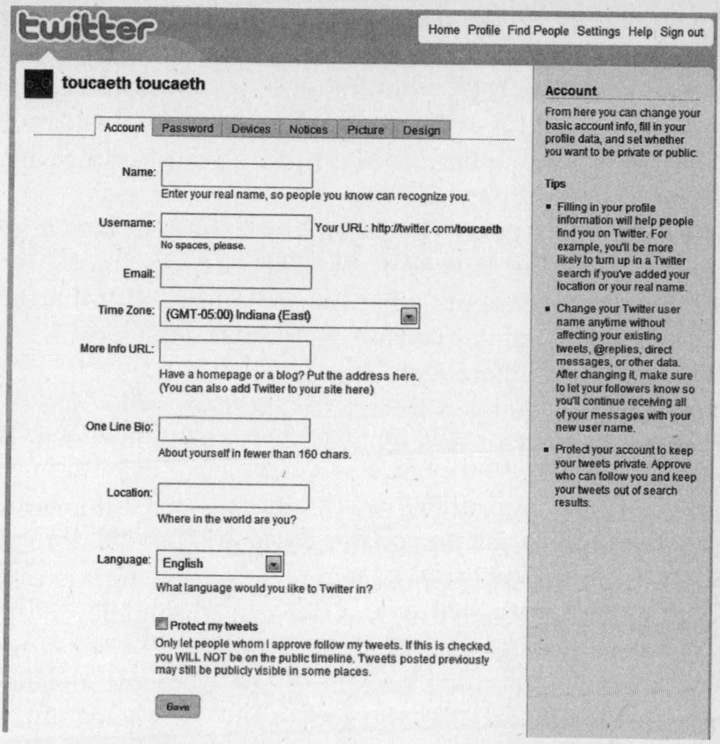

Figure 3.9   What Twitter calls "settings" actually offers a lot more than technical choices. It's one of the most important pages for successful Twitter marketing.

NAME AND USERNAME

That starts with your name.

Yes, you should know your name, and that question shouldn't be hard. But it might be.

You probably have more than one name. You have a name. Your web site might have a name. Your business might have a completely different name.

And that's assuming you just have one business and one web site.

I've already pointed out the importance of choosing a username that can be typed directly into the browser. That's vital, and even though it's going to appear at the top of your profile page, it's never going to be pretty.

Because it's also a URL, whatever phrase you choose is going to appear as one word.

Your "name" will appear on the right of your Twitter page and reveals who you *really* are.

So before you type in your name, *you have to decide which brand you want your Twitter page to represent.*

Will the tweets be about what *you're* doing now or will they be about what your company or your web site is doing now?

Do you see the difference?

It's a vital one, and it will help to determine who follows you, what they're looking for, and what sort of community you're going to build.

The username you choose is as important as the domain name for a web site. It tells readers what to expect.

My followers tend to be people who want tips and advice about Internet marketing. When they look for that advice, they don't turn to my company, Infomedia. They look for me.

My Twitter profile then uses both my username and my real name so that I'm easy to find and so that anyone reading my tweets understands that they're coming directly from me.

They're getting information that they can trust.

In addition, my company also has a timeline to promote our iPhone app. You can find it at @ifart. That's a very different kind of timeline. It's still very interactive. The person who writes it spends a lot of time answering questions from followers and engaging with the community. That's an important part of just about every timeline. But it's a timeline dedicated to a product, and it attracts people who are interested in that product. My followers might be interested in it, too, but they're also interested in topics that have nothing to do with iPhone apps. I get to keep both communities engaged with my company by creating two different timelines for two different timelines: one for me, and one for a product.

Bear in mind that if you do want to create more than one timeline, you will need to use a different email address on each account. That can be a problem if you only have a small number of addresses, so here's a work around: Create a Gmail account and you can place a period in any part of the address. To Gmail, john.doe@gmail.com or even j.oh.nd.oe@gmail.com is the same as johndoe@gmail.com. To Twitter though, those are different addresses, allowing you to use the same Gmail address on multiple accounts.

Note that on the right of this page Twitter points out that you can change your username without affecting the tweets and messages you've already sent and received.

That doesn't mean you should just enter the first username you think of.

Although your current store of messages will be safe, you will have to tell your followers about the change. When you've got a lot of followers—and use the strategies in the next chapter and you *will* have a lot of followers—that's always going to be a real pain.

In fact, one good strategy when you join Twitter is to open multiple accounts so that you can tweet about different subjects on different timelines. Twitter doesn't allow cybersquatting—and Twitterers who have tried it have had their accounts suspended—but if you think you might need more than one account, then it's worth reserving your usernames sooner rather than later.

Twitter is becoming a popular place!

EMAIL

Your choice of name and username isn't going to be too difficult. If you have more than one identity or brand, it might take a little thought, but usually the choice should be fairly clear, and you can always create more than one account. You'll need to use a separate email account for each timeline, so the only limit will be the number of email accounts you can rustle up.

That means your choice of email is a lot easier.

This isn't an email address that anyone is going to see.

If people want to contact you through Twitter, they'll have to do it either by replying to one of your tweets or by sending you a direct message.

But they won't see your email address.

The address you enter here will only be used to receive information such as Twitter's newsletters and to change your password.

If you're the kind of person who tends to forget passwords, that second use can be pretty helpful! Make sure then that you choose an email address that you actually use.

#Elevate 2008 is over! A truly amazing event and I'm now ready for vacation :-)
about 7 hours ago from web

Did you miss Saturday Night Live from Elevate 2008? The replay is now available! http://tinyurl.com/62elhh *1:30 AM yesterday from web*

30 minutes to Elevate LIVE! There's never been a live show like this... http://tinyurl.com/jclive 10 pm EDT, 7 pm PDT! *10:27 PM Oct 25th from web*

Figure 3.10   Three different kinds of time stamp on my tweets as seen by a follower. One of them was right, but at least they're in the right order—and that's what counts!

Time Zone

Time on the Internet tends to be a pretty strange thing. Check your email client and you might find all sorts of strange times attached to the emails you've received, and often they look like they have no relationship at all to the time the message was sent.

Usually, that doesn't matter at all.

On Twitter though, because tweets describe what you're doing *now*, time is important. (See Figure 3.10.)

So for the most recent posts, Twitter displays how long ago the tweets were sent. If a tweet is a day old, though, the time stamp refers to the time the tweet was sent based on the time zone *the follower* entered on the settings page.

I think that's a bit confusing. I'd rather know what time of day the person I'm following sent his tweets according to *my* time zone.

Again, it's not a hard question, but I think this is one that Twitter got wrong.

More Info URL

And now we come to something that's really crucial.

Twitter's profile appears to provide space to promote just one web site. In fact, as I'll point out later in this section, with a little creativity it's possible to promote all the web sites you want.

But even then, one web site—the link that appears beneath your name on the right of the screen—will always be the most prominent.

It's the one that people will click to find out exactly who you are and what lies behind this Twitterer.

That makes the link very, very powerful.

Usually, you'll want to link to your main web site. Sometimes, though, you might want to change this link to suit a particular promotion. If you were promoting a new ebook or affiliate product, for example, you could tweet about it on Twitter and link from your profile to a landing page.

Your tweets then would become another channel to bring potential buyers to your store.

Do you see how useful this can be?

But don't use a shortened URL in this space. Because Twitter leaves such a small amount of room in the text box, you will need to use shortened links in your tweets. But you want the full address in your profile page. That should help to generate curiosity, and even if it doesn't generate a click right away, it should increase name recognition for your web site.

One-Line Bio

So far, all of the fields I've discussed have been very, very simple.

They're very important—and you should know that they're much more important than they look—but none of them should have you scratching your head for more than a few seconds.

Your bio will take some effort and a fair bit of thought, too.

Writing about yourself is never much fun. That's especially true when you're doing it for business. You have to find the things in your life that are interesting to others, make yourself appear a professional, and do it all without boasting or sounding vain.

Usually, that's pretty hard.

Twitter makes it a real challenge.

It only gives you 160 characters.

That's right, you get just 20 more characters than you have to write a tweet to describe your entire life history.

What a relief!

That means you can't go into detail, talk about all the things you've done and what you do for others. All you can do is choose one or two of the most important facts about you and write a sentence. (See Figure 3.11.)

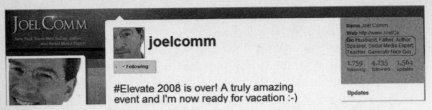

Figure 3.11 My bio as it used to appear on Twitter. Should I include my location here? Maybe, but it's not critical and might localize my brand too much.

For a long time, my bio, for example, used to say:

"Husband, Father. Author. Speaker, Social Media Expert, Teacher. Generally Nice Guy."

That's a very simple structure to follow, and you could use exactly the same model or produce your own. If you publish a sports web site, for example, you could write something like:

"Football fan, youth coach, and all-round sports nut with dodgy knees."

The format is three one- or two-word phrases that describe who you are or what you do, followed by a short joke to finish it off.

If you wanted to create a bio like this, you don't have to do any more than fill in these blanks:

"[Professional description 1], [Professional description 2], and [Professional description 3] who likes to [Personal description]."

A professional photographer looking to use Twitter to promote his services could easily use that format to create a bio that said:

"Wedding photographer, portrait pro, and creative artist who likes to photograph his kids at embarrassing moments."

A landscape contractor could come up with a bio that said:

"Tree surgeon, garden expert, and green-fingered designer who likes to smell freshly cut grass."

And someone who blogs about sports could use that format to create this bio:

"Lakers fan, Mets nut, and fantasy football coach who likes to tailgate downwind of the barbeques."

Do you see how bios like these leave room for just two or three basic facts about you while still allowing space for a little personal touch? That's all you have room for on Twitter, and it's all you need. It's a strategy that many people on the site have chosen to follow and for good reason: It's easy and it works.

And if people want to find out more they can always come to your web site. (I told you that link was going to be important!)

So one way of writing your Twitter bio is to summarize yourself in 160 characters. That's the approach I've chosen, and it's a very simple one.

An alternative approach is to write a bio that discusses a particular project.

This is a very different use of Twitter. Instead of tweeting about you in general, you'll be tweeting on one theme, which you can then change when that project ends.

British comedy actor and writer Stephen Fry (@stephenfry), for example, is known for being tech-savvy. He has a web site that he updates frequently and on which he blogs, vlogs, and podcasts. He also tweets several times a day, even when he's working.

He probably does that mostly because he enjoys it—tweeting is fun, after all—but there's no question that his tweets also help to generate interest in his latest projects so that when they're released, they already have an audience.

In the fall of 2008, for example, the BBC sent Stephen Fry around the world to film a documentary series about endangered animals. Fry constantly changed his location to reflect where he was tweeting from and updated his bio to describe what he was doing at the time. (See Figure 3.12.)

His tweets still helped to promote his personal brand. They were still about what he was doing at the time (and yes, that included

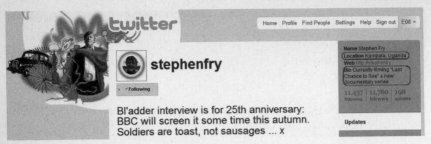

Figure 3.12 With about 800,000 followers, British celebrity Stephen Fry is one of Twitter's top users. Look at how he uses his bio and his current location to promote his latest project.

descriptions of what he was eating for breakfast at the hotel). *But because the bio placed them in the context of a large project, those tweets were easier for new followers to understand and they had a very strong promotional effect.*

This is something that any marketer could do. (See Figure 3.13.)

A photographer sent to Alaska for a week to shoot oil wells could change the location to reflect where he is now and alter his bio:

"Currently shooting oil wells in Alaska for Shell."

A landscape contractor could edit his bio to describe a big project he's been hired to complete:

"Now designing the flowerbeds for Ventura's new Ben Sheffer Park."

And someone who was writing an ebook about fantasy football could write this in his bio:

"Now working on the ultimate guide to real success with fantasy football."

Since putting this book together, for example, I've changed my bio to emphasize my work with Twitter:

Tweets describe what you're doing at one particular moment. They can't describe what you're doing over a period that lasts days,

Figure 3.13 Bios like these look like tweets themselves, but they're not.

weeks, or months. Your bio can do that, and when it does it focuses your tweets onto that one project.

When you have a lot of followers, it can be a very powerful way of promoting your work.

LOCATION

After asking you to sum up your life in 160 characters, Twitter then asks "Where in the world are you?"

We've already seen how changing your location to reflect where you happen to be working on a particular project can be very helpful.

Usually though, you'll be working in the same place most of the time so you should be a little careful here.

I don't try to hide the fact that I live in Loveland, Colorado. In fact, I talk about it quite a lot on my blog. It's a beautiful place, and I feel very blessed that I'm able to live here.

But my products have nothing to do with my location. When I attend conferences, I meet people from around the country, and I know that my books, courses, and products are used by people around the world.

I don't think that placing my location on my bio would really affect my branding, but I don't want people to feel that my work is somehow connected to Colorado. It isn't, so I chose to leave it off.

If there's a chance that your location could localize your work, then you might want to leave the location off, too.

PROTECT MY UPDATES

I'll skip the language setting because that's pretty self-explanatory. The last option on this page, though, is perhaps the most important of all.

Twitter's last question is whether you want to keep your tweets confidential so that only the people you approve see them, or whether you're prepared to let anyone at all see them.

If you're using Twitter for marketing, do not click this box.

You want to let anyone see your tweets who wants to. You want as many people as possible to come to your Twitter page, realize that you have fantastic, interesting tweets that they want to read, and sign up to be your followers.

If people can't see your updates, they're not going to sign up. You'll be restricted to tweeting to the friends, family, and contacts that you've chosen.

That's like a store owner hanging a "closed" sign on the door and only dealing with her friends.

If you want to tweet only about personal stuff, that's fine. But it's a different use of Twitter. If you want to use Twitter to build your brand and grow your business, then leave that box unchecked.

Choosing Your Twitter Picture

All of your profile information is reached by clicking the Settings link at the top of the page, and then the tab marked "Account."

There are seven settings tabs altogether, but initially you'll only see six. (See Figure 3.14.) The Connections tab is only added when you choose to work with certain APIs—services that extend the power of Twitter (I'll talk about those later). For now I also want to skip past the Password, Devices, and Notices settings and continue with the tabs that relate to your profile—the way you'll appear to followers.

I believe that you should first prepare your page before you start sending and receiving tweets. Once you've completed your bio (and yes, you can change it later if you're not completely satisfied with it), your next step should be to upload a picture.

Account	Password	Devices	Notices	Picture	Design	Connections

Figure 3.14 You won't see the Connections tab when you join Twitter. But you will find that the site places your bio information under the Account tab and separates Picture and Design.

You will need to upload a picture to your Twitter profile.
There's no getting around this step.

If you don't add a photo to your profile, you'll appear on the page as two strange circles. That's not very attractive, and worst of all, it makes you look like you're not serious about your time on Twitter.

When people have added their photo they'll expect to see yours in return.

And it has to be a good picture, too, one that portrays you as both professional and personable—exactly what your tweets should be doing.

Remember though that the picture itself is going to appear very small. While the image is clickable and can be seen in full size, few people bother so it's a good idea to use a close-up of your face that makes you recognizable, even when you're no bigger than a thumbnail. Try to include a full-body shot and your expression will probably appear no larger than a couple of millimeters on someone's screen.

You'll usually be better off with a good portrait that shows you smiling and at ease.

That's easier said than done, and in practice people make a lot of mistakes here.

Spend any time at all on social networking sites and you'll see photograph after photograph that look blurry, unfocused, or are just plain inappropriate. Here are number of guidelines to follow when adding your picture to any social media site, including Twitter:

♦ Don't hold the camera yourself.

Showing your arm doesn't look cool. In fact, it looks like you couldn't find a friend to hold the camera for you, or you don't know how to work the camera's self-timer. Neither of those creates good impressions—and neither creates good pictures either.

The pictures that I use on my social media sites have all been professionally shot. If you're serious about marketing with social media, that's something you might want at least to consider, too. You can either visit a local photography studio or use BetterTweetShots.com, a service that will send you to a local hand-picked photographer who will shoot a selection of portraits specifically for online use at prices that start at $99.

Alternatively, you can just ask someone to lend you a hand so that you don't have to show your arm.

♦ Use a good camera.

Many laptops today come with built-in webcams. Desktop Web cameras are almost as standard as a keyboard and mouse, and even the cheapest mobile phone comes complete with a lens, email facility, and practically a portable photography studio, too.

Don't use them.

Cameras like these tend to produce low-quality images that have lots of distortion. They're hard to focus and often produce images that are grainy rather than clear.

If you want to video conference with a friend or a business partner on the other side of the country, your webcam will do a fine job. I use mine all the time.

If you want to snap your friends at a birthday dinner, your mobile phone is just the ticket.

But when you're creating a portrait that will represent you on a social media site, use a real camera. Nothing else is good enough.

♦ Keep the backgrounds to a minimum.

Because you have such a tiny amount of space to squeeze your picture into, anything in the background is going to interfere with the most important item in the frame: you.

Ideally, your features should fill most of the frame. And behind you there should be just about nothing.

You might be able to get away with a horizon line, the sea or the sky, but if the background is busy in any way—if it shows trees, parts of buildings, or your car—it's going to distract from your portrait and look unfocused.

Find a nice white wall or a good high balcony and stand your friend, with the camera, directly in front of you.

♦ Show yourself.

And finally, use *your* picture, not a photograph of your cat, your dog, your hamster, your favorite comic book hero, or some squiggle that you feel might do a good job of representing you.

If you're tweeting on behalf of your company, then you can get away with using your company logo. Other than that, though, you'll need to use your photograph.

Social media is all about personal branding. It's about the connections you build as an individual and how you work that network.

To create those connections, you can't be a wallflower. You need to show your face. So shy or not, you need to upload a picture to your profile.

And it has to be a good one!

Designing Your Twitter Profile

Now we really get down to business.

When it comes to choosing your profile picture, there's really only one option. You want to make it a close-up of your face and make it fill the frame so that no one has to squint to look at you.

Your profile design is a lot more complicated.

I've pointed out that Twitter leaves you very little room for creativity in your bio. You're not going to be able to say too much when you only have 160 characters.

And the site is very tight-fisted with the links, too. Most of us have more than one site we'd like to promote, and it would also be good to bring Twitter's users into our Facebook network, Flickr streams, and even MySpace pages.

Why restrict your followers to just one marketing channel?

Being forced to place just one link on your profile is like taking a kid to a candy store and telling him he can choose only one piece of candy.

The background image gives you a chance to have it all.

But you'll have to do a bit of planning.

Figure 3.15   Twitter's profile design options are a lot more flexible—and much more useful—than they look.

Twitter gives you a selection of 12 background images to choose from. (See Figure 3.15.)

You don't want to choose any of them. *You want to create your own background and upload it by clicking the "Change background image" link beneath Twitter's designs.*

Instead of leaving the left side of your Twitter page blank or filled with some strange design, you want to use that space to promote your business. (See Figure 3.16.)

That strip is valuable real estate, and not using it is as good as leaving money on the table.

Figure 3.17 shows what my Twitter profile looks like.

It was created for me by TweetPages, a design firm that specializes in Twitter backgrounds. You can find them at twitpwr.com/tpjc. I think they do fine work, and I've negotiated a discount for Twitter Power readers. Use coupon code TWTPWR to save 10 percent on your order.

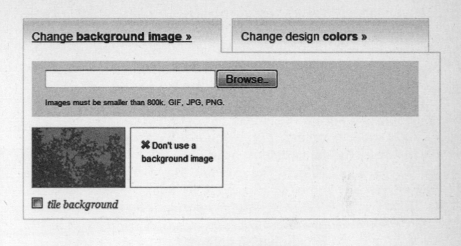

Figure 3.16 Change your background image and start building on your Twitter real estate.

Figure 3.17 My specially constructed Twitter background explains who I am, promotes my sites and my books, and tells people how to get in touch. It's also got a fun approach. What will yours do?

Take a look at the left side of the screen. You can think of it as having four separate sections.

The first section is the top-left hand corner. This is where the page begins so it needs to function as an introduction. It should say who you are and indicate with a glance what you do.

On my profile, I've done that with a stylized version of my name. You could also put your logo here.

Remember that unlike a conventional Web page, this won't be the first place the user will look. Your latest tweet will always be far more prominent and draw the eye first. The user will then look at the top left-hand corner to see who is providing these tweets.

That means this corner should contain an image or text that's visually enticing and that draws the viewer down the column.

Then there's the information column.

On most Twitter profiles, this is just a vertical bar that runs alongside the tweets and tells followers basic information about the Twitterer and—even more importantly—where they can go to find out more. It might even be a list of URLs.

TweetPages designed my info column to show on the right side of the background, rather than the traditional left side. In fact, the background is designed to view nicely in the most popular resolutions. (See Figure 3.18.)

Figure 3.18 TweetPages designed my background so it would look great in just about every browser viewing resolution. Clever, huh?

Pictures of me. Now it's your turn.

I opted to go with a playful design for my Twitter background. With the recent success I've had in developing iPhone applications (yes, I am creator of the now world-famous iFart Mobile application!), I feel like it reflects my personality and stands out from the rest of the crowd.

Of course, one of the beautiful things about having a custom Twitter background is that you can change it whenever you like. So I'll probably use the current background for a few months and then try something different. You don't have to place a picture of yourself on your background if you don't want to. It depends on the nature of your business and what you're promoting with Twitter.

If you're promoting your personal brand, using an image—or a series of images—that's larger than the tiny box provided for your profile can be very helpful.

People will see your profile thumbnail on someone else's Twitter page then click it to see who you are. They'll reach your profile and by seeing a second photo will feel that they're getting more than the simple introduction the thumbnail provides. They'll feel that they're getting a peek behind the scenes of your business.

If you're promoting a product or a brand, though, you could place a picture of that product here or simply go straight into the text on the information bar.

That begins with a brief introduction. One option is simply to thank people and tell them how they can learn more about you:

I can understand why Twitter shied away from calling connections "friends" in the way that Facebook does. The contacts you make online aren't like real-life friendships. They're important, they're valuable, and some of them might be your friends as well. But this is a whole new kind of relationship. It's lighter, faster, and less demanding. You're not going to be picking up your followers at the airport at three o'clock in the morning. Your friends shouldn't be afraid to ask.

But "followers" isn't right either. Communities might have leaders, but the other people in the group rarely regard themselves as followers—not outside church anyway.

I prefer to thank people for connecting with me, rather than for following me. (See Figure 3.19.)

Thanks for connecting with me on Twitter! Here are other places you can find me online:

Figure 3.19 If you are going to thank someone on your profile page, thank them for "connecting" with you. Don't thank them for "following" you.

You can use that format too if you want. Or you can use a format that I used on a previous version of my profile. That version said:

> *"Follow me and learn as I tweet about marketing, social media, and much more."*

It's a very simple model to copy that provides information about the benefits of becoming a follower, says something about what you do, and also functions as a "call to action," encouraging people to hit that "Follow" button.

So if you wanted your Twitter page to promote a blog about your travel experiences, you could write:

> *"Follow me as I travel the world, visit ancient sites, and eat some very strange food."*

It's very simple, and it can be very effective.

The bulk of the information bar is just a list of links that tell followers where they can go to discover more. Again this is very simple *but it could well be the most important part of your Twitter presence.*

You can have all the followers you want. You could have tens of thousands of people reading your tweets every day and telling all their friends about you. But if that's all they do, they're going to be of no use to you.

You need them to come to your other web sites. You need them to click your ads or buy your products.

You need them to help you make money—and that's not going to happen directly on Twitter. It can only happen by sending them to your other sites.

This sidebar is the place to tell them where they can find those sites.

Note how I provide lots of different options, and how I use headings to make the differences between those options clear.

This is a very different strategy to one that you might be using on your web site. There, you're more likely to use just a few external links so that you can control where your users go and so that those links don't compete with your ads.

Here's the secret: Your sidebar is actually an ad. It functions just like a Google AdSense unit, but it's *your* Google AdSense unit.

AdSense is probably the most used advertising network on the Internet. Operated by Google, the system's ads, delivered automatically and contextualized to match the page content, are what turned the search engine company into a multi-billion-dollar corporation.

And I've done very nicely out of them, too.

You can't put AdSense units on your Twitter page. But you can create your very own AdSense-type unit that promotes you. (See Figure 3.20.)

The design is different, but the principle is exactly the same. You're tweets are your content—good content, of course—and the ad runs alongside it. Naturally, it looks nothing like an ad so that people actually want to look at it, not run away from it.

Figure 3.20   It's not AdSense, but it works like AdSense ... almost.

That's the foundation of smart AdSense implementation, and it works in exactly the same way with these homemade "ads" on Twitter.

And just as an AdSense unit usually includes lots of different links so that readers have a choice and are likely to find at least one of them interesting, your sidebar is more likely to tempt your readers if it's filled with lots of different URLs.

So the headings tell people what sort of content they can find on those sites, and directly beneath those headings are the URLs themselves.

There is, however, one very important difference between your Twitter sidebar and an AdSense unit: You can't click the links in your sidebar.

It's just an image. It doesn't do anything except provide a background to your tweet timeline.

Clearly, that's a huge weakness. You can do something to get around it with some smart design work. I've made the headings and keywords in my information bar blue so that they look like links.

They might not function as links, but they will be as eye-catching as links.

And finally, at the bottom of the page, I've highlighted one particular item that I really want to emphasize. In the past, that was a survey I used to write the first edition of this book and understand how people were using Twitter. Now I place an image of this book there. (See Figure 3.21.) It helps to build trust, and it shows off a product too!

But the beauty of that last section of the information bar is that I can continue changing it.

Whenever you want to promote a new product, all you have to do is edit your background image and change the item at the bottom.

Now, if you're thinking that I should have put that promotion at the top of my information bar, then think again.

Your most important product should go at the top of the information bar—the brand that you want most to promote. In the case of my Twitter page, that's my personal brand.

My Twitter page isn't about my book or whatever product I happen to be promoting hardest at the time. It's about me, so my brand goes at the top of the page. The product is the second most

Figure 3.21 The bottom of my information bar gives a final kick to my promotions.

important item I'd like to promote so that goes at the bottom of the page, together with an image, so that it stands out.

Simple!

One other piece I have included on previous backgrounds is a message at the bottom of the page that tells people I don't answer direct messages. These are tweets that only the sender and the recipient can see. It's a great idea that should have been very useful, but it just hasn't panned out. I get dozens of them every day and most of them are automated. If someone sends an important message to me by direct message, it's just going to get buried. There are better ways to contact me, and I mention one of them here.

Designing a Commercial Background Image for Twitter

Or rather the design is simple, because creating your background image can be a little technical.

It's not *very* technical, but if, like me, you know absolutely nothing about graphic design you might want to outsource the image production itself to a professional designer.

Supply the mock-up, explain what you want the image to include, and let the designer do the hard work of making sure all the figures add up—because your design will need to have all the right dimensions if it's going to succeed.

Hugh Briss, for example, offers customized Twitter backgrounds through his web site TwitterImage.com. Prices start from $100, and he's already created beautiful backgrounds for some of Twitter's biggest users, including Chris Pirillo (@chrispirillo) and blogging expert Darren Rowse (@problogger).

However, I have recently become a huge fan of Matt Clark and his work at TweetPages (twitpwr.com/tpjc). They do great work with prices that range from $23 for the sidebar to $103 for a custom-made design. They also have plenty of free options and 99-cent designs that you can download right away. They're well worth a look. Remember to use coupon code TWITPWR for 10 percent off your order.

That's the easiest option. But actually, there is a whole bunch of different ways of creating a background image for Twitter, and some of them are very easy indeed.

If I can do it, no one has an excuse!

1. DO IT ALL YOURSELF

The hard way is to open up Photoshop (or Gimp or Paint.Net, if you prefer to use a simpler graphics program that doesn't cost anything) and get designing.

Here's what you need to know:

♦ The maximum size for the image is 800kb.

♦ The image dimensions can be flexible. Mine is 1200 × 650, which does the job. You can make it bigger though if you want to make sure that it fills even the biggest screens.

♦ The dimensions of the sidebar on the left are 80 pixels × 587 pixels.

♦ The top of the Twitter logo is 14 pixels from the top of the page. Place the highest point of your first image on the same line and it will be level with the logo.

Note that while you can put a sidebar—or anything else—on the right side of the page, too, there's no guarantee that it will appear on screens with different sizes; on small screens, it could be hidden by the Twitter timeline. If you're putting the sidebar on the left, adding information on the right might also be distracting; you just want your users to see your links and your tweets then surf on to find more. Hugh Briss, though, has come up with some pretty neat designs that use both sides of the screen.

If you've got skills with colors, shapes, and design programs, then you can use these figures to get creative. If you don't, you can keep things simple.

2. USE A FREE TEMPLATE

Twitterer Wayne Sutton (@waynesutton) has uploaded a free template that anyone can download and use as a foundation for their own backgrounds.

You can download the template file from Box.net at www.box.net/shared/lgw2pz4gso. Having saved the file, you'll be able to open it and start making the changes you want to the picture and the text.

That will give you the sidebar, but it won't give you a unique background design for the rest of the page. Fortunately there are a number of ways to deal with that too.

3. USE A FREE BACKGROUND DESIGN

Designer Natalie Jost (@natalie) is giving away a bunch of beautiful background patterns at TwitterPatterns.com. You can only use them on your Twitter page—so no using them on your web site without paying Natalie for her work first—but there are some beautiful choices there. (See Figure 3.22.)

Alternatively, GrungeTextures.com also offers a big selection of textures and backgrounds that you can use under a Creative Commons license.

Figure 3.22   Natalie Jost's Twitterpatterns.com provides a huge range of beautiful background designs . . . and all for free!

Choosing the Right Colors

Creating a tempting background image can be a lot of fun. It might look a little technical, and if you really find it daunting—or want to get something truly unique—you should be able to find a designer who can build something for you.

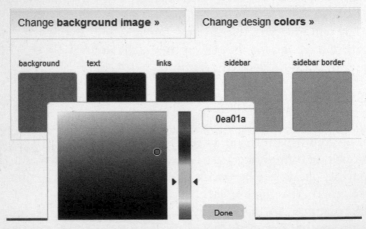

Figure 3.23   Colors are an important part of your Twitter design success. You can choose from a color palette or type the code numbers in manually.

But it's really not necessary. You should be able to knock up something very effective within about half an hour, especially if you're using a template.

Twitter though also lets you choose your color scheme, and this can be a little tricky. The most important thing to bear in mind here is clarity. (See Figure 3.23.)

You want your users to be able to read the text and find the links without having to squint, search or generally become frustrated.

You can set the colors for five of the elements on your Twitter page:

BACKGROUND

If you've created your own background image—and, of course, you should have done—then you won't need to worry about this setting. The color will only appear on the right of the screen where your image ends.

Be sure to make the image large enough to fill even the biggest screen and this color won't be visible.

Just to be safe though, it's probably best to choose a color that matches the color of your background image. The color will be plain and without any design, but the fact that your image is too narrow will be less obvious.

TEXT

The text setting refers only to the color of the words on the sidebar on the right. The Twitter timeline itself will always be black text on a white background.

Unless you've got some fantastic design in mind, make the text black—or some other dark color—and the background of the sidebar a relatively light color so that the text stands out.

Remember that design on the Web is all about results, not effects. You can have the most beautiful color combinations in the world, but if no one can read what you've written or find your links, the design has failed.

LINKS

And that's why your links should always be blue.

Just use the default color that Twitter provides for this setting. It should be absolutely clear to your followers that the reference to your web site is a link and that they can click it to learn more about you.

Confuse them and you'll lose clicks—and possible sales, too.

SIDEBAR

I've already mentioned that your bio sidebar on the right should be a light color so that the text that describes your bio information stands out. But it also needs to complement the design of your background image, so this might require a bit of experimentation.

Gray works well, so if in doubt, choose that.

SIDEBAR BORDER

And finally, the color of the borders in the right sidebar is the least prominent color that will appear on the page. It runs around your bio sidebar and between each of the bio's sections.

In fact, you'll probably only notice it if you get it wrong. Choose something garish, like canary yellow, and you'll see what I mean.

The safest bet is often black but it will really depend on how you've set up your design. Make the sidebar border the same color as the sidebar background and you can get rid of the border altogether—another good choice.

Creating the right background design on Twitter is hugely important. It's a vital opportunity not just to make your Twitter page look good but to broadcast some valuable marketing information, too.

It's worth making the effort to get it right.

Notices to Notice

Once you've created your background image, you'll be ready to start tweeting. Or almost ready, because there are just a couple more small things you still have to do.

The first is to set your notices.

This lets you choose how often you want Twitter to bother you.

If you let it, Twitter will bother you a lot. You want it to bother you sometimes and in ways that help you to build followers and enhance the site's marketing power.

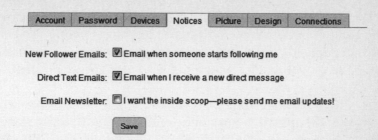

Figure 3.24 Twitter's notices can be a touch confusing.

When Twitter started, one of the options related to @replies. This setting determined whether other people's responses to the tweets they read appeared in your timeline, and if so, which people's. You could choose between showing everyone's replies, only replies sent between people you're following, and showing no replies at all.

That's no longer the case. In a controversial decision, the people at Twitter decided that the only replies that you'll see are those between people you're already following. (See Figure 3.24.)

So if you're following my tweets and I reply to someone else you're following, you'll see that message when you log in to Twitter. But if I reply to someone you're *not* following, you can only see that message by looking at my timeline.

That's both good news and bad news.

The bad news is that you'll be missing opportunities to make new contacts. The benefit of Twitter is that you're able to connect with other people in your industry. And the best way to see who on Twitter is in your industry is by following the conversations and looking at who is talking to whom. If all you do is read the tweets that reach your Twitter page, you're going to be missing out on lots of chats you could join and contacts you could make.

That's why there's also good news. It means that to get the most out of Twitter, it's no longer enough to read the tweets that the site pushes to your Twitter page. You also have to read the tweets on Twitterers' timelines. And when people come to your timeline to see who you're talking to, they'll see your bio, your background, and your link.

Limiting the @replies option might have reduced networking opportunities but it's improved your marketing power.

You should also choose to receive emails when you pick up a *new follower* and when someone sends you a *direct message*—at least initially.

As you're building your follower list, you'll want to see who's joining your community. But once your community really starts to take off and you're getting dozens of new followers a day, those emails will get a bit annoying and will stop being useful.

The same is true of direct messages. As I mentioned, these have become just about worthless. Because so many people use them as autoresponders, thanking others for following them, your inbox will quickly look like a spam folder. And with no search or filtering, it's impossible to find an important message should you receive one. Keep the notification on at the beginning just so that you can see how direct messaging works, but as soon as you get the idea turn it off too.

Auto Nudge will only appear if you've already added a mobile device. It sends a text message to your phone or to your instant messaging account if you haven't sent a tweet in 24 hours. Frankly, I'd rather receive a message telling me I'm tweeting too much. Once you get started, that's a bigger danger than going a day without sending an update.

And finally, receiving the *Twitter newsletter* can be interesting, but not as interesting as reading the Twitter blog, which should become part of your regular Internet browsing. It's always full of useful stuff.

Tweeting with Your Mobile Phone

The last thing you should do before you start sending tweets is to set up your mobile phone.

Twitter began with mobiles in mind, so it's not too surprising that while you can have a lot of fun—and a lot of benefits—with Twitter just using your computer, being able to send and receive tweets from your mobile phone makes the whole experience so much better. (See Figure 3.25.)

You can send out an update while waiting for your meal in a restaurant, while you're standing in line at the DMV, or while you're

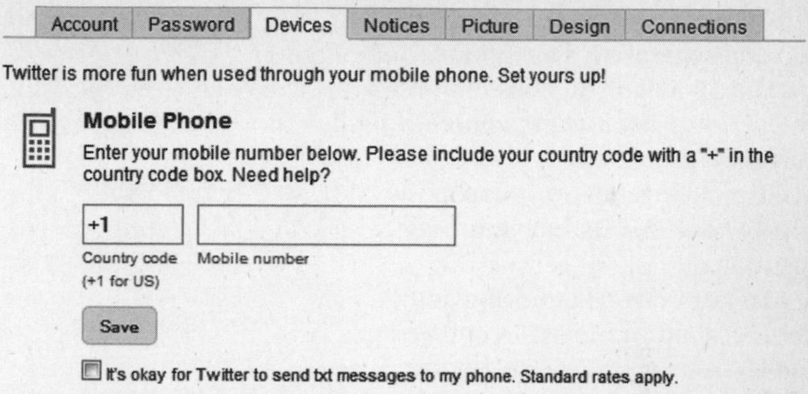

| Account | Password | Devices | Notices | Picture | Design | Connections |

Twitter is more fun when used through your mobile phone. Set yours up!

Mobile Phone

Enter your mobile number below. Please include your country code with a "+" in the country code box. Need help?

| +1 | |

Country code   Mobile number
(+1 for US)

Save

☐ It's okay for Twitter to send txt messages to my phone. Standard rates apply.

Figure 3.25   Twitter also lets you tweet to and from a mobile phone. You can be connected and computer-free.

sitting in the audience at a conference listening to a speaker and sharing what you're hearing with your followers.

It makes the whole thing so much more convenient, and it means that you're much less likely to forget to update.

To send and receive tweets on your mobile, press the Devices tab under "Settings," enter your phone number and click the checkbox that allows you to receive tweets on your phone as SMS messages.

You'll then receive a code. Send that code to 40404 in the United States, 21212 in Canada, 49 17 6888 50505 in Germany, 46 737 494222 in Sweden, 5566511 in India or +44 7624 801423 everywhere else, and your phone will be set up to send and receive tweets. Vodafone subscribers in the United Kingdom can also tweet by texting to 86444.

Twitter Mobile Commands

@username + message

Sends a tweet to another Twitterer. Your message appears as a reply in their timeline.

D username + message

Sends a private message to a Twitterer's device, and saves a copy in their Web archive.

WHOIS username

Lets you read a Twitterer's profile information.

GET username

Retrieves a Twitterer's latest tweet.

Figure 3.26   Twitter Mobile Commands

Because you've agreed to receive tweets on your mobile, though, you are at risk. When you're following lots of people—and to build up followers, you will need to follow lots of people—your phone will be going off all the time.

So before you start following people, send the word "stop" or "quit" from your mobile phone to Twitter's number. That will leave your phone set up to send messages but stop you receiving messages.

Later, you can choose to follow selected Twitterers by sending the message "on username" (e.g. "on joelcomm") so that only the Twitterers you feel are the most important turn up in your phone.

NUDGE username

Asks a Twitterer to post an update.

FAV username

Marks someone's most recent tweet as a favorite.

STATS

Lets you see how many followers you have and how many people you're following.

INVITE phone number

Sends an invitation to join Twitter by SMS to someone's mobile phone.

Figure 3.26 (continued)

That's just one of a bunch of useful commands that you can send to Twitter from your mobile phone once it's set up to send and receive tweets. (See Figure 3.26.)

And that's it!

Once you've done that, you're ready to send your first tweet.

Sending Your Very First Tweet

Hit the home link at the top of the page to return to your Twitter page.

There, at the top of the screen, is Twitter's constant question "What are you doing?"

Beneath it is the space for you to write—in 140 characters—an answer.

So off you go.

Type whatever is going through your mind and hit "update." (See Figure 3.27.)

Figure 3.27   Love your tweet or hate it, once it's up,
Twitter gives you options.

Don't worry if you can't think of anything very smart and witty to write. At this stage, you just want try writing something so that you can see what happens. "Joining Twitter!" is good enough.

Now anyone will be able to read that tweet.

If that sounds like a terrible idea, click the tweet and you'll get a time stamp. Click that time stamp, and you'll get the tweet itself. On the right of the update will be two icons: a star and a trash can.

The star saves the tweet so that you can easily find it again and the trash can deletes the tweet. There's a good chance that you'll find both of those useful.

Becoming a Follower

And the last thing you need to do before you're ready to start building up your Twitter presence is to follow people.

This is the easiest part of Twitter and really the most enjoyable. There are so many amazing people on the site that you shouldn't have any trouble at all finding people whose tweets you want to read and who you want to follow.

If you already know who you want to follow on Twitter, just surf to their Twitter page and hit the "Follow" button. If not, there's a stack of people in the directory at the back of this book who post very interesting updates.

You're welcome to go to @joelcomm and follow me too!

A Word about Security

You're almost ready to start building your followers. Before you head out into the Twitterverse though, a word about security. Twitter's incredible growth has attracted the attention of all sorts of bad guys.

There have been incidents of accounts being hacked and taken over, phishing scams, and password theft. President Obama's account was hijacked by a hacker, as was Rick Warren's. Occasionally, you'll see messages flying around Twitter warning you against clicking a link or following a particular person.

In general, it's a good idea to follow those warnings.

Many apps, too, require you to enter your Twitter username and password. Requests for passwords always give me the creeps, but in practice, so far 99 percent of those requests have been fine. It's no surprise, though, that Twitter is moving towards using OAuth, an open source identification system that keeps data secure and doesn't require that an app user enter a password. That should nail that issue.

Much more of an issue, especially for well-known Twitterers, are fake accounts. Anyone can set up a new account and start Twittering in someone else's name. Sometimes the account is clearly fictional, done with honest intentions, and often very well, too. @darthvader, for example, is a hilarious satire of the evil Star Wars character. The Don Draper timeline (@don_draper), which tweets on behalf of a character in AMC's *Mad Men* television show, was originally created by Paul Isakson (@paulisakson), director of strategy & insights at digital relationships company space 150. He wanted to find out what would happen if people could actually engage with a TV character and then hand control of the timeline over to the company. AMC wasn't happy and shut him down, but now—smartly—it uses the timeline to market the show.

Those uses are fine, and as long as the owner of the rights to the name doesn't complain—and when the Twitterer is helping to promote the brand, why should he?—then Twitter will turn a blind eye.

Much more worrying is when someone tweets deceptively in the name of an individual or a business, using their trust to sell their own goods.

This is a problem that I've been battling with for some time.

I have one account. You can find me on @joelcomm and nowhere else on Twitter. And yet, I've reported dozens of fake accounts Twittering as @joel_lcomm or @joel_m_comm and all sorts of other odd combinations that are designed to defraud followers by suggesting that I recommend products that in fact I've never heard of.

Of course, it's not just me. This is a danger for celebrities, and it's a danger too for companies. If someone starts Twittering in the name of your business, they're stealing your customers—and worse, they're stealing your reputation.

Twitter is pretty good about this. Report someone for identify theft on the site by sending the username to @spam and they'll shut them down fast. But there's nothing stop them from starting up again with a slightly different username.

That's why Twitter has also introduced "verified accounts." You can see them on the accounts of very well-known Twitterers such as Ashton Kutcher (@aplusk) and Oprah Winfrey (@Oprah). At the top right of the timeline, you'll be able to see a check mark in a blue cloud background and the phrase "Verified Account." If you think you'll need one of these, you can apply at twitter.com/account/verify_request.

So that's the basics. You now know how to set up your Twitter account and create an attractive profile that acts as a marketing tool. And you know too how to send tweets and follow people.

Now you can start building up your own followers.

4

Building a Following on Twitter

Web sites have users, Facebook has friends, and Twitter has "followers." They follow your messages—and, in the process, they follow your life.

Unlike users or Facebook friends though, followers don't have to make any effort to enjoy your content. The tweets that you write can come to them, even directly to their mobile phone if they want.

But like users and Facebook friends, followers are valuable. The more followers you have, the further your messages will reach and the more influence you'll have. (See Figure 4.1.)

As always on the Internet, it can take time to build a large community of readers—certainly more time than most impatient publishers like to commit. But it's worth the effort, and there are a number of things that you can do to reduce that time and build your list quickly.

The most important is the piece of advice that remains golden whatever you're doing on the Internet: Produce content that's interesting, fun, and valuable.

Tweets are supposed to describe what you're doing right now, but they can also include opinions, announcements, and conversations. You can write anything you want. You can even include links in your tweets to send people for further reading. Clearly, *that* can be very useful!

Figure 4.1 It's nice to be popular. This is how my followers look to other followers on Twitter. Browsing follower lists is a good way to find people with updates that you want to read. The button on the left allows you to follow other people's followers directly from their list. The button on the right also lets you block them and mention them in a tweet.

But if all you do is tell people about your new product or try to send them to some affiliate site, you'll soon find that you have no followers at all.

Don't forget that some of your followers will be receiving your tweets on their mobile phones. That means that they might be paying for them. If they don't think that they're getting value for their money—whether that's entertainment value, advice value, or any other kind of value—they'll stop following.

You might not have to pay money for followers on Twitter. But you do have to pay with good content—written in 140 characters or less.

In this chapter, I'm going to explain how to build your followers. As you follow these strategies, though, bear in mind that the best way to create a long list of followers—*and the only way to keep them reading and engaged*—is always to create great content, and on Twitter that means generating interesting conversations that other people want to join.

Quantity or Quality: Choosing the Type of Following You Want

If you want masses and masses of followers, there's really nothing to it. It's a breeze. It's simple. It's almost foolproof.

Simply browse Twitter and follow everyone you see.

Some of those people will follow you in return automatically. Others will follow you out of manners.

In one experiment, Stefan Tanase (@stefant), a Romanian security researcher, created a Twitter account with the username Osen Komura (@osen). He found that simply following almost 50,000 people give him nearly 8,000 followers in return, a follow-back rate of about 17 percent.

It's possible. You can do it. And if you're desperate to have a large Twitter following, you could try it.

But I wouldn't recommend it, and I wouldn't do that for a number of reasons.

The first is that it's going to take you a huge amount of time. It's going to be very tedious, and it's going to stuff the tweets that you see on your home page with messages from people you really don't care to follow.

In effect, you're agreeing to be spammed in return for doing some spamming yourself.

That's going to turn what should be a really fun experience into something that you're really not going to want to do for very long.

The second reason is that Twitter will make it hard. If there's a large gap between the number of people you're following and the number that follows you, Twitter will stop you following any more people until more readers start taking your tweets.

There's no single number or ratio that triggers that block. According to Twitter's Support pages, "[t]he number is different for everyone, and is based on a ratio that changes as the account changes."

But the most important reason for not building your followers by following as many people as you possibly can is that the marketing effect will be about as strong as spam.

Only a small number will actually read your tweets. A small fraction will want to join your conversations. And when you send out a tweet about your new product, your new blog post, or the release of your new ebook, only a tiny number of your followers will pay attention.

That doesn't mean that you shouldn't want a large Twitter following. Obviously, lots of interested followers are always going to be better than a few interested followers. But the price to be paid for having a large number of followers is often a less-targeted market and a lower conversion rate of followers to customers or users of your own site.

On the other hand, choose to target only those people with a direct interest in your topic and, while you should be able to keep many of them active and engaged, there will be relatively few of them.

And you'll be missing other people who might be interested in what you have to say.

So what should you do? Should you attempt to build as large a following as possible? Or should you try to make it as targeted as possible?

In general, you want a core group of followers who are very interested in your topic, as many people as possible with a mild interest in your topic, and a few people who might be interested in some aspects of your topic if you get lucky.

In practice, level of interest is not easy to measure, and the chances that you'll turn a vaguely interested follower into a loyal customer will depend on your topic. If you're using your Twitter membership to drive people to a web site and products about fantasy football, for example, you might be able to convert many people who have an interest in sport, even if they don't play fantasy football.

If you tweet about lacrosse, though, you'll probably struggle. A more focused group of followers would then be much more valuable than a large one.

One factor in deciding whether to go for as large a group as possible or focus on a select group is the broadness of your topic's appeal.

♦ If your topic is very popular—sport or cars, for example—you could do well with a large group of followers.

♦ If your topic appeals only to a small crowd—polo, for example, or solar-powered cars—then you might do better narrowing down your followers.

Note that the broadness of a topic's appeal isn't the same as the size of its niche. A marketer who had a web site about Corvettes, for example, would be operating in a small niche. But the topic could be of interest to anyone who likes cars.

When you're considering who to target for your followers, begin with those most interested in your topic. Then expand to bring in people who might be interested in some of the topics you'll cover in your tweets.

Clearly, there's no scientific formula here.

The balance that you create between a highly targeted group of Twitter followers and a more general crowd will usually be down to a feeling that you have about your chances of bringing in people with only a slight interest in your topic.

That feeling comes from experience and from an understanding of your subject and its audience. But it is important to also understand the difference between those two types of followers and try to include both in your follower list.

So how do you go about finding high-quality followers?

Quality: How to Be Intentional about Creating Your Own Network of Experts

High quality followers can do different things. Some will be the type of followers who hang on to your every tweet, follow all your links, and buy your products.

You certainly want to have lots of those . . . but identifying them isn't easy.

Few Twitterers write on their bios that they're looking to buy lots of products about Corvettes or football—or anything else.

What you can find very easily on Twitter though is *experts*.

This is really Twitter's strength. The site is stuffed with people who have great information about particular subjects and who are willing to share it.

Find experts on a topic related to yours and encourage them to follow you, and you'll be giving yourself a massive and very valuable network.

The first thing you have to do though is find them.

Twitter has never had a very good search engine. If you were looking for a particular user on the site, you could toss their name into the search engine and hope something came up.

Figure 4.2   To search deeply on Twitter, you have to get off Twitter and use search.twitter.com.

But that was about it.

Looking for keywords was always a huge pain, and the results just weren't up to scratch. These days, you can also use Twitter's lists feature which lets Twitterers categorize their followers by subject. But few people do, so the lists are rarely comprehensive or helpful.

One of the best things about Twitter, though, is that it lets developers create their own tools for the site. As we'll see later in this book, some of those tools can be very valuable. One tool was so valuable that Twitter decided to buy it. Summize's search engine is now a part of Twitter and can be reached by surfing directly to search.twitter.com or by clicking the search link at the bottom of a Twitter page. (See Figure 4.2.)

You'll find a bunch of trending topics—a list of the most popular subjects that people are currently discussing—and search field in which you can enter your keywords and pull up tweets that contain that phrase.

You'll then be able to see who's talking about your topic and, by looking at the bios and reading their tweets, see which of those Twitterers are the leading experts.

Search is also now integrated into Twitter itself. On the right side of the page, you'll find a search field and, more importantly, have the option to save your searches. That makes it very simple to follow the conversations around your most important topics.

If you want to keep track of what people are saying on Twitter about your company or your products, simply search for that keyword then save the search. *You'll be able to monitor those conversations with just one click!*

You can do exactly the same thing when you're looking for experts to follow. There's nothing wrong with searching from your Twitter page instead of from Twitter's search engine. But the search engine is much more powerful. The Advanced Search feature lets you define your search much more powerfully. You can search for complete phrases, tweets by certain people, with a specific area, within a certain time period, containing links, and even tweets with smilies.

At some point, it's likely that you'll find many of those search features useful, so while you can search from your Twitter page to find the experts in your field, it is worth taking the time to get used to Twitter's search engine.

Whichever search field you use, though, finding the experts in your field is both easy and important.

If you wanted to tweet about fantasy football, for example, then all of the people who came back in the search results for that phrase would be potential followers. You could try following them all and hope that they follow you back, but that's going to take a while. (See Figure 4.3.)

It's much more efficient to identify the key Twitterers on the topic and get them to follow you.

If other people see that the expert is following you, they'll assume that you're also an expert and want to follow you, too.

Do you see how that works?

Figure 4.3 Search for "fantasy football" on Twitter Search and you get a huge list of responses. Clue: experts usually put pictures on their profiles.

One way to succeed on Twitter is to hang out with the influence-makers. Find the top people in your topic on Twitter and become a part of their circle.

When you're one of the prominent Twitterers on the site, you'll find it's much easier to persuade people to read your tweets. In fact, you won't have to do anything but make sure that your tweets are interesting, informative, and entertaining.

And the best news is that getting in with the expert crowd on Twitter is much easier than becoming part of the in crowd at high school.

There are three simple steps.

1. IDENTIFY THE EXPERTS

Once you've got your list of people who have mentioned your topic in their tweets, you'll need to narrow them down to find the key influencers.

Good signs to look out for in the search results include a picture in the profile and frequent posts.

Experts understand the value of both of those things.

You can also try tweaking your search to include terms such as "guide," "guru," "expert," or "author" to help identify leaders.

And when you find someone, check to see how many followers they have and when they last updated. There's no minimal number of followers a Twitterer must have to become an expert—too much depends on the topic—*but there is one sign that marks out the experts on Twitter and it's crucial to your understanding of the site.*

I've described Twitter as being the Internet's watercooler. But hang out at your company's watercooler and you'll find that some people are always more influential than others. They're the ones who set the topics, build groups around them, and direct the conversation. It's a dynamic that happens whenever people get together. Whether it's based on charisma, knowledge, confidence, energy, enthusiasm, motivation, or who knows what else, it doesn't matter. At every party and every gathering communities form around particular individuals. (See Figure 4.4.)

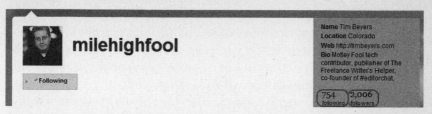

milehighfool

✓ Following

Name Tim Beyers
Location Colorado
Web http://timbeyers.com
Bio Motley Fool tech
contributor, publisher of The
Freelance Writer's Helper,
co-founder of #editorchat.

754 *following* | 2,006 *followers*

Figure 4.4 Tim Beyers is a writer for investment site, The Motley Fool (www.fool.com), but his tweets about freelance writing have made him a must-follow for professional writers. That expertise is reflected in the ratio between the numbers of people Tim is "following" and the number of his "followers." At almost 3:1, it's clear that people are coming to Tim to read what he has to say about his topic.

That happens on Twitter, too. And on Twitter you can spot the individuals around whom those communities form by comparing the number of people they follow to the number of people who follow them.

I've pointed out that most of the tweets posted on Twitter come from a small minority of Twitterers. That's no different to a party where most of the talking is often done by a small number of people—the people with the best anecdotes, the most outgoing personalities, and the easiest way with small talk.

Those are the people you want to find in your topic. They're the nodes around which your community operates, and they're a group of leaders you want to join.

Whatever your topic, it shouldn't take you too long to produce a list of at least a dozen people who are experts to some degree in your field.

Read their tweets and follow them.

2. GAIN THEIR FRIENDSHIP AND RESPECT

So far, all you've done is identify an expert and followed his or her updates.

That's going to be interesting, but it's not always going to turn that expert into your follower. It's only going to turn you into their follower.

To be seen as an expert yourself, you need to stand out both on the list of people they're following and on their timeline.

That happens only when you turn that Twitter connection into a friendship and a relationship cemented by respect.

Twitter provides a couple of tools to do that.

You can hit the reply icon next to one of their tweets. Or you can send them a direct message.

In general, replies are better. All of your followers will be able to see them. Even if the expert himself doesn't respond, other people will see that you're following that expert and that you have something to contribute to the debate.

That already starts to make you look like an expert.

And if the expert responds to your reply, then you've hit the jackpot. All their followers will see that tweet and stop by to see who they're talking to. You can start to pick up a ton of followers that way, especially if you then continue the conversation with those new followers.

Direct messages are useful only if you have a special request, and you should only use them once you've already attracted the expert's attention through your tweets and your replies, and ideally after letting that expert know that you're sending them a direct message.

Otherwise, it's too much like sending a cold email to someone and hoping they respond. If they don't, it's also unlikely that they'll respond to a reply so you'll have lost the opportunity to start a conversation in public, too. And that's if they see the direct message. With so much spam in direct message mailboxes, many good requests get lost.

However you plan to make yourself noticed, do be careful. No one is going to appreciate being bothered by everyone who follows them. Twitter might be a very friendly, open place where it's remarkably easy to exchange messages with the kind of people you'd really struggle to meet anywhere else, but if you want to build a friendship you still have to pay your dues.

3. GIVE BACK MORE THAN YOU TAKE

To do that, you have to give the expert you're hoping to add as a follower information that's truly valuable.

You can tell him something he doesn't already know.

You can point him in the direction of a resource he might find helpful.

You can even try sending him a link if it really will make a difference to what he's doing. (Links are a dime-a-dozen so if you're going to reply with a link as a way of attracting attention, the content of the link has to be really good.)

And you need to hand over this valuable information as often as you can.

Twitter works because people are prepared to share valuable knowledge for free. Some of that knowledge might look worthless, but if it really is worthless, no one will follow them.

When you show anyone that you have valuable knowledge to share, you'll stand out—even to other experts.

Building up a collection of experts as followers will take a little time. Some of that time will be spent searching. Some of it will be spent reading tweets—that can be very addictive. Some of it will be spent updating your own tweets so that you look like an active member of the community.

And some of it will be spent replying to other experts in your field, and messaging them.

As you're doing it, though, you should find that the number of followers starts to grow—first with people you respect and then with the people who respect them.

Quantity: Seven Killer Strategies to Reaching Critical Mass on Twitter

I pointed out that there are two kinds of follower lists. There are targeted follower lists made of a few people with a strong interest in your topic, and there are general follower lists made up of lots of people with a weaker interest in your topic.

I also pointed that while you'll want your list to have a mixture of both types of followers, the balance between them will depend on the nature of your topic.

We've seen that adding targeted people can be difficult. It's enjoyable and interesting. You'll learn a great deal reading the tweets of other important people on the site, but it can take time, and it does depend on good tweet content and good replies.

Creating a large, general follower list can be a lot easier.

Beyond creating great content, there are a couple of important principles you need to keep.

The first is that you have to participate—you have to become a follower.

You can follow all sorts of people on Twitter. You can follow people you know, people you don't know, and people you'd like to know.

Each time you become someone's follower, you turn up in their list, which means that they can see who's following them and so can everyone else.

You don't have to ask their permission—all tweets are public unless the Twitterer restricts them—and you don't have to wait for them to approve you. All you have to do is hit the "Follow" button and that person's tweets will appear on your page, and if you want, on your mobile phone, too.

Once you've found someone to follow on Twitter, you can see who they're following and who's following them. If any of those people look interesting, you can add them to your follow list—and continue.

As I mentioned, that could be all you need to do to win followers, but that would be slow going and inefficient.

The other principle you need to keep is to join the conversation.

So far, I've been describing Twitter as though the information flow was only one way. That isn't the case at all. While the main use of Twitter is to let other people know what you're doing, thinking, or listening to at any moment in time, the service also acts like a public slow-motion instant messenger. (See Figure 4.5.)

You can ask questions and provide answers to the questions other people ask.

In fact, the ability to get great answers on Twitter is one of its biggest strengths. The entire site acts like a giant forum in which experts on all sorts of subjects are willing to lend their advice to almost anyone who asks for it.

It's something that makes Twitter a very valuable resource. Every time you respond, you contribute to someone else's conversation. That makes you a valuable part of the community,

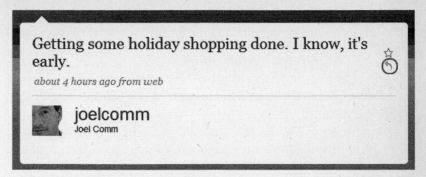

Figure 4.5 Go ahead, make my day. Tell me what you think.

and it increases the chances that other people will follow you too.

Building a long list of followers doesn't happen overnight. It comes as a result of networking on the site, of providing good tweets that other people want to read, and being active in other people's discussions.

It's the reward that comes from participating on Twitter, and best of all, it's a lot of fun to do.

But it is important. Twitter really took off once it achieved a critical mass of users—when enough people were using it that the tweets were interesting to read and there was a good chance that you could find someone you wanted to follow.

Critical mass is important to your follower list, too.

You need to have enough followers to enable your tweets to spark a conversation.

You need to have enough followers to be able to convert at least some of them to customers, users, or clients.

And you need to have enough followers to spread word of your tweets and inspire other Twitterers to tell their friends about you.

Although there aren't any foolproof shortcuts to creating your list, there are a few things that you can do to cut the time and build your list faster.

Here are seven different ways to do it.

1. LOOK FOR PEOPLE YOU ALREADY KNOW

Let's start with the very easiest method.

Look for people you already know.

' Twitter is popular enough now for there to be a good chance that at least some of the people in your address book are already Twittering away.

As we've seen, Twitter lets you find those people on the site by taking a leaf out of Facebook's page. It can scan your Web mail and compare your contacts to the people in its own database.

Initially, I recommended that you do *not* do this. I believe that it's a better idea to wait until your profile has been created and you've started posting tweets.

Once you've done that though, you're free to go.

Just hit the "Find People" link at the top of the page, enter your email address and password, and let Twitter do the searching. The site will then return a list of all the people in your contact book who are using Twitter. Follow them, reply to some of their tweets, or send them a personal message to make sure that they see you're following them and there's a good chance they'll follow you, too.

That's the good news.

The bad news is that this only works for Web-based mail.

At the moment, there is no simple way to search your Outlook contacts for Twitterers.

So you'll have to cheat.

Open a free Web-based email account such as Gmail or Yahoo! Mail, if you don't have one already, then export your contact list from Outlook and import it into your new account. Your new mail service will explain how to do it, but it shouldn't take more than a few minutes.

You won't have to actually use that account, but you will now be able to search your contacts automatically on Twitter to see if any of them are Twittering.

How many followers will this method give you?

It depends on the size of your contact list and the chances that a large part of it will be on the site. You're unlikely to pick up thousands of followers right away, but there is a good chance that you'll be able to add a few new readers and there's an even better chance that those people will follow you in return.

2. TWEET YOUR BLOG

One of the most common goals of a good Twitter presence will be to direct followers to a web site. (See Figure 4.6.)

Once they reach your site, your followers will be able to read posts that are longer than 140 characters. They'll be able to click on your ads, and they'll be able to buy your products.

They won't be able to do any of those things on your Twitter page.

But another of your aims will also be to build a closer connection with the users you have, so that you become a part of their lives. That means your users will return to your site more often and they'll be more likely to take you up on your special offers.

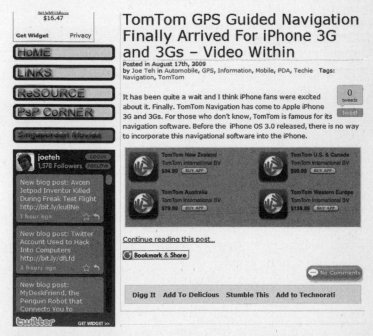

Figure 4.6   Joe Teh puts his tweets on his blog, techielobang.com/blog.

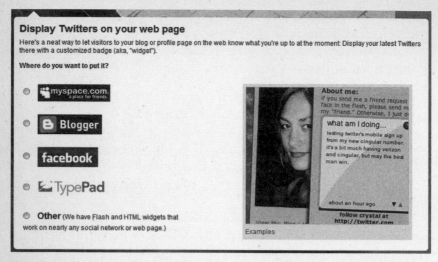

Figure 4.7 Twitter's own widgets make publicizing your tweets as simple as click, cut, and paste.

Those users then are a valuable pool of potential followers.

If you can show your users your tweets and bring them to your Twitter page, you'll be able to massively increase the number of your followers.

And Twitter makes it very easy to post tweets on a web site.

If you want to add your tweets to a blog, surf to twitter.com/badges and select the kind of page on which you'd like to put your tweets. The site offers MySpace, Facebook, Blogger and Typepad as automatic options, but it also provides widgets that work just about everywhere. (See Figure 4.7.)

Once you've chosen the type of badge you want, you'll be able to customize it and copy the code. Insert the code where you want the tweets to appear on your site, then upload and check to see it's all looking the way it should.

If you're looking to show your posts on any other kind of web site though, an even easier option is to click the "goodies" link at the bottom of Twitter's pages. Choose "Widgets" and you'll be able to select a module to place on your Web page. Again, these work for Facebook and MySpace, but if you click the "My web site" link, followed by "Profile Widget," you'll be able to optimize a module that you can place on your site.

As always, it's a good idea to make the customization match the design of your site as closely as possible. You want your tweets to look like they're part of your site so that readers see it as extra content, not something that's been brought in from outside—like an ad.

The result should be that you'll have some extra content on your site, your users will be able to see your tweets on your page and they'll be tempted to click through to your Twitter page to see all the tweets they missed.

If you're getting thousands of users to your web site every week and only a small fraction of them actually follow you on Twitter, you can still end up with a massive number of followers using this method.

Note that Twitter also allows you to place a module showing tweets about a particular topic. Twitter calls these Search Widgets, and while they can add some valuable free content to a web site, they won't increase your followers on Twitter. They might, though, increase someone else's following on Twitter.

For WordPress users, the news doesn't look quite so good.

In fact, it's even better.

You'll probably have noticed that WordPress isn't listed as one of the badges that Twitter offers. While you can select "other," a better option is to use the Twitter Tools plugin. You can download it for free from alexking.org/projects/wordpress.

This plugin won't just show your tweets on your site, it will also let you send tweets from your blog, turn your posts into tweets and issue alerts, complete with a link, whenever you write a new blog post. (Alex, a Web developer in Denver, Colorado, has a bunch of other very cool WordPress plugins and themes that you can check out on his site, too.)

And, of course, you can ask your web site users to follow you on Twitter.

Or rather, you can *tell* them to follow you on Twitter, because according to Dustin Curtis (@dcurtis), an interface designer, the way web sites tell users to follow them on Twitter has a dramatic effect on the clickthrough rate.

Saying simply "I'm on Twitter" produces a clickthrough rate of 4.7 percent—a respectable figure. Ordering users to "Follow me on twitter" increased that clickthrough rate by 55 percent, pushing

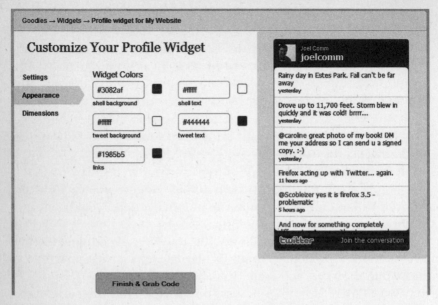

Figure 4.8   Twitter's "goodies" include widgets that let you place your tweets on any web site. Just be sure to match the design of the widget to the design of your site to help it blend in.

it up to 7.31 percent. Making the phrase more personal by saying "You should follow me on twitter" increased the clickthrough rate to 10.09 percent, and providing a link for people to click in the phrase "You should follow me on twitter <u>here</u>" was the most effective of all with a clickthrough rate of 12.81 percent.

Interestingly, the last three figures were only true when Dustin wrote the name of the site without a capital letter—"twitter" rather than "Twitter." Capitalizing the name of the site reduced the clickthrough rate by as much as 6 percent.

So if you want almost one in eight of your site's users to become your Twitter followers, just tell them where to go.

3. Pay Your Followers!

This might not sound like the smartest—or the cheapest—way to bring in large numbers of followers, but you could just consider paying people to follow you.

Giving away freebies is a marketing standard. You create goodwill, let potential customers try your products before they buy, and build a list of clients that you can draw on in the future.

As long as you follow the simple rule that what you give away should cost you little but have high value to the recipient, you should find that offering freebies can have a fantastic effect on your revenues.

I've given away hundreds of thousands of dollars' worth of goods through my web sites and seminars, and I've received many times that in return.

The principle can work in exactly the same way on Twitter to incentivize Twitterers to follow you.

Angie Jones (@fitbizwoman), who produces a subscription-based fitness newsletter, for example, once used her Twitter bio to promise a free recipe ebook to anyone who follows her. (See Figure 4.9.)

Emailing that recipe book would have cost her nothing. In fact, when she asked her new follower for an address, she was building up an email list of people interested in exactly the sort of information she offers.

Giving away that recipe book actually paid her by giving her something more valuable in return: a targeted list.

It also showed her followers what she can do, what her customers will receive, and it gave people a great reason to follow her tweets.

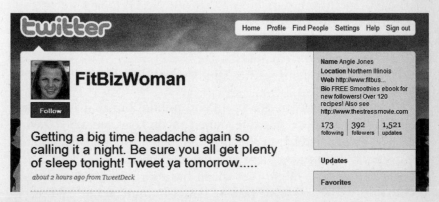

Figure 4.9 Angie Jones's bio promised smoothies to followers—although they did have to make them themselves.

shop

El Jumpino Jalepino!
TokyoGoGo

SeeWorthy

> http://buy-tees.net is the first international tshirt blog to ask for their customised springleap coupon code to give to their readers. *7:41 PM Oct 16th from web*
>
> http://www.imod.co.za is the first blog to display their customised springleap coupon code. Don't wait till your coupon code name is taken! *7:27 PM Oct 16th from web*
>
> remember that the springleap 40% OFF Sale is now ending at 10am TODAY. Use coupon code G71RB84 for FORTY PERCENT DISCOUNT on everything! *3:01 AM Oct 13th from web*
>
> like our profile image? it's the featured designer for september - the amazingly talented Colwyn with "Tiger Hug" *8:53 PM Oct 12th from web*
>
> the 40% off Sale on springleap.com has been extended to 10am Monday morning (South African time) - DON'T MISS OUT ON THIS ONE *8:46 PM Oct 12th from web*
>
> @nickjackson we did send you an email replying to yours. did you get it? *3:59 PM Oct 12th from web in reply to nickjackson*

Figure 4.10   SpringLeap pays its followers to keep in touch—and generates sales, too.

SpringLeap (@springleap), a South African designer T-shirt company, takes a slightly different approach. Rather than rewarding Twitterers immediately when they follow their tweets, SpringLeap offers constant rewards in the form of time-limited discount codes in its tweets. (See Figure 4.10.)

For anyone interested in SpringLeap's unique T-shirts, following the company's tweets pays. And the company gets to make sure that people read its company news, are aware of new designs, and revisit to shop often.

4. RESPOND TO REQUESTS

One topic that I'm going to keep coming back to in this book is that successful Twitterers use Twitter to do more than make announcements.

They use it to spark conversations. And they use it too to *join* conversations.

Those conversations are open and public, but that just means that they're even more valuable. When anyone can see who's saying what in a Twitter exchange, anyone can follow the links back to the Twitterers who impress them and follow them as well.

Sometimes that might just mean hitting the reply button and coming up with a good response. Often though, other Twitterers offer golden opportunities to jump into a chat by asking a question.

Provide a good answer, and you get to look like a bigger expert than the original Twitterer.

There are a couple of rules to follow here though.

The first is that any information you provide has to be genuinely good. Saying, "Yeah, I'm having trouble with that too . . ." or quoting from Wikipedia is not going to do you any good.

People will follow your tweets only if they feel that you have information that's worth reading. That's one reason it's a good idea to answer questions about your subject rather than any question you happen to see.

You'll pick up people with an interest in your topic, but you'll also get a bigger opportunity to show off your expertise.

The second rule is that the more popular the questioner, the greater the benefits of lending them a hand—or even providing them with a good reply. (See Figure 4.11.)

Not sure @don_draper goes to work today. Strange, but he owes us. Maybe we should all do something when Sally gets back from school. *10:54 AM Oct 27th from web*

@JodiJe Simply had plenty of practice advising Don on these issues. *10:52 AM Oct 27th from web in reply to JodiJe*

@dossy What does that mean, Eliza-style? *10:51 AM Oct 27th from web in reply to dossy*

@andij1967 Thank you for being next to me. It'll take both of us a while for that news to sink in... *10:50 AM Oct 27th from web in reply to andij1967*

@mikepratt Rather: was it something I said that kept you from returning my gesture initially? *10:49 AM Oct 27th from web in reply to mikepratt*

@trench Sorry, drop what? *10:49 AM Oct 27th from web in reply to trench*

@danperry I was hoping we become friends. It seems you opted not to. *10:48 AM Oct 27th from web in reply to danperry*

@dustindk Thank you. Somehow, he didn't seem more excited that me, though. *10:47 AM Oct 27th from web in reply to DustinDK*

Figure 4.11 Betty Draper (@betty_draper) is a character on the AMC show "Mad Men." She also tweets—or rather a fan does it on her behalf—and has over 10,000 followers. Reply to her tweets or answer her questions and when she comments back you'll be putting your name in front of thousands of people. Who else can you find with a large following?

When they thank you or comment back, lots of people will see their response, wonder who you are, and stop by your Twitter page to find out.

This is a strategy followed by Dan Perry (@danperry), a search engine optimization expert at Cars.com.

5. MOBILIZE YOUR SOCIAL NETWORK

Here's one I really like! Twitter is extremely powerful, but it becomes even more powerful when it's used as one part of a marketing strategy that uses different elements of social media.

Because each social media site offers different features and works in a different way, by making them all work together you can be sure that you're sharing the audience between each site.

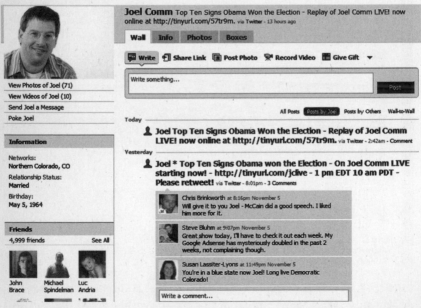

Figure 4.12 My Facebook page is stuffed with Twitter content. With 5,000 people to bring to my Twitter timeline, why not? And check out how those tweets spark conversations here. On Facebook, tweets turn followers and friends into a community.

Facebook, for example, gives me much more flexibility than Twitter. It lets me post photos, run groups, and interact with my friends in all sorts of different ways. I have 5,000 friends on Facebook—the maximum the site allows. By placing my tweets on Facebook, too, I'm able to show all of those 5,000 people my Twitter content and give them a reason to follow me there, too. They'll want to make sure that they're not missing anything. (See Figure 4.12.)

And this can work the other way, too. If you see someone on MySpace or Facebook with lots of friends and who tweets as well, follow them on Twitter and comment on their wall. There's a good chance that they'll follow you back and their friends and followers will want to check you out as well.

6. PUT YOUR TWITTER NAME IN YOUR SIGNATURES

Such an easy thing to do, such an old idea, and so often forgotten.

As soon as a new technology comes along, there can be a tendency to forget about all the old standards, like the value of including your URL on your business card and your email and forum signatures.

Just as that strategy can drive plenty of interested people to your web site, adding your Twitter URL to those signatures can have exactly the same effect.

Twitter might let you search your contact list for people who are already Twittering, and it might let you send those who aren't on the site an invitation to join up, but if all you want to do is alert people on your email list—in forums, and anyone else you chat with online—that you're Twittering, then this is a very simple way to do it.

7. RUN A CONTEST

I pointed out that one way to build up followers is to reward them for following you. We also saw that some Twitterers are doing that by giving them a freebie as soon as they hit the "follow" button.

Another way is to include discount codes in the tweets to keep people reading.

Jason Cormier (@jasoncormier), who runs a search marketing and social media agency, takes a very different approach for his clients.

He helps them to organize contests on Twitter.

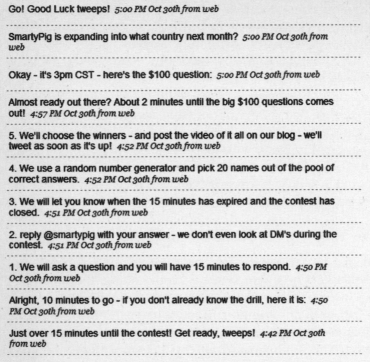

Go! Good Luck tweeps! *5:00 PM Oct 30th from web*

SmartyPig is expanding into what country next month? *5:00 PM Oct 30th from web*

Okay - it's 3pm CST - here's the $100 question: *5:00 PM Oct 30th from web*

Almost ready out there? About 2 minutes until the big $100 questions comes out! *4:57 PM Oct 30th from web*

5. We'll choose the winners - and post the video of it all on our blog - we'll tweet as soon as it's up! *4:52 PM Oct 30th from web*

4. We use a random number generator and pick 20 names out of the pool of correct answers. *4:52 PM Oct 30th from web*

3. We will let you know when the 15 minutes has expired and the contest has closed. *4:51 PM Oct 30th from web*

2. reply @smartypig with your answer - we don't even look at DM's during the contest. *4:51 PM Oct 30th from web*

1. We will ask a question and you will have 15 minutes to respond. *4:50 PM Oct 30th from web*

Alright, 10 minutes to go - if you don't already know the drill, here it is: *4:50 PM Oct 30th from web*

Just over 15 minutes until the contest! Get ready, tweeps! *4:42 PM Oct 30th from web*

Figure 4.13   SmartyPig (@smartypig) runs contests on Twitter to keep its followers reading and to make sure that all of its customers follow its tweets.

SmartyPig, for example, a kind of online savings bank, asks a question on Twitter at a specific time. Followers have 15 minutes to reply. Three winners are then selected at random from those who sent in the correct answer and receive a $100 gift card. (See Figure 4.13.)

One contest generated almost 100 correct answers in the space of 15 minutes.

The big advantage of a competition like this is that it's happening in real time. The company could just as easily have asked the question on its blog and said that it would be announcing the winners a week later.

By running the contest live, through Twitter, it collects all of its customers together in one place at one time, turns them into a community and creates a party atmosphere, too.

And, of course, it also makes sure that all of its customers are following its tweets.

Twitterank and Page Rank

So there are all sorts of different strategies that you can use to build up your follower list. But the number next to your follower list is just one measure of success on Twitter.

No less important—and perhaps even more important—is the extent to which you are the focus of conversation.

Because Twitter is like a giant open chat, the more people who reply to your tweets, the more influential your posts. It's a great sign that people are interested in what you have to say and want to take part in the discussion.

That's the theory, at least, behind Twitterank (twitterank.com), a service that uses the number of incoming replies to give each Twitterer a score that is supposed to represent their popularity. The theory is similar to Google's page rank, which rates the importance of web sites based, among other things, on the number and quality of incoming links the site receives. (See Figure 4.14.)

joelcomm's **twitterrank is:**

199.66

approx. 99.77 percentile
(23.13% confidence) wtf?

URL: http://twitterank.com/view/joelcomm
Get your twitterank!

Figure 4.14 According to Twitterrank, I'm pretty popular—maybe.

Twitterank lets you see your own score, and you can toss in the usernames of other Twitterers to see their scores, too.

Twitterank was created by programmer Ryo Chijiiwa and caused a bit of a storm when it first came out. Because Ryo asked for username and passwords, a rumor spread that he was hoarding personal data and that the service was a giant phishing scam. That appears not to be true—Ryo has since made clear that all passwords are automatically deleted as soon as the Twitterank has been calculated—but it was a pretty good example of the speed with which information (and a good idea) can spread across the Twitterverse.

The real question, of course, is how useful this stuff is. The service was created as a bit of fun. Unlike Google's page rank, Twitterank isn't going to affect where you turn up in search results or how much traffic you're likely to receive.

It certainly won't affect the amount of money you receive in advertising revenues.

You might consider it as one way to measure how well you're managing to motivate discussions in comparison to other Twitterers. You can also take a look at the list of the top 50 Twitterers to see what they're doing to get those replies coming in. For many, it seems to consist of being a well-known mover and shaker off Twitter as much as the type of tweets they're posting.

Interestingly, though, tweets also receive page ranks.

Paste a tweet into Google and you'll find that it's been indexed in the search engine. (See Figure 4.15.)

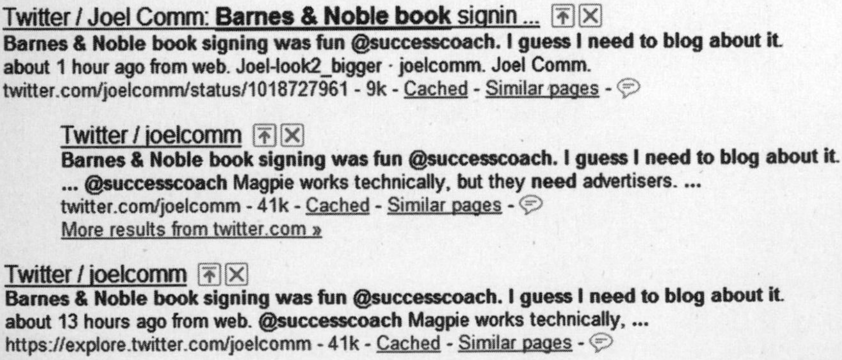

Twitter / Joel Comm: **Barnes & Noble book** signin ... 	[↥][X]
Barnes & Noble book signing was fun @successcoach. I guess I need to blog about it.
about 1 hour ago from web. Joel-look2_bigger · joelcomm. Joel Comm.
twitter.com/joelcomm/status/1018727961 - 9k - Cached - Similar pages - ⌐

    Twitter / joelcomm 	[↥][X]
    Barnes & Noble book signing was fun @successcoach. I guess I need to blog about it.
    ... @successcoach Magpie works technically, but they **need** advertisers. ...
    twitter.com/joelcomm - 41k - Cached - Similar pages - ⌐
    More results from twitter.com »

Twitter / joelcomm 	[↥][X]
Barnes & Noble book signing was fun @successcoach. I guess I need to blog about it.
about 13 hours ago from web. @successcoach Magpie works technically, ...
https://explore.twitter.com/joelcomm - 41k - Cached - Similar pages - ⌐

Figure 4.15 Hey look, I'm on Google, too.

My suspicion is that this works the same as any Web page. Since I have links going to my Twitter page from other authority sites, Google raises the page rank of my Twitter page and the value of my outgoing links. Whether that's worth anything to me is hard to say. I can't imagine that anyone's going to look for a tweet from me on Google, and trying to target keywords so that your Twitter page will turn up at the top of search rankings is unlikely to be worth the effort.

But it is an interesting quirk of Twitter.

Creating a long list of followers is always going to be one of the most important tasks that you do on Twitter. It's a challenge that requires first deciding what kind of followers you want—an audience that's niched and mostly targeted, one that's large but general, or a balanced combination of the two.

It will then involve a great deal of following and reading. You'll have to reply to tweets that other people have posted, place tweets of your own, and track down the people you know—and would like to know—on the site.

It's a process that takes time. While there are strategies to make that process faster—and I discussed several of them in this chapter—no one ever builds a four-, five-, or six-figure follower list overnight.

That's because, above all, creating a large following on Twitter requires writing good tweets—the kind that people actually want to read and which make them feel that you're going to have more good information for them in the future.

That's what I discuss in the next chapter.

5

The Art of the Tweet

The moment it became clear that the Internet could be a good way for businesses to make money, one simple rule stood out.

Sites with good content succeeded; sites with poor content failed.

That didn't mean that lots of people didn't try earning money with poor content. They did. They still do.

And they still fail.

Sure, a web site owner can find a wordsmith in Mumbai to churn out articles for $5 each so that he can have somewhere to put his ads, but even at those low rates, he's still going to lose money.

If the content isn't good, no one will want to read it.

Instead of putting effort into creating good articles, the publisher will have to put even more effort into dragging people to his Web pages.

And he'll have to keep doing it because when a user has visited a poor site once, he won't come back.

That rule holds true on Twitter, too.

To build followers and keep them engaged, you have to produce good content.

The only difference is in the nature of good content on Twitter.

Because you only have 140 characters, you can't create long list posts that are so popular in social media sites.

You can't create in-depth how-to articles that give people valuable knowledge and help them to complete important tasks.

And any interviews you wanted to run would have to consist of very short questions and one-word answers.

Good content on Twitter needs to be entertaining. It needs to be informative. It needs to be valuable.

And it needs to be short.

In this chapter, I'm going to look at some of the ways to produce great Twitter content, the kind of tweets that build followers, keep your readers coming back for more and engage them in your conversation.

I'm going to start though by talking about the rules.

Tweet Etiquette

Every conversation has rules. We know not to interrupt someone when they're talking. We know not to use bad language when we talk. We know not to talk too loudly.

And we know too how and when to break all of the rules.

Exactly the same is true for a Twitter conversation.

The site hasn't been around for long, but Twitterers have already tried to figure out something like a Twittering etiquette

Some of those etiquette rules are smart, sensible, and should always be followed. Others are smart, sensible, and should usually be followed.

While it's important to know the rules, it's just as important then to know when to break them and what happens when you do.

1. DON'T SPAM

This is one rule you can't break. Spammers don't survive for long on Twitter. They don't build followers. Any followers they do get don't read their tweets, and the number of conversions they can generate will be so tiny that, as a marketing method, you'd probably be better off printing a thousand flyers, folding them into paper airplanes, and tossing them out of your office window.

There are all sorts of different ways to spam on Twitter.

As we've seen, one way is to follow lots and lots of people in the hope that some of them follow you in return. That's not just ineffective, it also turns up clearly in your bio.

Whenever someone's bio shows that they're following several thousand people but only being followed by a handful, that's a pretty good sign that they're looking to spam. They're trying to build up followers who will follow them out of politeness rather than because they have interesting content.

Twitterers often steer clear of people like that.

The spamming itself though is done by constantly sending out tweets that say things like "I've just up a new blog post—check it out!" or "Sign up for my RSS feed!"

You can send out tweets like this occasionally. But as we'll see later in this section, they have to be mixed in with other tweets, too. Otherwise, you're just spamming, and that's annoying.

Worse, it doesn't work.

Another method popular with spammers is to add popular hashtags or keywords associated with trending topics to their tweets, even if those topics aren't relevant. While that will bring in plenty of eyeballs, it's also a very quick way to get your timeline closed down.

Spamming isn't just bad manners, it's also terrible marketing.

2. Follow Style Rules

Twitter's founders may have had mobile phones in mind when they designed the service, and plenty of users may be typing their updates from their handheld devices, but Twitter isn't exactly the same as SMS messaging.

That means the language needs to look more like real words than the usual SMS-style abbreviations.

It goes without saying that typing in uppercase letters looks like you're shouting, but you should spell out words completely and avoid using numbers instead of letters whenever possible. (So "late" is not spelled "l8" and "to" is two letters, not one number.)

That might mean more typing, but the reasoning is sensible. "Heading 2 town l8. Dont no wot 4" is hard for the reader to understand. It's only good manners—and good marketing sense—for you to put in the work so that your readers don't have to.

There are exceptions, of course. If you're really strapped for space then this is a rule you can break, but understand that you're forcing your followers to make an effort.

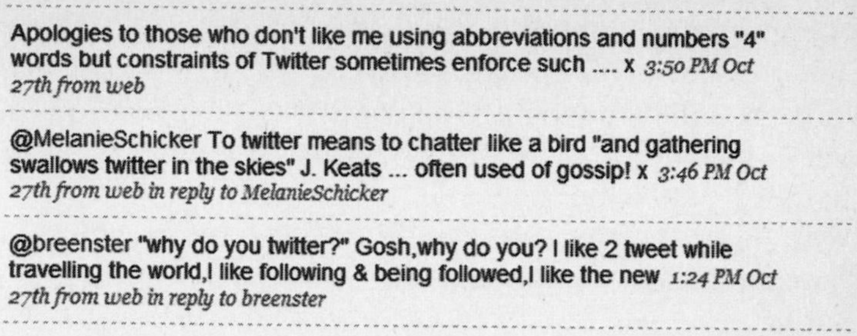

Apologies to those who don't like me using abbreviations and numbers "4" words but constraints of Twitter sometimes enforce such .... x *3:50 PM Oct 27th from web*

@MelanieSchicker To twitter means to chatter like a bird "and gathering swallows twitter in the skies" J. Keats ... often used of gossip! x *3:46 PM Oct 27th from web in reply to MelanieSchicker*

@breenster "why do you twitter?" Gosh,why do you? I like 2 tweet while travelling the world,I like following & being followed,I like the new *1:24 PM Oct 27th from web in reply to breenster*

Figure 5.1   Stephen Fry apologizes for his lack of style.

What is permissible though is to use symbols such as "@" and "=", and to skip some of the grammar. The question Twitter asks might be "What are you doing?" but you don't have to begin your answer by saying "I am . . ." (See Figure 5.1.)

Sentence fragments such as "About to start watching the football. Can't wait." are fine.

3. GIVE CREDIT FOR RETWEETS

One of the things that makes Twitter such a powerful tool is the fact that information placed on the site can quickly go viral. When one person spots a good tweet, they can pass that message on to their own followers and soon it's spreading right across the Twitterverse and beyond.

For a marketer, that's like hitting the jackpot.

On Twitter, it's done by retweeting.

Twitterers can simply copy someone else's tweet and tweet it themselves . . . but they must give credit to the original Twitterer by adding "RT" or "Retweet" together with the username of the original Twitterer. At the moment, the format for retweets then looks like this:

"RT @username: original tweet."

So if you wanted to retweet this post from my timeline

"Spontaneous LIVE broadcast! join me now with special guest! - http://tinyurl.com/jclive"

then you would tweet:

"RT@joelcomm: Spontaneous LIVE broadcast! join me now with special guest! - http://tinyurl.com/jclive"

Any comments you want to add to the retweet can go at the beginning or in brackets at the end:

"Not missing this! RT @joelcomm: Spontaneous LIVE broadcast! join me now with special guest! - http://tinyurl.com/jclive"

"RT @joelcomm: Spontaneous LIVE broadcast! join me now with special guest! - http://tinyurl.com/jclive (Not missing this!)"

The etiquette is simple enough, but it changes a lot. Not everyone uses brackets or places their comments in the right place, so it's not always easy to see what's comment and what's part of the original tweet. And as a tweet spreads across Twitter—when a retweet is retweeted—the original Twitterer can become lost.

That's why Twitter has rolled out a new way of posting retweets. In addition to being able to fave and reply to a tweet, you can also press a retweet button. That places the tweet on your followers' home pages, even if they're not following the person you're retweeting. The tweet will look like any other message, complete with avatar, so the identity of the original Twitterer is clear. (See Figure 5.2.) But it also says who retweeted it so that you know it was sent by someone you follow. You will be able to retweet the message in turn or reply to it. Very easy.

And I don't like it. While it's nice to find the odd surprising Twitterer in my timeline, I like being able to add comments to tweets and offer my own take. For that I need to do it manually.

The value of sharing tweets though is easy to understand. It might not be original content but if your followers would find the original tweet interesting, why shouldn't you share it?

The tricky bit is to get other people to retweet for you, and there's a whole bunch of things you can do to increase the chances that that will happen. I'll talk about those a little later in this book but for now bear in mind that if your tweets are interesting enough,

Figure 5.2 Dave Baldwin (@highonbeingdave) shares the love—and a tweet.

people will share them with their friends and followers—and those friends and followers will come to your page to find out who you are.

4. STICK TO 140 CHARACTERS

You *have* to stick to 140 characters, right? That's all they give you, and they do it for a good reason. Being starved of space stops you waffling and sparks your creativity. It's what Twitter is all about.

Well, yes and no.

Twitter gives you 140 characters because that's all that can fit through SMS systems. If mobile phone companies could handle messages of 200 characters then that's probably how long our tweets would be.

Even though the limit is fairly arbitrary, it does make sense to keep to it as much as possible.

The alternative is to show half-complete tweets and offer links for people to continue reading or break messages up so that they're sent over several tweets. There are even services such as TwitLonger (www.twitlonger.com) that allow people to post messages as long as they like with the first 140 characters appearing as a tweet.

You can see all of these things happening sometimes on Twitter, and they rarely look good. Readers expect the content on Twitter

Later, after playing tourist, we'll meet at @web2asia 's offices to see a bunch of cool startups. The #china20 tour... http://ff.im/eg6 *12:11 AM yesterday from FriendFeed*

Back in Shanghai, about to go play tourist with @christinelu and @rocmanusa. Damn the pollution here is extreme. My... http://ff.im/ef6 *12:09 AM yesterday from FriendFeed*

Video of Seagate hard drives being tested: http://www.viddler.com/expl... more video coming in... http://ff.im/aGE *4:41 PM Nov 7th from FriendFeed*

Figure 5.3 Tech expert and super-blogger Robert Scoble (@scobleizer) wrote some of the rules for tweeting and says that they should be broken. Here, he turns his tweets into teasers for FriendFeed, a service that links together social media sites.

to be small. They expect to be able to read and absorb it in one bite. These are content snacks, not three-course meals with coffee.

Writing a thought that takes more than 140 characters and spreading it over three or four tweets is giving people more than they want. It also makes you look like you're dominating the conversation.

Chat with a friend, and you'll take turns speaking. You'll speak, your friend will respond, and then you'll continue. Keep talking without giving your friend a chance to offer his response and you'll start to sound rude.

Multiple tweets can have the same effect upon Twitter.

Again, this doesn't mean you should *never* break up a long tweet. And it certainly doesn't mean that you shouldn't post one tweet after another. (See Figure 5.3.)

What it does mean is that you should be aware of the effect you can create in your timeline when you do either.

5. FOLLOW PEOPLE WHO FOLLOW YOU

How many people you should follow on Twitter can always make for a great discussion point. Follow thousands of people and you're not going to be able to read all of their tweets. Inevitably, you'll miss tweets you'd really like to read and you'll look like someone who has lots of acquaintances but no real friends.

When I started using Twitter I would follow almost everyone who followed me. The idea was that in giving everyone the benefit of the doubt I would meet many new people and enter into discussions that I might otherwise have missed. Even then, more were following me than I was following back so I invariably missed a lot of tweets. Still, it was great to look at my Twitter page and see a huge variety of different conversations taking place.

It was a bit like strolling through the networking room during a break at a conference. I could choose which conversations to join and which to walk past. I have always found it very valuable but it's impossible to follow everyone back.

As my numbers have grown I have had to reevaluate the way I follow others on Twitter. With tens of thousands of follows, I discovered that it had become nearly impossible to use Twitter without it dominating me! Since one of my key tenants for using Twitter is to use it in a way that fits your lifestyle, I made a radical move. I unfollowed everyone and started over. You can read more about my controversial "Twitter purge" on my blog at http://twitpwr.com/purge/.

As of this writing, I only follow 433 people. For me, it means that I will have conversations with fewer people but they will be more frequent and meaningful. And with over 65,000 people following me, I still have an opportunity to share my tweets and have people respond to them as desired. Essentially, it just means that my main Twitter stream is now more manageable for my lifestyle.

You might want—at least at the beginning—to reward everyone who follows you by following them in return. There are plenty of top Twitterers who do this.

Similarly, you might prefer only to follow close friends and people you already know. That will make you look antisocial and cliquey, which is not the best image for a marketer, but it's possible.

Ultimately, I think this is one place where eventually you have to skip the etiquette and do what works. As your follower list grows, you'll have to start being a little bit choosier about who you follow in return, and your followers will just have to understand that you're being selective, not rude.

Spend any time on Twitter and you're going to come across plenty of other rules, too. Some purists, for example, have argued that your tweets should only describe what you're doing, not what you're thinking or planning to do. I think that's far too restrictive and judging by the way that Twitter has developed, other people seem to agree: If it sparks a conversation and entertains your followers, it's a fair topic. If they don't like it, they should read someone else's tweets.

And that's really the ultimate test of tweet etiquette: how other people react and how you would react to the same kind of thing.

If you're building followers and they're responding to what you're writing, you're following the right rules.

The Benefits of Following before Twittering

One of the results of flexible Twitter etiquette is that it's inevitable that every Twitterer ends up making and following his or her own rules.

Some follow everyone who follows them; others don't.

Some reply to everyone who replies to them; others don't reply to anyone.

Some ask questions and expect followers to answer; others never do.

That means before you dive into a conversation—and even before you get your own tweeting career fully under way with regular tweets that spark conversations and market your products and your services—it's important to spend time following others and reading their tweets.

Clearly that's going to take a little time, but the advantages are important.

First, you'll get to see the etiquette rules that they're following. If you can see that someone you'd like to add as a follower has 1,000 followers but only follows 40 people, you shouldn't be too upset if he doesn't add you the minute you add him.

You'll also see whether he thinks using numbers instead of letters is annoying or acceptable (based on whether he does it himself) and what he likes to tweet about.

No less important, you'll be able to see who's following him so that you can follow them, too, and understand who might follow you if you turn this Twitterer into a follower.

But perhaps most crucially, if you spend time following and reading tweets before you dive into a conversation you'll be able to see what caused the Twitterer to respond to one of his followers.

joelcomm

> ✓ Following

@Christinahills wait till we release
TextCastLive.com - gonna be earthshaking
in the marketing world!

about 3 hours ago from web in reply to christinahills

Figure 5.4   What did Christina Hills (@christinahills) say to get her name and link in front of tens of thousands of people?

This is what you want to happen when you tweet directly to other Twitterers by hitting the "reply" button. Your timeline will look as though you're in conversation with all sorts of interesting people. When those users reply to your replies, your name and a link to your Twitter page appear in their timeline. All of their followers can see it and will want to know who you are.

It's fantastic marketing.

By looking at the questions that other repliers asked and the responses they posted, you'll be able to understand what you have to reply—or post—to win that prize.

How to Join a Conversation

One of the things that makes Twitter so appealing is that it's such an open community. There might be several million people on the site talking about what they're doing and chatting with other Twitterers, but you really do feel that every one of them could be your friend if you wanted them to be.

That's a remarkable feeling, and it's something you can't find on many social media sites. Facebook, for example, requires a potential friend to confirm that he or she knows you before you can even see their profile, let alone add them as a contact.

Twitter is much more communal. Everyone on the site seems to be available to provide information, swap a tip, or hand over some valuable piece of advice.

On one condition: you give them something valuable in return.

That means when you want to take part in a conversation that you can see happening on Twitter on a topic that looks interesting, you can't simply introduce yourself and expect to be welcomed.

Twitter might feel like a giant networking room, but it doesn't work in the same way.

If other people on the site want to know who you are, they can stop by your profile, read your bio, and surf through to your web site.

What they really want to know is what you have to contribute to the debate.

And that can't be a plug for you.

Or rather, it can't *just* be a plug for you.

If all you do is say something like "I covered this topic in my blog! Check it out here: tinyurl.com/sdsdsf" then you're going to sound like a salesman.

If, on the other hand, you provide one solid piece of information that you drew out of that post *and* provide a link to a place where readers can learn more, then you're paying for the return reply.

Do you see the difference?

The first type of tweet is an ad; the second type is a contribution to the conversation.

But you don't have to do anything as blatant as including a link in your tweet to get the benefits of joining a conversation if you do it right.

Christina Hills (@christinahills), for example, is an entrepreneur who helps other business owners with their marketing. I know that many of her followers would be interested in the sort of information that I provide in my timeline, and I'm sure that she recognizes that some of my followers would find her strategies helpful, too.

By joining each other's conversations we each get to learn new things and we expose our followers to the others' expertise. (See Figures 5.4, 5.5, and 5.6.)

It's a technique that can only work through conversation.

That's just one way to join a conversation, and as you can see, it's incredibly simple. In fact, you can think of it as a little like a

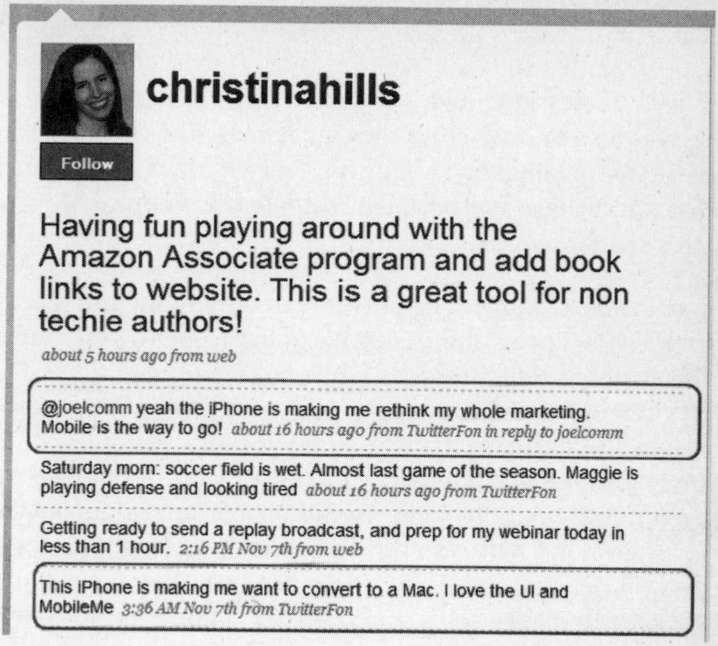

christinahills

Follow

Having fun playing around with the Amazon Associate program and add book links to website. This is a great tool for non techie authors!

about 5 hours ago from web

@joelcomm yeah the iPhone is making me rethink my whole marketing. Mobile is the way to go! *about 16 hours ago from TwitterFon in reply to joelcomm*

Saturday morn: soccer field is wet. Almost last game of the season. Maggie is playing defense and looking tired *about 16 hours ago from TwitterFon*

Getting ready to send a replay broadcast, and prep for my webinar today in less than 1 hour. *2:16 PM Nov 7th from web*

This iPhone is making me want to convert to a Mac. I love the UI and MobileMe *3:36 AM Nov 7th from TwitterFon*

Figure 5.5 Joining a conversation on Twitter. Christina Hills had written a tweet about the iPhone. I replied with my own contribution to the discussion, and she responded. We get to talk about the iPhone and our followers get to follow a quick chat between two marketing coaches about a tool we're both using.

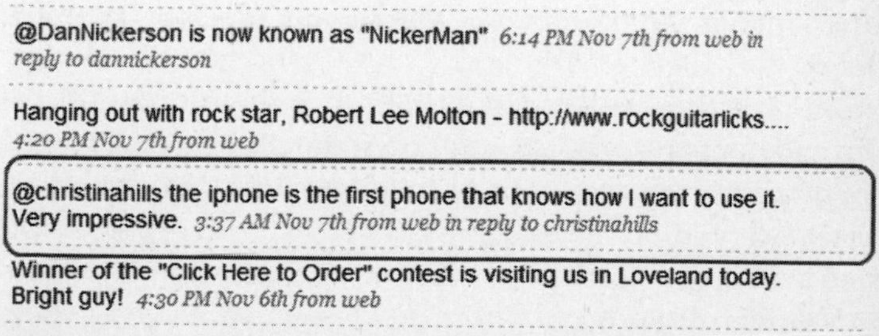

@DanNickerson is now known as "NickerMan" *6:14 PM Nov 7th from web in reply to dannickerson*

Hanging out with rock star, Robert Lee Molton - http://www.rockguitarlicks.... *4:20 PM Nov 7th from web*

@christinahills the iphone is the first phone that knows how I want to use it. Very impressive. *3:37 AM Nov 7th from web in reply to christinahills*

Winner of the "Click Here to Order" contest is visiting us in Loveland today. Bright guy! *4:30 PM Nov 6th from web*

Figure 5.6 My reply to Christina's tweet. I add my opinion—we're talking!

@problogger Good deal. Having such a huge reputation has its value. *8:10
AM yesterday from twhirl in reply to problogger*

@problogger How did you secure those Twitter accounts? How to go about
it? Through $$$? *8:05 AM yesterday from twhirl in reply to problogger*

@Spartz I secured the twitter usernames with a trade - some of my time for
the names *8:07 AM yesterday from TweetDeck in reply to Spartz*

Figure 5.7   Professional blogger Darren Rowse keeps his community close by answering their questions. Here he answers Spartz's (@spartz) question about his acquisition of a Twitter username for his new Twitter blog Twitip (www.twitip.com).

traditional link exchange. The better your tweets and the more popular your Twitter page, the easier it's going to be to get your name on other people's timelines.

Providing information isn't the only way to join a conversation though. An alternative method is to ask for information.

This is another good reason to read someone's timeline before you join the conversation. Some Twitterers are fantastic at answering people's questions. Others aren't so hot. That might be because they don't have the time. It could be because they have too many followers. Or it might just be because that's not what they want to do with their Twitter presence.

Read the old tweets first, and you'll be able to see how often the Twitterer answers and what kind of questions they're likely to answer, too. (See Figure 5.7.)

How to Be Interesting on Twitter

This is what it all comes down to. You can follow etiquette, offer great tips in replies to other people's tweets, and ask questions that get your name in the timelines of the most important Twitterers on Twitter.

But none of that will mean a thing if you don't have the sort of content and conversations on your own timeline that will turn those visitors into followers—and your followers into customers, clients, or regular users.

Even though Twitter asks a very specific question, there's a huge range of different kinds of content that you can write as tweets. In this section, I'm going to describe the most important and the most effective kinds of tweets.

In general, you can divide your tweets into two types: broadcasts and conversations.

It should be clear now that Twitter can be used in two ways. One way is to convey information—to tell your followers what you're doing, thinking, or have been doing until now.

That's a one-way stream. Tweets like these don't always expect replies. They're meant to be informative and entertaining, and while people might reply to them, their first function is to enable the Twitterer to tell his followers something they don't know.

It's little different to the way that a television station works.

The second types of tweets are those that are intended to spark discussions, or which form a part of a discussion. Questions and answers to other people's questions and replies are obviously conversation tweets, but they can be much more subtle than that. Just tweeting something controversial or even just writing the sort of thing that people will want to know more about can make for a good conversation tweet, too.

And having a conversation brings all sorts of benefits.

We've seen that when someone replies to one of your tweets, your name and link appear on their timeline, winning you more followers. Each discussion starter then can act like a viral ad.

You can reply to their replies, giving you easy additional content and an enjoyable conversation.

And the discussion as a whole can help to build a community and bring your followers—and potential customers—closer to your brand.

Ideally, a Twitter timeline should contain a good mixture of both kinds of tweets. If you're busy replying and chatting to your followers, you might start to look a little too cliquey. You'll probably find that you'll be talking to the same group of people and, worse, that you won't have complete control over the conversation. Instead of saying what you want to say, you'll feel obligated to discuss the topics that your followers want to ask you about.

If that's what you want your timeline to do, that's fine. Lots of people use Twitter in that way—much like a large, open instant messaging board—but if you're using Twitter for marketing, you will need to keep control of the message and the subjects of the discussions.

> Book signing at Barnes and Noble next Saturday! - In Northern Colorado? Come meet me at 12 noon - http://tinyurl.com/joelbook
>
> *about 22 hours ago from web*
>
> **joelcomm**
> Joel Comm

Figure 5.8   Link Tweets—"This is what I'm working on now." Read all about it here...

On the other hand, if all you do is broadcast, then your timeline is going to look a little dull. Although there are some very successful Twitterers who do nothing but broadcast—President Obama's campaign tweeting picked up almost 125,000 followers but did little more than tell people which rallies he was addressing—most Twitterers find it pays to combine the two approaches.

Use broadcast tweets to make sure the information you want to share gets across.

And use conversation tweets to turn those followers into a community, keep them coming back, and make sure that the issues they want discussed are addressed.

These are some of the most effective types of tweets that you can send:

This is probably the most common type of broadcast tweet, if only because there are a number of Twitter apps that let bloggers turn their posts into tweets automatically. (See Figure 5.8.)

It's also very useful.

If you've put up a new blog post, then you'll want people to know about it and read it, and many of your followers will want to do just that. Darren Rowse, for example, has a second Twitter account at @digitalps to promote his digital photography web site, Digital Photography School (digital-photography-school.com/blog/). (See Figure 5.9.)

Even though this timeline does nothing but announce automatically new posts that have been published on Darren's photography

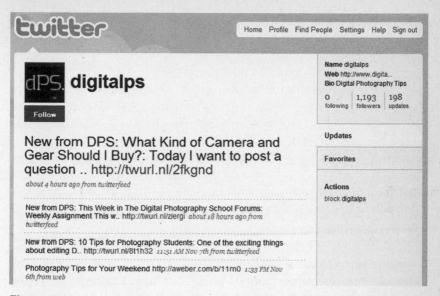

Figure 5.9 Could Darren Rowse's photography tweets be simpler? And yet they're making him money.

blog, it has a five-figure follower list and *a 10 percent clickthrough rate from doing absolutely nothing at all*.

In fact that means you can actually guesstimate how much each of those tweets is worth.

Now, I don't know what Darren's figures really are but if he's converting 3 percent of his users into revenue through advertising, and generating, let's say, one dollar from each ad click (he has a very well-respected site in a high-value field), then each tweet read by 15,000 followers could give him about $45 in direct revenue.

With 20 tweets visible on one page and representing four days' worth of new content, each Twitter page then could represent about $900 worth of income in the space of just a few days.

I doubt that Darren is making that much from this Twitter time-line. As follower numbers grow, clickthrough and conversion rates start to drop even if the overall figures get bigger. But it does show that it is possible to measure the value of a tweet that links to a web site and that the potential for earning with tweets that link to high-earning sites can be very rewarding indeed—especially when it's completely effort-free. Once the Twitter account has been opened and the Wordpress plugin installed, Darren doesn't have to do anything more and he could be picking up an extra $200 or so a day in direct revenue.

So how do you create tweets like these?

The easiest method is to do exactly what Darren did. He uses Twitterfeed, a service which checks his blog's RSS feed at set times and sends the title, description or both of any posts uploaded since its last check, together with a shortened link, through Twitter.

You can sign up for Twitterfeed at Twitterfeed.com. It's completely free and very easy to use, but you will need to have an RSS feed already set up on your site. (See Figure 5.10.)

Once you've logged in—the service uses OpenID, so you can sign in using the same username and password that you've created at any one of a number of different sites—you'll be asked for your Twitter username and password, the URL of your RSS feed, how often you want Twitterfeed to check for new content, and how many updates you want to add at a time.

You should be a little careful here. If you have the sort of blog that has new RSS content shooting out several times a day, then your timeline is going to be filled with posts. It's going to look like a broadcast station.

Figure 5.10 Twitterfeed turns your blog posts into tweets automatically.

Posting one article to your blog a day and letting Twitterfeed send one link tweet each day should be enough, especially if you're surrounding those tweets with other types.

Twitterfeed will also ask whether you want to include the post's title, description or both; how to shorten the link; and whether to order the tweets according the site's publication date or Globally Unique Identifier (GUID).

Include both the title and the description. Yes, it means that your tweet will be more than 140 characters, and that's bad etiquette. But the content itself is more than 140 characters, so by offering the first few words of the article you'll create curiosity. If your followers want to find out what the rest of the sentence says, they'll have to click the link.

It's harder to generate that sort of interest with just a title that fits into the tweet space.

There are a number of different services that shorten URLs so that you don't end up filling the tweet with your post's address. They all do more or less the same thing, so choosing TinyURL keeps things nice and simple, and unless you have a good reason to do otherwise, publish your posts by publication date. Twitter's users expect updates to be chronological so it's a good idea to keep to that format.

Finally, you have 20 characters to introduce the title, description, and link. Darren Rowse uses "New from DPS," which is straightforward and effective, but you can also try leaving this blank and just deliver the RSS text as tweet content together with the link. (See Figure 5.11.)

Test both approaches, track the results, and see which produces more clicks.

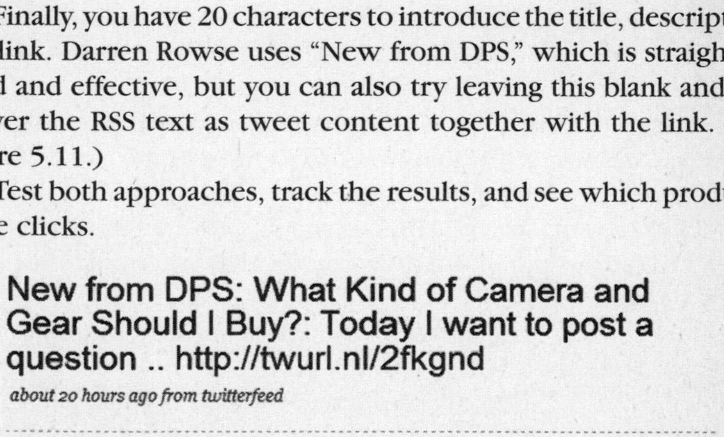

New from DPS: What Kind of Camera and Gear Should I Buy?: Today I want to post a question .. http://twurl.nl/2fkgnd

about 20 hours ago from twitterfeed

Figure 5.11   Darren Rowse's Twitterfeed tweets are longer than 140 characters and are cut in mid-flow. But they do create curiosity.

And Twitterfeed also lets you filter content so that it only tweets about posts that contain certain keywords. You might want to use this if your blog's topics are broader than the interests of your followers, but bear in mind that you can only include content, not exclude it. It's almost inevitable then if you do choose to filter your content that you'll miss at least some posts.

The alternative to using Twitterfeed—or a similar service—is to write the tweets manually. That will give you complete control over when you update, but it will require a little more effort. And be sure to use a URL-shortening service to keep the link short and memorable.

There is a risk involved in using this method though. Darren's photography blog is interesting enough—and well-known enough—for people to want to follow his automated tweets just to stay informed. It's little different to following an RSS feed. But you can't rely on this method if the site doesn't have its own pulling power already. Few people are going to be attracted by a headline from a firm it hardly knows.

Dell, for example, which is believed to have made over a million dollars using Twitter, has multiple accounts allowing each of its business branches to target separate markets. Whether you're following Direct2Dell (@direct2dell), Dell Cloud Computing (@dellintheclouds), Dell Small Business (@DellSmallBiz), or Dell Your Blog (@dellyourblog), most of what you'll receive will be Twitterfeed headlines from that business's blog.

The result is that even a company the size of Dell struggles to gain large followings on each of its Twitter accounts.

Of course, your own blog URLs aren't the only kind of links you can include in your tweets. You can add links to any sites that you've found interesting and, more importantly, that you think your users would find interesting.

You can even send links to the articles you're reading at the moment. (See Figure 5.12.)

I'm afraid! I'm so very afraid! - http://tinyurl.com/4m2ejk - Click at your own risk *about 17 hours ago from web*

Figure 5.12   Giving my followers fun with a link tweet.

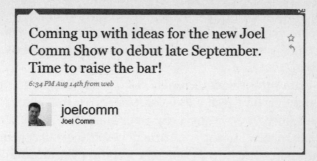

Coming up with ideas for the new Joel
Comm Show to debut late September.
Time to raise the bar!

6:34 PM Aug 14th from web

joelcomm
Joel Comm

Figure 5.13 Don't just tell us what you're doing; tell us what you think about what you're doing, too.

This will mean that you're sending people away from your timeline, but they're going to leave anyway. It's much better that they leave with the impression that you're up to date with the latest news on your topic and that you're a source of great information.

CLASSIC TWEETS—"THIS IS WHAT I'M DOING NOW"

It's unlikely that you're going to get many replies to link tweets. Your followers will click the link, leave, and by the time they remember they want to tell you what they think of the post, they're already long gone.

You might receive a few replies, but on the whole these are broadcast posts that are intended to be informative rather than updates that you can expect to provoke discussion.

But these could well be the only type of tweets that are purely one-way. As long as your followers are staying on your timeline, there's always the chance that someone will have a comment to make.

That's true even when you write the most basic of tweets—the one that Twitter suggests and that the site was created for: when you tell people what you're doing right now.

These are always going to be among the easiest types of tweets to create, and they're not hard to make interesting. Try to steer clear of describing what you're eating. Too many people do this and—unless you're traveling through the Sahara desert and dining on camel meat and toasted scorpions—that's going to get old very quickly. Focus on the various activities that you do during the day.

But here's the thing.

Don't just say, "Heading to the library" or "About to take a nap." *Also say what you think about what you're doing or explain why you're doing it.*

That makes the tweet so much more interesting.

The benefit of these kinds of tweets is that they let your followers follow you through the day. That's the idea of Twitter. It's a bit like reality TV, but you can choose from millions of lives to follow instead of the odd people the producers cram into the Big Brother house.

Just telling people exactly what you're doing then can be interesting, but talking to your followers about what you're doing is a little like stepping into the video booth and taking them into your confidence. (See Figure 5.13.)

It has a much more powerful binding effect and is far more entertaining.

So a tweet that might have said "Heading to the library" becomes "Heading to the library to grab two kids books for E. If I read The Gruffalo one more time, my head will explode."

And even "About to take a nap" would become "About to take a nap. Fingers already half-asleep. Summertime always does this to me."

Do you see how posts like these add personality to your timeline?

They don't just announce what you're doing. They describe who you are, too. They're the small talk that builds the connections and the trust on which all relationships—including business relationships—are built.

When you're competing for the attention of followers from among millions of other Twitterers, it's these little details that can help you to stand out.

OPINION TWEETS—"THIS IS WHAT I'M THINKING NOW"

Okay, Twitter doesn't actually ask this, and there are even some Twitter purists who feel that tweets should only be about actions, not opinions. (See Figure 5.14.)

I think they're wrong; that's my opinion.

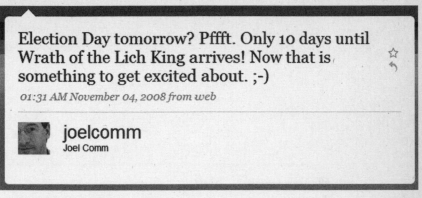

Election Day tomorrow? Pffft. Only 10 days until Wrath of the Lich King arrives! Now that is something to get excited about. ;-)

01:31 AM November 04, 2008 from web

joelcomm
Joel Comm

Figure 5.14   Sheesh ... it's just an opinion.

Just as you can make tweets about actions more interesting when you also state your thoughts about those actions, so you can make your timeline more personal when you include tweets that describe what you think.

Anyone who has read my tweets and my blog knows that I'm not someone who is afraid to state my opinion. I have lots of them, they're strongly held—and lots of people don't agree with them.

That's fine. They don't have to read them.

I understand that telling people what I think about the various issues that concern me deeply might put some people off following me and reading my blog posts. It could cost me customers.

I'm prepared to accept that, but I don't think it's happening. On the contrary, I think that my openness and the fact that my readers know where I stand and what I think—even if they don't always agree with me—has a positive effect on the whole. The people I lose by expressing my opinions are made up for by the close connection I have with the readers and followers who remain.

That's always a choice you have to make when expressing an opinion, especially on controversial issues and especially when you're using Twitter for marketing. If you're marketing a corporate brand rather than a personal brand, for example, it might be a good idea to keep the opinions focused on topics that affect your industry.

People without opinions look impersonal; companies without opinions look impartial.

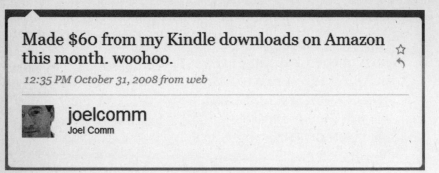

Made $60 from my Kindle downloads on Amazon this month. woohoo.

12:35 PM October 31, 2008 from web

joelcomm
Joel Comm

Figure 5.15 Mission accomplished!

If you are using Twitter to reinforce your personal brand, feel free to share your thoughts on anything that comes to mind.

Tell people what you think of something that affects your industry.

Tell them what you think of something that's happening in the news.

Tell them what you think of something someone else posted.

Use tweets to tell people what you think about anything, and you'll be putting your personality into timeline.

MISSION ACCOMPLISHED TWEETS—"THIS IS WHAT I'VE JUST DONE."

Share your thoughts and you're almost guaranteed to get people sharing theirs. Few things can start a discussion faster than saying something that you know lots of other people feel strongly about.

Telling people what you've just done can have the same effect. (See Figure 5.15.)

These kinds of tweets look like broadcasts. They're really little different to tweets that announce that you've just uploaded a new blog post.

Both talk about activities that you've already completed.

But while your followers can see the results of your link tweets, they won't always be able to see the results of your Mission Accomplished tweets. They'll only be able to comment on them.

Announcing that "I've just done this" is also another way of saying "What do you think of this?"

And the result is often answers to a question you didn't know you were asking. That's particularly true when the task you've accomplished is particularly interesting or impressive.

Tell people that you just broke $1,000 in monthly AdSense earnings, for example, and you can be confident that one of your followers will congratulate you—and ask you how you did it.

Tell them you just powered up a level in World of Warcraft, and you could get a similar response.

And tell them that you've just baked a chocolate cake and that you're about to get stuck in with a cup of coffee and the newspaper, and you'll probably get people asking you if they could have some, too.

Tweeting about what you've done might be an odd way to answer the question "what are you doing now?" but it can be a very good way to fill your timeline.

ENTERTAINMENT TWEETS—"I'M MAKING YOU LAUGH NOW."

Followers follow people whose tweets they find informative, but they also follow people whose tweets they find entertaining. Stephen Fry's tweets, for example, are filled with the sorts of witty comments and insights that gave him a career as a comedy actor. Reading them is like watching one of his television shows—in 140 character bites.

If you can come up with tweets that are fun and entertaining to read, as well as being genuinely helpful, then you'll never struggle to find followers. (See Figure 5.16.)

Figure 5.16   Okay, so I won't give up the day job . . .

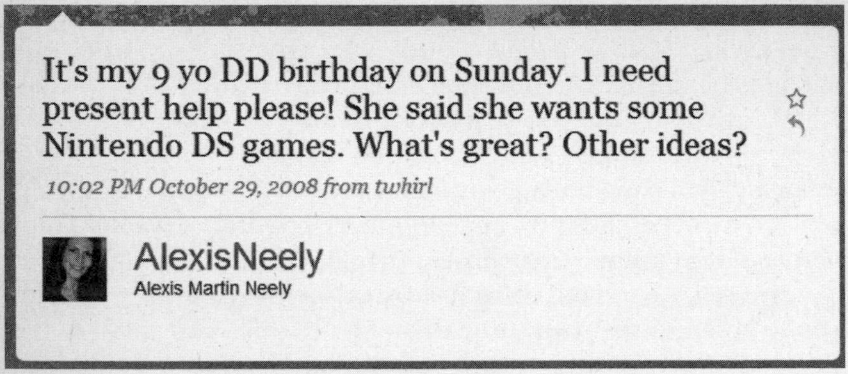

> It's my 9 yo DD birthday on Sunday. I need present help please! She said she wants some Nintendo DS games. What's great? Other ideas?
>
> *10:02 PM October 29, 2008 from twhirl*
>
> **AlexisNeely**
> Alexis Martin Neely

Figure 5.17 Legal expert and marketer Alexis Martin Neely (@alexisneely) puts out a call for help.

Ideally, of course, all of your tweets would be filled with jokes, humor, or wit. If you can't manage that, though, then depending on the subject of your timeline—and your ability to crack jokes—tossing in the odd humorous tweet can help to lighten the mood and make your Twitter page a fun space to hang out.

QUESTION TWEETS—"CAN YOU HELP ME DO SOMETHING NOW?"

One very easy way to turn your followers from readers into contributors is to ask a question. Twitterers do this often, tossing out requests for help from anyone in their follower list who might have some good advice.

Often, the questions will be very simple—ideas for birthday presents, recipes for tonight's dinner, and so on. Sometimes, they can be fairly complex and demand expert help from people with specialized knowledge. (See Figure 5.17.)

But questions don't just have to be requests for information. They can also be discussion starters. Ask your followers what they think about a topic, and you'll soon know just how engaged your followers really are—especially if you throw in your opinion first.

Tweeting "I can't stand violent video games" could you get a discussion started in response.

Tweeting "What do you think of violent video games?" could have a similar effect.

sims

Follow

check out my new disney park wall: http://twitpic.com/nxb1 now i need maps from the international parks!!

9 minutes ago from TweetDeck

Figure 5.18 Andrew Sims (@sims) shows off his desk.

But getting the discussion rolling by tweeting "My son plays violent video games. I can't stand them. What do you think?" increases the chances that your followers will hit the reply button and toss in their two cents.

PICTURE TWEETS—"LOOK AT WHAT I'VE BEEN DOING"

The short text updates that Twitter offers make both reading and contributing quick, letting users dip in and out. The investment in time and effort is small, but the rewards can be much, much bigger.

Not surprisingly, Twitterers have been looking for ways around those restrictions. Including a link that takes the follower to a web site is one simple way to do that, but you can also add a picture to your tweets.

Or rather, you can put a picture on the Web and send a tweet about it. (See Figure 5.18.) True, that's not quite the same thing as attaching a photo to a message in the same way that you can do on Facebook or MySpace, but it can still be a neat way to add content to your timeline and show people what you've been doing rather than tell them in 140 characters and create new discussion points.

In theory, you can do this any way you want. There's no reason why you couldn't post an image to your Flickr stream then add the link to a tweet. But TwitPic (www.twitpic.com) does make it all a great deal easier.

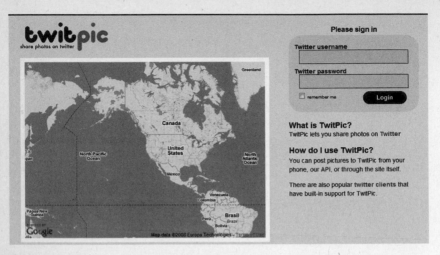

Figure 5.19   TwitPic lets you put pictures on Twitter—well, almost.

Sign in with your Twitter username and password, choose an image to upload, describe and tag it, then add a message on the same form that will be broadcast as a tweet. The tweet then appears in your timeline with a link to the image on TwitPic. (See Figure 5.19.)

It's very neat, very simple, and a very good way to share one more type of information with your followers.

DIFFERENT TYPES OF TWEET

As I look back on my own tweets, I can see that many of them can be easily categorized. This list isn't exhaustive, but it can supply you with models of the various kinds of tweets that you might want to include in your timeline.

The Mundane

Full of self and without any apparent redeeming value, the Mundane tweet is the backbone of Twitter. Narcissistic and banal, it's all about me. But don't think for a second that the Mundane tweet is not without merit. On the contrary, it's those Mundane tweets that help to build the foundations of a relationship. They're the first two steps that take you from "Like me" and "Know me" to "Trust me" and "Pay Me."

Here's a typical Mundane tweet: "In the New Zealand Air lounge at Sydney airport. Nice digs. Waiting for flight to SFO."

The Communicator

Instant messaging is mostly for person-to-person communication. Forums allow more people to enter the conversation, but the process is slow. The immediacy of Twitter has facilitated dialogue in a completely new way. Not only can you respond to someone else's tweet instantly, but others can enter the discussion just as easily. The Communicator tweet is nothing more than a public reply to another member. Many of the relationships formed via Twitter find their roots in this simple interactive tweet.

This is a typical Communicator tweet: *"@nprscottsimon so what's the difference between the NPR and @ifart app again?;-)"*

The Inquisitor

The Inquisitor tweet answers Twitter's question with a question of its own. It doesn't state what you are doing but seeks to use the massive Twitter member base to derive solutions, opinions, or any other response that can be gathered by polling the public. Asking a question is a great way to not only find an answer, but also to stir up your followers. After all, people love to be the one who provides the solution.

Here's a typical Inquisitor tweet: *"I am looking to hire a smart and energetic affiliate manager to join me in my Colorado office. Any entry-level people got what it takes?"*

The Answerman

The Answerman tweet can be as simple as responding to a trivia question or as serious as helping someone locate a dry cleaner in New York City. If you are able to answer a question for someone, why not lend a hand? It's instant recognition for you and a big help to them.

This is a typical Inquisitor tweet: *"@angiemeeker yes, check out @omNovia Web Conference, DM and I can answer some of your questions:)"*

The Sage

Want to tweet but don't have anything particularly important to say? Looking for something more significant than "Watching Three Stooges reruns. Gosh I love Curly!"? Simply find a quote from a famous author, lyrics from a favorite song, or line from a classic film to share with your followers. Pithy sayings and little tidbits of information are always a useful and entertaining way to keep your timeline ticking over—and they often get retweeted, too.

Here's a typical Sage tweet: *"'Only PASSIONS, great passions, can elevate the soul to GREAT things!' - Denis Diderot"*

The Reporter

Twitter has made citizen journalists out of all of us. From the terrorist attacks in Mumbai and the US Airways plane going down in the Hudson to the election sham in Iran and the death of Michael Jackson, more people are getting breaking news on Twitter than anywhere else. If you've got news—accurate news, of course—why not share it and inform your followers?

This is a typical Reporter tweet: *"Michael Jackson has died. A sad and tragic life. Now come the movies, books and tv specials . . . sigh. R.I.P. MJ. I hope you made your peace."*

The Kudos

Giving compliments is a fantastic way to show appreciation for someone. It's even more impactful when done on Twitter because it's public forum. Not only does the person or business receive the Kudos, but all of your followers see it as well.

Here's a typical Kudos tweet: *"Don't you look beautiful today @marycomm."*

The Critic

Some people just love to criticize—and sometimes that can be a good thing, especially on Twitter where companies are watching for negative comments.

This is a typical Critic tweet: *"United lost my luggage. Surprise, surprise."*

The Advocate

Every Friday on Twitter is FollowFriday, the day when Twitterers recommend that their followers follow selected people they follow. Just add the hashtag "#followfriday" to your tweet and list the usernames of the people you're recommending. Don't recommend more than about half a dozen people at a time, though, otherwise the introduction loses its shine. And of course you don't have to wait until Friday to do this.

Here's a typical Advocate tweet: *"#followfriday @dannickerson @cameronjohnson @marycomm @michelletrent @brianwillms @gaildoby @briankmeans @ksurritte - great peeps!"*

The Benefactor

People love free stuff. They also enjoy winning things. The Benefactor tweet is used for contests or giveaways. Designed to be retweeted, the goal is have your tweet go viral so that more people are aware of your contest. The Benefactor tweet is known to receive many retweets and can help increase your follower count quickly and legitimately.

This is a typical Benfactor tweet: *"I'm giving away the 4th edition of AdSense Secrets for FREE! No strings attached. http://adsense-secrets.com"*

Twitter asks a very simple question, and the answers it receives to that question have turned it into an Internet phenomenon. But one of the reasons that the site managed to expand so quickly is that its users have expanded the scope of its activities, too.

Top Twitterers don't just explain what they're doing now. They also reveal what they've *been* doing, would like to do, and what they're thinking as well. They make their followers laugh, think, read, and above all, respond—and they do it with a variety of different kinds of tweets.

In this section, I've described some of the tweets that I use to keep my followers engaged, and some of the tweets that I've seen other Twitterers using, too.

You don't have to use all of these different kinds of tweets. Darren Rowse's digital photography school timeline does fine with just one or two types. On the whole, I think you're going to get the best results when you mix things up.

That should give you a social atmosphere in which you're the host and free to make announcements and share your news.

There is one type of tweet that you *shouldn't* post though: the kind of tweet that gets you in trouble.

We've all heard about people who have created videos of themselves doing stupid things then posted them on YouTube for everyone—including their boss—to see.

The same thing has happened on Twitter.

When PR executive Steve Rubel (@steverubel) tweeted that he had a free subscription to *PC Mag* but always tossed it directly into the trash, the publishers weren't too happy.

As they were his clients, they were also in a position to do something about it, and that short tweet left a big hole in his income.

Twitter may sometimes feel like a private space in which you're just shooting the breeze with your pals, but it's not. People read it, so if there's anything you don't want everyone and their uncle to know, don't tweet it.

There are plenty of other ways to write enticing tweets without landing yourself in hot water.

How to Drive Behavior

So far I've been focusing largely on one particular type of follower response to your tweets. While some tweets simply provide information, others will spark a discussion in which your followers will provide information of their own in return, spreading your name across the Flickrverse and giving you a community.

But sometimes you want your followers to do other things.

Usually, that means clicking a link, but it rarely stops there. Once your follower has reached the web site, you'll need to do something to monetize them, or at least start the process of monetizing them.

Your ability to do that will clearly depend far more on what that web site says than on what a 140-character tweet says, but what you say on Twitter can have an effect on what the follower does eventually. Especially if you write the right kind of tweets.

We've already seen, for example, how T-shirt firm SpringLeap gets its users not just to visit its online store but to buy something when they get there by handing them a discount code on the way to the link. And they create urgency by making it clear that the code has a limited lifespan, increasing the chances that the follower will actually use it.

Discount cards and a time-limited offers are just two classic ways that you can influence follower behavior though.

Another method is to use spontaneity. Because Twitter happens in real time, you can decide to interact with your followers on the spur of the moment.

Anyone who's following your tweets at that particular moment gets to join in the fun and feel the benefits.

Anyone who stops by later will feel that they missed an opportunity and realize that they should be following you more often.

Sometimes, for example, I'll decide to do a live uStreamed broadcast from my office. (See Figure 5.20.) During a visit from another marketing guru, we'll turn on the video camera and bring our Twitter audiences into our discussion by announcing it on the site.

When followers understand that this is a one-off surprise chance to pick up some valuable information, there's a good chance that they'll tune in.

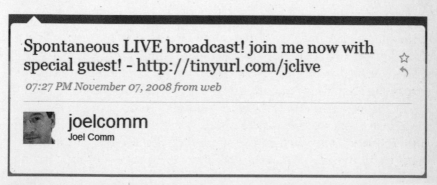

Figure 5.20   And on today's special edition of The Joel Comm Show . . .

Ultimately though, while your tweets can create interest, excitement, and anticipation, they can only do so much. The real conversion work comes when they reach your Web page, which is why you must have your sales channels ready and set up before you drive your followers towards them.

But direct sales aren't the only way you can benefit from a long list of engaged followers. In the next chapter, I'm going to look at what talking to your customers on Twitter can do for you.

6

The Magic of Connecting with Customers on Twitter

When you produce interesting tweets, your followers benefit.

They find their way to your site where they can pick up some valuable information.

They enjoy the benefits of special offers and discount codes.

They gain a greater understanding of the sort of products, services, and information you provide.

They feel part of a community that shares even more useful information and which provides support too.

And they can have a good time as well.

But a solid group of followers is also a resource for you, and not just because some of those followers will go ahead and make purchases either from you or from your sponsors. They're valuable because they're a giant source of information.

They're a source of information about your market and your products.

They're a source of information about who's talking about you, spreading your name, and winning you referrals.

And they're a source of information about all sorts of things that can help you to improve your products and grow your business.

In this chapter, I'm going to explain how Twitterers are using the site to build a focus group of customers that they can draw on to increase their bottom line.

We're releasing 3 new podcasts next year! Does anyone want a sneak peek at the show to be released in January?

about 6 hours ago from web

waltsnider
Walt Snider

Figure 6.1 Podcaster Walt Snider (@waltsnider) rewards his followers with a sneak peek and puts himself in line for some valuable feedback, too.

Identifying Problems and Soliciting Feedback

The people who choose to follow you on Twitter are your most dedicated customers. They're the ones who want to be the first to know when you release a new product. They want to know what you're planning next, to pick up discounts that will cut the cost of their next purchase, and to lend you a hand, too.

Many of your followers will be such enthusiasts that they'll want to have an influence over your products, your blog posts, or the direction of your company.

They want to contribute.

All you have to do is take advantage of that offer of help.

One way to do that is to give your followers a sneak peek before a major release and ask what they think. (See Figure 6.1.)

Your followers will love this. They'll understand that they're being told about a new product before anyone else. That will make them feel part of an exclusive club.

When they tweet you back with their comments, you'll get to identify problems, bugs, and areas of improvement before you take the product public. You'll also get to build up interest so that when you do hit the release date, you've already primed the market, and you'll be able to use their praise as testimonials that you can include on your sales page.

Is the sales copy a disaster, or does it rock? Go ahead, do your worst! *about 3 hours ago from web*

Go look at www.blogflippingfool.com and tell me what you think of the new site. Is it compelling? Good? Bad? Please check it out! Thanks. *about 3 hours ago from web*

Hello Twitters! Who's out there who can do me a really quick favor? I want you guys to tell me what you think of something. *about 3 hours ago from web*

Figure 6.2 Marketer Thomas C. Gajdjis puts his followers to work.

When Internet marketer Thomas C. Gajdjis (@tommygadget) wrote a sales page for his ebook about blog flipping, for example, he wanted to know whether his copy looked compelling. The usual way to do that is to put up different pages and compare the results over time. Thomas though, was able to ask his followers what they thought about his copy so that he could iron out any bumps before the launch. (See Figure 6.2.)

He was also sending his followers to his sales page, making them aware that he was about to release a new book on a topic that they or their own readers might find interesting, and perhaps most important, when those followers replied, their followers would be alerted to his sales page, too.

That's very simple. You don't have to do any more than make what you want examined available and then send out a tweet. You'll get a ton of very valuable feedback.

But this is another time to remember that Twitter is a public forum. When your followers hit the "reply" button to tell you what they think, they're also going to be telling their followers what they think.

That could be valuable marketing. It will help to spread the word about your launch. But that word-of-mouth marketing is only going to be helpful if your product is almost ready anyway. If you need to make a lot of corrections before you start selling, then that second ring of followers is going to see a great deal of criticism and very little praise. That's not likely to lead to sales.

If the product you want feedback about is almost ready, then ask your followers to "reply." Everyone will see their response.

If you think the product or the sales page might still need a lot of work, ask them to direct message or email you. You won't get the viral marketing, but you will get some valuable, relatively confidential feedback.

The drawback to picking up comments in this way is that any feedback you receive is likely to be short. If you're asking people to reply, they're not going to do more than identify one or two elements that could be changed and point them out in 140 characters or less.

If you're asking them to email you, you might get a longer report but you're still not likely to get a huge amount of detail. Your followers will want to be helpful, but few of them are going to invest a huge amount of time into improving your product or your sales copy.

Unless you ask them a heap of detailed questions.

When I was putting together the first edition of this book, I wanted to know how people were using Twitter and what they wanted to do with the site. I could have simply sent out a tweet that asked, "Thinking of writing a book about marketing with Twitter. What would you like to see in it?" but I don't think I would have received many replies. (See Figure 6.3.)

Instead, I used my company's survey software, InstantFormPro (www.instantformpro.com), to create a short questionnaire that guided my followers' responses and gave me exactly the information I was looking for.

Obviously, I promoted the survey through tweets, and I even included it on my Twitter background.

That survey gave me a huge amount of data, and it also provided me with a valuable list of people who had expressed an interest in the subject.

As a method of generating detailed feedback as well as increased marketing range, surveys can be very powerful.

Discovering Your Top Fans, Promoters, and Evangelists

Read someone's Twitter timeline and it's going to feel a little like walking into a private party. The Twitterer will be replying to

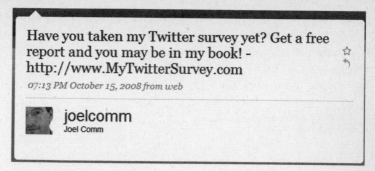

Have you taken my Twitter survey yet? Get a free report and you may be in my book! - http://www.MyTwitterSurvey.com

07:13 PM October 15, 2008 from web

joelcomm
Joel Comm

Figure 6.3 How to get masses of feedback for a project in the works.

followers who have replied to his tweets and addressing issues that other followers have raised.

There should be plenty of other interesting content there, too, but much of the timeline of a good Twitterer will be directed at individuals.

Why those individuals? How do Twitterers choose which people to address and which to mention specifically, drawing the attention of all of their followers in turn to that Twitterer?

How *should* they choose them?

Often, a reply that drops a name in front of every other follower on a list will be a direct response to something that Twitterer said. Hit "reply" to a tweet, and there's a reasonable chance that the Twitterer will hit "reply" back. That's especially true if you've done your homework, read the timeline, and paid attention to the sorts of things that might catch a Twitterer's attention.

Spot that someone you follow tends to reply to questions, for example, and should get a response with a good query. If they respond to praise, then a pat on the back could win you a place on their timeline.

But there's another reason that a Twitterer could—and should—mention one of his followers in his timeline: if that follower is one of his key marketers.

Every good business has people like this. They're your most loyal customers, the ones who rave about your products to their friends, send links to your articles to their contact list, and are always getting in touch with questions, suggestions, and feedback.

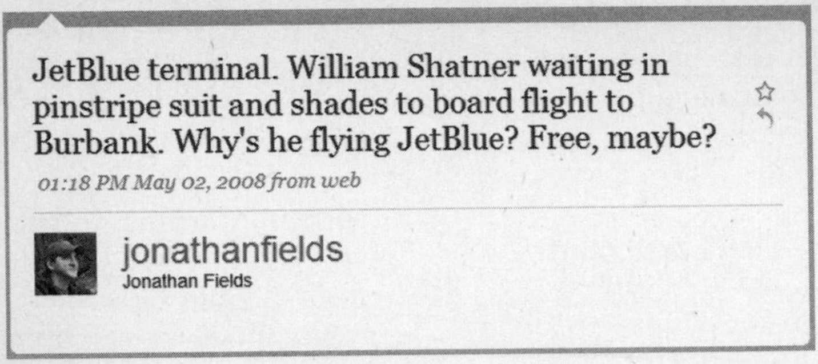

> JetBlue terminal. William Shatner waiting in
> pinstripe suit and shades to board flight to
> Burbank. Why's he flying JetBlue? Free, maybe?
>
> *01:18 PM May 02, 2008 from web*
>
> **jonathanfields**
> Jonathan Fields

Figure 6.4　Jonathan Fields spots Captain Kirk boarding a JetBlue plane. JetBlue spots the reference and hones in on a customer.

Those people are worth gold to any business and every good marketer will want to do everything they can both to keep them happy and to make the most of them.

Twitter lets you do both. And it helps you to find them, too.

In fact, there are all sorts of ways to discover who is talking about you the most on Twitter—and companies are using them.

In September 2006, for example, *BusinessWeek* described how Twitterer Jonathan Fields (@jonathanfields) had spotted William Shatner boarding a JetBlue flight at New York's JFK airport earlier that year. He sent out a tweet that wondered aloud why the actor was flying a budget airline and immediately received an email saying that JetBlue was now following him on Twitter. (See Figure 6.4.)

The company had been alerted to its name in a tweet and responded by following a customer who had already shown that he was prepared to talk about the airline.

There are a number of ways to do that.

One method is simply to toss your username into Twitter's search engine at search.twitter.com or in the search field on your Twitter page and see who comes up. You will be able to count who has mentioned you the highest number of times in their tweets and who is giving you the most praise.

But search will only tell you who has been talking about you in the past. Unless you leave it open in your browser and refresh the page constantly, it won't tell you who is talking about you now.

Twitter does have a tracking system that can do that. Type "track [keyword]" into your instant messenger or mobile device and every time someone types that keyword—such as your "@username"—in a tweet, you'll receive a message telling you what they said. (See Figure 6.5.)

You'll then be able to check out who they are or reply to their tweet.

That's one useful way to stay informed about what people are saying about you, but not everyone uses a mobile device with their Twitter account, and when you're tracking to discover who are your biggest evangelists, you also want to be able to keep records of what people are saying.

That will enable you to create detailed lists of who is generating referrals on your behalf, which topics interest them the most, and what is most likely to spark a retweet or a reply.

A better method is to use a service called Monitter (www .monitter.com). This lets you keep track of a number of different

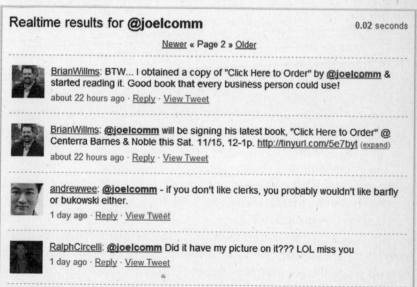

Realtime results for @joelcomm   0.02 seconds

Newer « Page 2 » Older

BrianWillms: BTW... I obtained a copy of "Click Here to Order" by **@joelcomm** & started reading it. Good book that every business person could use!
about 22 hours ago · Reply · View Tweet

BrianWillms: **@joelcomm** will be signing his latest book, "Click Here to Order" @ Centerra Barnes & Noble this Sat. 11/15, 12-1p. http://tinyurl.com/5e7byt (expand)
about 22 hours ago · Reply · View Tweet

andrewwee: **@joelcomm** - if you don't like clerks, you probably wouldn't like barfly or bukowski either.
1 day ago · Reply · View Tweet

RalphCircelli: **@joelcomm** Did it have my picture on it??? LOL miss you
1 day ago · Reply · View Tweet

Figure 6.5 Twitter's search engine gives me a list of people who have been talking about me. Brian Williams (@brianwillms) is the CEO of my local Chamber of Commerce. He's a very nice man, and it looks like he's very well read, too.

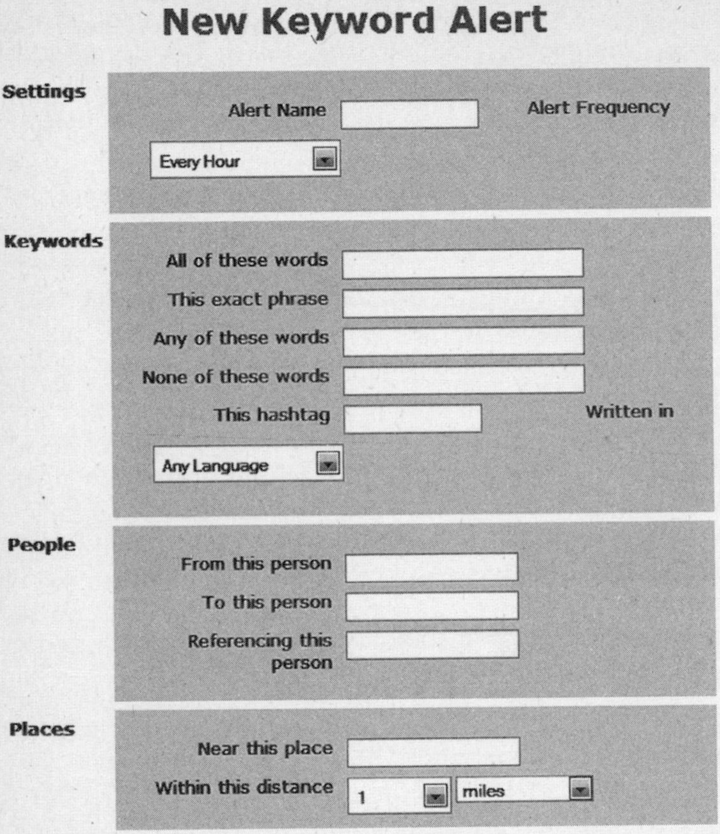

New Keyword Alert

Settings

| Alert Name | [ ] | Alert Frequency |

Every Hour [▼]

Keywords

All of these words [ ]

This exact phrase [ ]

Any of these words [ ]

None of these words [ ]

This hashtag [ ]   Written in

Any Language [▼]

People

From this person [ ]

To this person [ ]

Referencing this person [ ]

Places

Near this place [ ]

Within this distance   1 [▼]   miles [▼]

Figure 6.6 TweetBeep keeps your ear to the ground, letting you know who's saying what about you.

keywords in real time. It's fun but you can't keep the tweets permanently, so unless you're watching it all the time and making notes you will miss some people.

The best way to keep track of what people are saying about you, your product, or even your industry then is to use TweetBeep (www.tweetbeep.com). (See Figure 6.6.)

This works in exactly the same way as Google's Alert service. Sign up and you'll be able to enter keywords that you want to follow. TweetBeep will search for them every hour or every day, depending on your choice, and send you an email every time it comes across a new mention of that term.

Set up filters in your email client and you'll soon have all of your keywords arranged into folders so that you can see which Twitterers are most interested in the topics your business covers.

So you could have one alert—and one folder—for tweets that mention your username. Another alert could cover mentions of your business's name. Another could look for mentions of your blog, and another the title of your ebook, your main product or your topic, and so on.

That will give you all the data you need to create list of the most important—and active Twitterers—in your field.

Now you have to act on that data.

Obviously, the first thing you should do is to make sure that you're following those Twitterers. They're going to be tweeting about all sorts of other topics, too, but because these people are of interest to you, you'll want to know what they're saying.

This is exactly what Twitter is for.

You'll then want to start bringing them into your conversation.

If they haven't replied to one of your tweets already, then start by introducing yourself. Find one of their tweets to reply to and offer some good information.

Even if they've only mentioned your subject rather than your name or one of your products, there's still a good chance that they'll know who you are, so it shouldn't be difficult to get them to follow you and to start building up a relationship.

And once you have that relationship, you'll want to make the most of it. Before you release a new product, reply to your top evangelists to ask them what they think.

Give them sneak peeks of what you're doing so that they'll rush off and tell their friends.

When you see that they've left a great recommendation for you in a tweet, direct message them to give them a bonus reward.

When they mention that they bought your latest product or that they're reading your blog post, drop them a line to ask what they think. They'll be thrilled, and you'll get a testimonial on their timeline.

When you can see who is saying nice things about you—and what they're saying—you can take all sorts of steps to encourage them and keep them spreading the word.

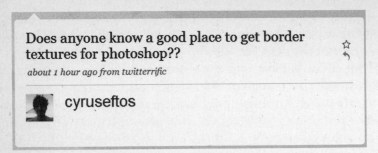

Figure 6.7   Cyruseftos (@cyruseftos) puts out a call for help.

If they're saying good things, it's like having a constant stream of referrals and recommendations right on your profile page.

Your Micro Help Desk

Your evangelists and promoters are people who are going to be helping you anyway. They do that because they like your business. They're excited about it, they enjoy the benefits it brings, and they want their friends to share those benefits, too.

Only a small number of your followers are going to fit into this category though. The rest are just going to be people who are interested in what you do and want to know what you're doing now.

But those people can still bring you a huge amount of value.

We've already seen how they can help you to spot problems before you launch products. But they can also help you in all sorts of other ways, too. Because the site is filled with experts who possess all sorts of specialized knowledge, Twitter can be a one-stop help desk for whatever you're struggling with.

The easiest way to find help is simply to ask the people you know if they can supply it. (See Figure 6.7.)

Obviously, this is always going to work best when you have a giant follower base. The higher the number of people following your tweets, the greater the chances that one of them will be able to lend a hand.

That means that as you're building your followers, it's worth paying attention to what each of them does and considering the sort of help they might be able to offer in the future.

Choose to follow a Web design expert, for example, and you should be picking up some interesting tweets that could help generate your own design ideas. But if you can get the designer to sign up as one of your followers, then when you ask a question about Web design, there's a good chance that you'll get a professional answer.

It's also worth looking at the number of followers your followers have. If you can get followed by a few people with large audiences, there's always a chance that your requests for help will be passed along or that their readers will click through to see your tweets.

Followers with lots of followers of their own can provide outlets to plenty of help.

So how do you ask for that help?

You could certainly come straight out and ask if anyone knows a skilled programmer or a great copywriter or where you can get a good logo designed.

That would be very simple, and depending on the size and make-up of your followers, there's a very good chance that it would give you results.

You could also ask your followers to retweet your message to help you find the assistance you need.

And again, every time you do this, you're spreading your name across the Twitterverse. People like to help and they like to show off their own expertise, too, so when someone tweets back with the information and advice you were looking for, you get to appear in their timeline and they get to look like an expert.

Everyone wins.

But Twitter isn't the best place to find the help you need for your business.

Conferences are much better.

I'm a huge fan of conferences. I think they're fantastic places to learn new skills, become aware of outstanding opportunities, and meet other entrepreneurs keen on starting joint ventures and bursting with ideas.

I don't understand why everyone doesn't go to a conference.

I do understand why everyone doesn't go to *every* conference. That would take far too much effort.

One of the most effective uses for Twitter then is to follow tweets from people attending conferences.

That's never going to be as effective as being there in person, but it is still valuable.

If you know someone—or even better, a group of people—who are attending a conference, make sure that you're following their tweets. You should be able to pick up an idea of what people are saying, the sort of advice the speakers are offering, and the questions people are asking.

It might even be possible to tweet back with your own questions for someone at the conference to ask on your behalf.

I still think that you should be attending conferences. But if there are some that you can't make, Twitter can help you to get a taste of what you're missing—and tap a truly expert source.

Both of these approaches, though, are about you extracting help from your followers. That's valuable, but it works the other way too.

Yes, you should be offering solutions whenever you see people asking questions in your field. We've already seen how that can be a great way to win followers and show off your own skills.

But it's even more important that you supply help that's directly related to your business.

This is where tracking keywords related to your business is so important.

It would be nice to believe that every tweet that mentions the name of your business is going say what a great company you have, how awesome your products are, and that absolutely everyone should buy absolutely everything you're selling. Then buy some more for their families.

But life isn't like that.

Inevitably, you're going to see tweets from people who just weren't happy.

Some of them won't be happy with the quality of the product. They'll find that it didn't do what they hoped it would do—even if their hopes were way off-base.

Others will complain about the customer service. For some people, if they don't get a refund because they're not still using a product four years after buying it, something's wrong with the company.

And others will have encountered a bug, a mistake, or an inaccuracy that they want to highlight.

@hephail please let us know what issues you
faced with Safari, it is one of our favourite
browsers and we do our best to support it

03:43 PM November 06, 2008 from web in reply to hephail

 cleartrip

Figure 6.8   ClearTrip (@cleartrips), an Indian travel firm, uses
its followers as an unpaid quality assuance team.

Whatever the reason, whenever you see a complaint that relates
to your product, jump on it.

Ask them what the problem is. Show that you're prepared to
work with them to try to fix it. And when you do fix it, let them
know by sending them a reply tweet so that everyone can see.

When you do that, you pick up a number of important benefits.

You stop that bad publicity in its tracks. If positive viral marketing can have fantastic effects on your sales, negative tweets can
seriously restrict your growth.

You also get to turn a complainer into an unpaid member of
your quality assurance team.

That old saying "the customer is always right" might not always
be right (sometimes the customer is just plain wrong, but it's right
not to tell him), but you can always learn something from a customer
complaint.

When ClearTrip, an online travel firm in India, noticed a tweet
that mentioned the site wasn't working in Safari, for example, its
staff were quick to ask what was going wrong so that they could fix
the problem. (See Figure 6.8.)

The risk here is that your Twitter account will morph into an
always-on customer help desk. Rather than broadcasting the messages you want to put out, you'll be spending much of your Twitter
time telling people how to solve their problems and following up
bug reports. (See Figure 6.9.)

But perhaps that's no bad thing. ClearTrip has both a corporate Twitter account and its staff have accounts, too. Twitter itself
sends out tweets that announce error reports and keep its followers

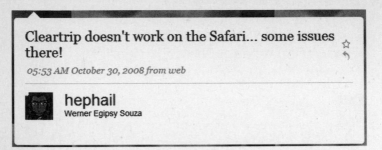

> ### Cleartrip doesn't work on the Safari... some issues there!
> *05:53 AM October 30, 2008 from web*
>
> **hephail**
> Werner Egipsy Souza

Figure 6.9   Hephail (@hephail) spots a problem with a product. The company spots his complaint and acts on it.

informed about what's happening on the site, while its staff are free to tweet their personal stuff without being disturbed.

Because there's no limit to the number of Twitter accounts you can set up, you could create a separate account that functioned as an online, real-time help desk.

Your customers would know where to come for help and everyone would see that you're dedicated to meeting their demands.

Twitter is as much a conversation tool as broadcasting device. Used carefully, you can have fantastic chats with your customers and your clients.

You can have conversations that help you to spot problems before your product is released and to win feedback and reviews.

You can follow conversations so that you can see what people are saying about you—and encourage them to keep on saying nice things about you.

And you can talk to those people who are less than completely happy, turning your Twitter account into the kind of open access help desk that your customers will love and your potential customers will appreciate.

But you can also use Twitter to talk to your staff and your team. That's what I'm going to discuss in the next chapter.

7

Leveraging Twitter for Team Communication

It's a conundrum. Twitter relies on tiny little posts and yet the effect is massive. It's certainly been massive for the people who created the site, but it's also huge for relationships between people. Now readers of my blog and followers of my tweets can see what I'm doing and what I'm thinking throughout the day.

Instead of relying on an occasional blog post, they get brief updates that, because they only take a second to write, come in on a regular basis.

Now I'm not a distant friend who sends occasional letters. I'm the guy in the next office they pass in the corridor.

That makes a huge difference to the way any online entrepreneur interacts with his customers but also with anyone else involved in his business.

I have a beautiful office in Loveland, Colorado, staffed with some great people. But I also employ freelancers scattered around the country and even around the world. It's one of the benefits of the digital age: I can hire the best people for the job wherever they may be.

Some of those people have been working with me for years. I've never met them, and I can count on the fingers of half a hand the number of times I've spoken on the phone to some of them. Lots of other entrepreneurs do the same thing, and plenty of people today consider their local coffee shop to be their prime working space.

These days you don't need to be in the same office as someone working on the same project to get the task done. As long as everyone has an Internet connection—and you can rely on them—your team members can be thousands of miles apart.

While telecommuting means you're not limited to your local labor pool, it does have its disadvantages. A team member you never see and never talk to can feel remote. The connection between you isn't the same as that between you and someone in the same building. They'll feel left out of the loop, and they won't be up to date with the changes happening in your company.

That means they'll be less able to help with those changes and there's always the risk that they'll be left behind.

When you're all Twittering though, it's much easier to see what everyone is doing.

You can see what they're working on, the team members can see what you're up to, and you'll all feel much closer.

Twitter for Virtual Team Leaders

That means those tweets don't even have to be work-related. While a tweet telling everyone on the team which aspect of the project they're building now will certainly be helpful, a quick note offering a prediction for the night's ball game or revealing what's in their grocery bag can be useful, too.

That's because of Twitter's power as a virtual water cooler.

It's a place where people come to hang out, shoot the breeze, and talk about things that aren't really business-oriented at all.

And just as those sorts of random conversations make people feel closer to each other, so tossing out random thoughts on Twitter can have the same effect.

You could say what you're doing, add a link to a blog you're reading, or reply to someone else's tweet. The frequent reminders keep everyone in each other's minds, and *the thoughts themselves let everyone understand who the writer is.*

This is important. Twitter has been criticized for posting a lot of pointless posts. One company even reported that 40 percent of all tweets are "pointless babble." What nonsense. Most conversation is pointless babble, but it's that small talk that deepens trust, builds relationships, and allows people to like each other. Employees and team members don't just work for money. They also work for the satisfaction of the job they're doing. They stay with their current companies and continue working on their current projects because they find the challenge interesting—and because they *like* the people they're working with.

Those connections are as much a part of incentivizing workers as bonuses and options.

When your team is scattered and the members never meet, those connections are very weak. It becomes very easy for a team member to drift away and be tempted by another interesting project.

If loyalty can no longer be taken for granted at bricks-and-mortar companies, it certainly can't be assumed at firms connected only by email.

On the other hand, when team members feel that they're working for a real person, alongside other real people—people who play video games, teach their kids soccer, cook lasagna at the weekends, and so on—they feel that they're part of a community. It becomes much harder to walk away. They're not betraying an email; they're leaving a friend in the lurch. (See Figure 7.1.)

You're likely to be sending these kinds of personal, informal tweets anyway.

You're also likely to be sending out tweets that announce blog updates or that invite your followers to check out your new release. But those non-business tweets can have strong business effects.

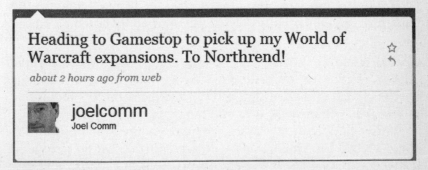

Heading to Gamestop to pick up my World of Warcraft expansions. To Northrend!

about 2 hours ago from web

joelcomm
Joel Comm

Figure 7.1   Now everyone knows I like video games.

Creating a Twitter Account for a Virtual Team

Making sure that your Twitter timeline includes at least some informal tweets will help you connect with your virtual team members. But it's not a strategy that's dedicated to the virtual team. Those team members will only form one part of your followers. As a result, they may feel a little like interlopers, watching the conversation from the outside.

If you want to really get them involved, you can try to bring them into your community by creating a dedicated Twitter account just for the team.

We've already seen how ClearTrip has both a corporate Twitter account and separate accounts that its employees use to communicate with customers.

There's no reason why a team leader couldn't create a Twitter account specifically for members of the team.

Each team member won't only feel that they're a member of an exclusive club. They'll also understand that they're working on something communal rather than building something alone.

The risk though is that communication that might best be kept secure will find its way into the public. Just as you can monitor the conversations of people who mention your products so your competitors would be able to follow what you're saying to your team members—unless you keep your tweets private.

Click the "Protect my updates" check button on the Settings page of your Twitter account, and only the people you approve will be able to follow your updates. (See Figure 7.2.)

You're not going to have many followers on a timeline like this. And you're not going to be driving people to your commercial sites

☐ Protect my updates

Only let people whom I approve follow my updates. If this is checked, you WILL NOT be on the public timeline.

Save

Figure 7.2 Protect your updates and your team chats will stay private.

or to your blog. But that's not the point. You will have created an online forum where your team members can talk, interact, and keep everyone updated on the progress of the project.

There are some disadvantages here though.

Not all of your team members are going to be familiar with Twitter or feel comfortable writing in 140-character posts. You're likely to find that this strategy works best with people who already know how to use the system and do it anyway.

And while it works in real time, you want your team members to be working on the project, not spending their time writing tweets! Use a team Twitter account to troubleshoot problems, request help, and provide updates, but this is one time when you want to try to keep the tweets as professional as possible.

Building a Team with Twitter

So Twitter can help to keep together a team that's already been established. It can do that by helping scattered members to understand that they're working alongside each other and that they're not alone. And it can do it by providing an online clubhouse where they can get together to keep everyone informed.

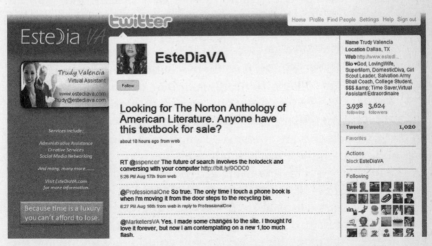

Figure 7.3 Virtual assistant Trudy Valencia (@estediava) uses Twitter to join the corporate team.

But the site can also be used to put those teams together in the first place.

When you need help with your business, there are all sorts of places you can look. I've had a lot of luck with Elance, a job site for freelancers, but word of mouth, personal web sites, and even friends and family can all be good sources of team members. (See Figure 7.3.)

In fact, you're likely to be spoiled for choice, which is not a good thing. Choosing the right person isn't easy so you could find yourself wasting time trying to break in new team members only to find that they don't make the grade and need to be replaced.

Twitter can make those hiring decisions a great deal easier.

The fact that someone is on Twitter is already a good sign. That shows that they're not scared of new technology and that they're used to communicating and staying in touch at a distance—all important considerations when you're building a virtual team.

But Twitter also reveals far more about that team member than you're likely to find on any resume or in any portfolio.

Of course, you'll want to read those, too. The Twitterer's bio page should contain a link to their web site, where you'll be able to see how they present themselves professionally. Need a designer, for example, and you'll be able to see their designs and gain an understanding of their style.

But there's more to working with someone than the quality of the work they deliver.

There's also the question of their reliability, their professionalism, their ability to keep to deadlines, their communication skills, and whether they're just a pleasant person to work with.

When you're hoping to work with someone over the long term, all of those elements are going to be important—and not all of them will be visible on their professional web site.

Read their tweets, however, and you'll be able to see not just what their work is like, but what they're like, too.

You can start with a search. Toss in a keyword that only a professional with the sort of skills you need is likely to use. If you were looking for a designer, for example, you could see who is using the term "raster." (See Figure 7.4.)

stereo_type: anyone know of a decent vector editor OTHER than illustrator for Mac? I'm using PixelMator for **raster** stuff, but need my vector goodness
1 day ago · Reply · View Tweet

raster: Note to self: do *not* plug the space heater into the UPS...
1 day ago · Reply · View Tweet

gabeboning: jeez... the horror of being trapped inbetween vector graphics and **raster** graphics
2 days ago · Reply · View Tweet

Figure 7.4   Don't know what these people are talking about; they must be designers.

If you were hunting for someone to help with your web site, you could see who's been tweeting about "ruby-on-rails."

If you were looking for a copywriter to produce a sales page, you could search for terms such as "copy," "headline," or "call to action."

Clearly, not all of those people are going to be available for freelance work. But some will be, and you can add terms such as "freelance" or "contract" to narrow down the search.

Once you've managed to find a few freelancers with the skills you need, the fun can really begin. You'll be able to read their tweets to see how friendly they are and what they like to discuss.

There are a couple of things worth paying particular attention to.

First, note how often they answer questions.

Asking technical questions is nice—just knowing how to ask requires some knowledge—but more important is knowing how to answer. That betrays an even higher level of knowledge, and even more important, it also shows a willingness to help people with less knowledge than they possess themselves—and that, after all, is why you're hiring someone.

But note, too, how they use jargon. Are they comfortable with the technical terms? Do they appear to be familiar with the latest technology.

And even more important, look at who they're following and who's following them.

The best experts in each field are likely to have created their own communities of similarly skilled professionals. They might not have done that deliberately, but if they're tweeting about their profession and providing good information, there's a great chance that other professionals will be following them.

If you don't want to approach that professional—or if they're not available for hire—then following their own follow list could lead you to others.

This strategy works in reverse, too.

Virtual assistant Trudy Valencia (@estediava) uses Twitter to trawl the site for possible clients. When she finds people who have expressed an interest in outsourcing, she follows them and makes it clear that she's available to lend a hand.

It's a very simple formula that requires little more than careful searching, a polite approach, and the understanding that you're not going to win a job with every follow.

Twitter works wonderfully when used by individuals to broadcast information about themselves and to keep in touch with other individuals across the Twitterverse.

It can also be hugely beneficial to businesses relying on scattered teams, allowing them to create the kind of bonds that previously could only be formed in offices.

But Twitter is also used to build brands.

8

Using Twitter to Help Build Your Brand

Online advertising has really spoiled everyone. Not only can advertisers now finely target where their ads appear, making sure that they're only shown to people most likely to find them interesting, they can also track what happens after those ads go up.

They can measure how many people see the ads, how many click on them to learn more, and most important, how many actually buy as a direct result of seeing their commercial.

With that kind of targeting and data, it's no wonder that Google, with its leading AdSense system, is worth billions of dollars.

But the old advertising system didn't disappear. Drive down any highway and you're still going to see giant billboards drawing your eye and advertising businesses.

Times Square still has its neon lights, and even TiVo hasn't rid television programs of commercial breaks every 10 minutes.

The Internet might have changed some of the ways that advertising works, but brand-building is still important. *If you want people to know who you are and remember the name of your business, you have to keep putting it in front of them and you have to continue to interact with your buyers*.

That's what traditional advertising has always aimed to do. An advertiser who bought a radio spot in the 1950s wasn't expecting to see a spike in sales immediately after his ad was broadcast. But he was expecting to see his product's name recognition increase.

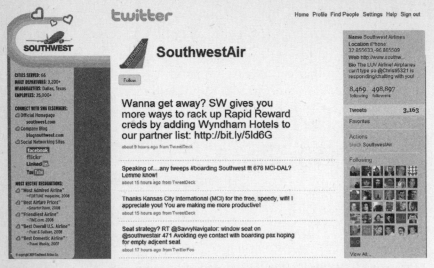

Figure 8.1   Southwest Airlines is just one company that uses Twitter to talk to customers and build a brand.

Customers would become familiar with the product, and over time, as they absorbed the advertising message, they'd trust it and they'd buy it.

On the Internet that's been done with banner ads that keep a product's name visible at the top of a Web page, and with campaigns that pay for each thousand views rather than for each click that the ad receives.

And it can be done now with Twitter, too.

Twitter has proven a very valuable branding tool, and it hasn't been lost on many big corporations. (See Figure 8.1.)

Just some of the companies you can find on Twitter include Carnival Cruise Lines (@CarnivalCruise), Delta (@deltaairlines), Jetblue (@JetBlue), Dell (@Direct2Dell), Amazon (@amazondeals), Forrester (@forrester), GM (@GMblogs), and my favorite, M&Ms (@msgreen and @mmsracing).

All of these companies (or products) are using Twitter to build a loyal following with their customers and promote their brand. In this chapter, I'll explain some of the most important things to bear in mind when you do the same thing for your business.

Create a Story

At its most basic, branding can simply mean putting the name of a product or a company where people can see it. That makes the name familiar so that a customer recognizes it on the shelf.

In practice, of course, branding does so much more than that. It also attaches the product's name to a story so that when the customer sees it, he trusts it and associates with it.

It's that trust and attachment that are key to successful branding, and both start with a story.

Before you begin using Twitter to brand your company then, you first need to think about what you want that brand to say. Do you want your product to look cool and streetwise or luxurious and exclusive? Do you want it be associated with ideas of health and nature, or would it sell better if customers considered it to be at the peak of technological development?

Take a look at how competing products sell themselves and decide how you want your product to appear in the market. Usually, rather than trying to create a brand from scratch you'll be able to create a variation on a general theme used in your industry.

Internet marketers, for example, might be a pretty mixed bunch, but many of us like to appear in suits. That shows that while we might spend our days writing Web content and creating products, we're really traditional business people who broker deals and negotiate partnerships. We'll then try to mark ourselves out within that niche with a brand that represents our own unique personalities.

My Twitter page uses a pretty straightforward picture of me, and my bio describes me first as a "husband" and "father." That down-to-earth image might accurately reflect who I am, but it's also a part of my brand. People know when they read my blog that I'm just a regular family guy with a good business who's prepared to share what he's learned.

Yanick Silver, on the other hand, who is one of the world's leading Internet marketers, is much more of a daredevil. His bio includes the term "adventurer" and his photo shows him hanging over a computer like Tom Cruise in *Mission Impossible*. That action stuff is part of his brand—and a part of his story. (See Figure 8.2.)

One product that does a very careful job of creating the right story for its market—and which also does it through Twitter—is

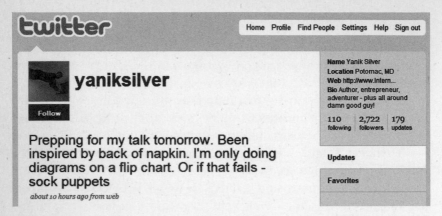

Figure 8.2   Leading Internet marketer Yanick Silver (@yanicksilver) creates an adventurous brand on Twitter.

M&Ms. By giving different colored candies a different personality, Mars, the manufacturer, is able to appeal to different kinds of buyers. (See Figure 8.3.)

Twitter, therefore, has a timeline for green M&Ms (@msgreen), which is targeted towards women, but it also has another timeline "written" by the red M&M (@mmsracing), which associates itself with NASCAR to appeal to men. (The mmsracing account has about 1,000 fewer followers than the msgreen account, which has been online just six months longer.)

It's likely that you already have a good idea of the kind of story you want your brand to portray. So how can you use Twitter to put that story across?

Figure 8.3   M&Ms uses two types of brand images on Twitter. The green M&Ms are more popular, but look at how the same product can tell two different stories and appeal to two different markets.

Portraying Your Brand with Your Profile

We saw earlier in this book how the background of the profile can be a useful way of providing your followers with more information than you can squeeze into a bio.

By creating a sidebar on the left of the page, you can send followers to your other web sites where they might be able to do a range of different things from clicking your ads to making purchases.

Those are direct results. When you're using Twitter to build a brand, though, you don't need your followers to type a URL into their browser or make a purchase right away. You just want them to remember you.

That means producing a design that makes your brand memorable and that sums up you or your company.

Southwest Airlines, for example, used to use an image of its planes' tail as its photo and chose the sky as its background image. Today, it has a sidebar with links and testimonials, but it also includes a logo showing the plane surrounded by hearts to emphasize its image as the "LUV airline." Either way, readers can see immediately whose page they're reading, and they understand what the company does. (And note too the bio on Southwest's Flickr page: "The LUV Airline! Airplanes can't type so @Christi5321 is responding/chatting with you!" Creating a personal touch is key to success on Twitter. For companies, that's difficult, but letting people know who's tweeting makes a corporate timeline human.)

M&M's old Twitter page used the green candy to push the brand in the run up to Valentine's Day. Mars matched the color scheme and graphics with the subject of the campaign.

Mars has gone a little further in its branding of M&Ms. Not only did they create two pages, but they also change their design so that the brand's image suits the current campaign. For Valentine's Day 2008, for example, the company used Twitter to promote the idea that green, not red, is the color of love—and that their green candies were symbols of love, too. The profile used a green background with a picture of Eros as a green M&M, and the company's web site linked back to the Twitter page where people could discover "love tips, quips and personal appearances." (See Figure 8.4.)

It was certainly memorable, and the image alone was enough to help the page to stand out.

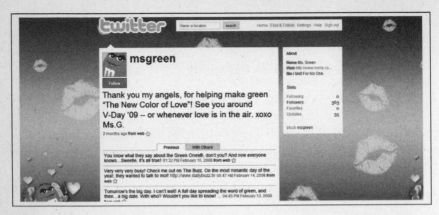

Figure 8.4 According to M&M's, green is no longer the color of money. It's the color of love.

But the profile doesn't have to be spectacular to convey the story of your brand, be instantly recognizable, and stick in the mind. For a long time, Whole Foods Market (@wholefoods), for example, simply used a plain green background to match its green image and its logo as its picture. Today, it also uses a sidebar. (See Figure 8.5.)

That's very simple—and still very effective.

When you're using Twitter for branding then, your background image is going to be important. You can choose an image that's

Figure 8.5 Whole Foods Market goes for green, pure and (almost) unadulterated, for its Twitter background.

complex and carefully designed—and change it as you change your marketing—or you can opt for something very simple but which still does the job.

More important is the style you use in your tweets.

Tweet Style—What to Say When You're Building a Brand to Create Value and How to Say It

Jonathan Fields' response to being followed by an airline company minutes after tweeting about them wasn't completely positive. *BusinessWeek* quotes him as saying that he was "totally startled" and says that, at first, he thought that JetBlue had noticed he was using the airport's wireless network.

The feeling was a mixture of respect for the company's diligence and use of technology—and general creepiness about the fact that they were watching him.

Clearly there is a danger for companies using Twitter to communicate with customers and build their brand. When they put themselves in the public arena, there's a chance that they can do more harm than good. Firms that get social media wrong look like interlopers, uninvited guests who have gate crashed the cool people's party.

That doesn't just mean that they're missing out on all of the opportunities that the social media site offers. It can also show that the company just doesn't "get it." That could have as negative an effect on their sales as good tweeting can have a positive effect.

There are a few things that a company needs to do to blend in on Twitter and make sure that the image it's putting across on the site strikes a chord.

The first thing it needs to do is to *be human*.

We've already seen how Southwest Airlines gets this by saying who is writing the tweets in the company's name. But the company that really stands out for maintaining a personal touch on Twitter is Comcast.

Comcast takes a huge amount of flack on Twitter. Twitterers are constantly complaining about the company's poor phone-based customer service. No one though seems to be complaining about its Twitter-based customer service at @comcastcares. Run by Frank

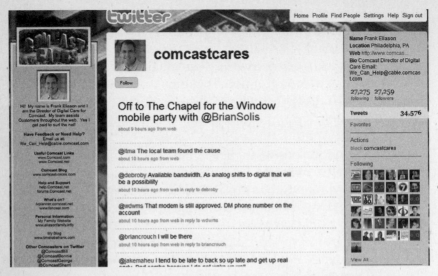

Figure 8.6   Comcast shows that it cares by giving its tweets a human face.

Eliason, the "Director of Digital Care for Comcast" puts his own picture rather than the company logo on the bio, includes an email address for people to write to, and broadcasts tweets that look like they're coming from a Twitterer, not some company rep. (See Figure 8.6.)

Note how the company puts together a whole bunch of different strategies here:

♦ It's chosen a name that doesn't just reflect the company but which refutes a common criticism made of the corporation on Twitter.

♦ It's used the background image to point people to places where they can get more information and talk to other company reps.

♦ Its tweets are written by a named individual who converses with the company's customers, and it doesn't just broadcast messages to them.

♦ And it follows about the same number of people that follow its tweets to show that it's listening as well as talking.

As we'll see, these are characteristics that appear in the time-lines of many other successful companies on Twitter. They're also characteristics that are missing even from companies that are really trying to make the most of Twitter—and failing.

BestBuy also used a real person rather than a logo to front its corporate Twitter page. Unlike Comcast, though, when BestBuy first started using Twitter, it made all sorts of mistakes that serve up a valuable lesson for any business thinking of using Twitter for branding.

First, the name was wrong. @bestbuy was snapped up early, but it had no updates, was following no one, and only had a handful of followers. Twitter doesn't allow cybersquatting and has been known to take away accounts from individuals who are trying to use a company name, so that URL should have been available to BestBuy if they wanted it. It's possible that there was a good reason that the company didn't complain and grab @bestbuy for itself right away, but I can't think of one. It's certainly done it now.

But not before playing around with @gina_community first—a terrible timeline. The first problem was the profile picture. (See Figure 8.7.)

While Frank Eliason looks happy, friendly, and approachable in his image, "Gina" looked like she'd been locked in a hotel room with a laptop.

Worst of all, the tweets themselves consisted of little more than cut-and-pasted statements made in response to alerts of the company name.

The overall impression wasn't that this is a friendly, helpful company that wants to improve its customers' experience, but that this is a company that just doesn't care.

The only consolation was that BestBuy only managed to gather around 166 followers before the company shut down the timeline and created a new (and much better) one on the BestBuy domain—but that's likely to be 166 customers who have been freaked out by the tweet they've received.

Having a human—rather than a corporate—presence on Twitter might involve actually showing a human face in the way that Comcast does. But it will always involve tweeting in *an informal, friendly manner*.

Figure 8.7   How not to build a brand on Twitter. BestBuy got it all wrong with a poor image and creepy tweets.

Twitter, after all, is a very personal place. It's a site that asks a personal question and lets people share their random thoughts with the world at large.

Businesses that tweet like a corporate executive addressing a board meeting will stand out on the site and scream that they have no idea what they're doing—or who they're talking to.

Starbucks, for example, has a number of timelines but its main Twitter presence, @starbucks, consists mostly of a customer representative answering questions. The company appears to be using the site as an extension of its customer service—one very simple corporate use for Twitter. It uses a logo instead of a personal image, but "Brad," the employee responsible for managing the account, isn't afraid to talk about his own personal experiences. He discusses the branches he's worked at and, of course, his own favorite drinks. (See Figure 8.8.)

Although it's clear that this is a corporate Twitter account, because the tweets are written in such a friendly, laid-back manner, it does create the impression that the followers are chatting with the barista in exactly the way they might do at the café itself—and that the café itself is a friendly, relaxed place to be.

That's good branding.

Figure 8.8   Starbucks shows that it's a relaxed place to hang out with friendly, easygoing tweets.

So your tweets should be friendly. They have to sound like they're coming from a real person, from another member of the Twitter community and not from some creepy company that's listening out for a mention of its name. (See Figure 8.9.)

But what should those tweets say to build a brand image that's positive and memorable?

In practice, corporate tweets that try to build brands tend to fall into four broad categories:

♦ Company News

♦ Customer Support

♦ Feedback

♦ Special Offers

NEWS

We've already seen that only posting news updates on Twitter can make for a pretty ineffective timeline. Dell's tweets can be dull

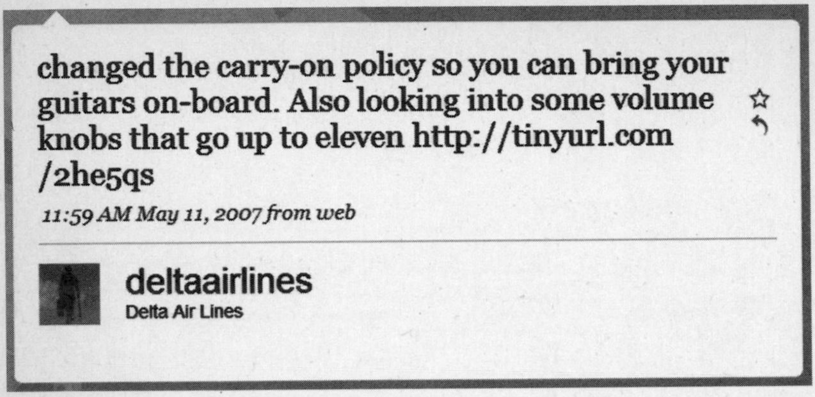

changed the carry-on policy so you can bring your guitars on-board. Also looking into some volume knobs that go up to eleven http://tinyurl.com /2he5qs

11:59 AM May 11, 2007 from web

deltaairlines
Delta Air Lines

Figure 8.9 Delta Airlines (@deltaairlines) disappeared for a while but then woke up. Its tweets have included important news about the company's carry-on policy, and its corporate Twitterer added an important human touch, too.

tweets. But including some carefully chosen news posts can have a positive branding effect. They reward the follower with useful information, and they also show that the company is enthusiastic about what it's doing.

That enthusiasm can be infectious.

Clearly, you have to be careful to make sure that you're broadcasting the right kind of news and that you're doing it in the right way.

Usually one of the most important rules for releasing news about a company is whether it passes the "Who cares?" test. (See Figure 8.10.)

In general, no one cares what companies are up to. If your local medical clinic had just repainted its waiting room, why would you care?

You wouldn't care unless that information actually affected you. If the clinic had changed its phone number or fired your doctor, then you'd want to know.

If it's changed its design, you probably wouldn't want to know.

On Twitter, that rule still holds to some degree. News announcements that affect the reader are always going to be the most interesting. But even an announcement that a company has changed

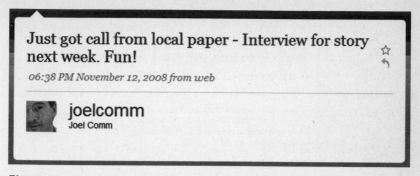

Figure 8.10   News about Joel Comm. Who cares about my interview? Well, I do and by showing that I'm excited about it, I hope my followers get excited too—and feel that if my local newspaper considers my work important enough to follow, it's important enough for them to follow as well.

its blog design or squished another bug in its program can be interesting if it looks like gossipy fun.

The best way to handle news for branding then is to mix it in with other kinds of content, and to add a personal comment so that it sounds like it's coming from a real person and not from a company.

CUSTOMER SUPPORT

Customer support on Twitter is often seen by companies as the only reason to use the site. Once they have someone Twittering away and answering questions, they feel that they've done their job and that there's nothing else to do.

That's a big mistake.

It's not just a mistake because doing it badly—like BestBuy did—can actually put people off. It's a mistake because good customer service itself can be good branding.

It shows that the company is available to anyone who needs its help and that it listens, too.

The Home Depot (@homedepot) does this very, very well. Its tweets offer short seasonal tips to keep people reading, but its real strength is the quality of its customer support. Even though one Twitter account can only address a fraction of the questions the

Figure 8.11   Sarah, The Home Depot's spokesperson, shows off the company's customer service.

company's customers are going to have, the impression it creates is that followers will find even better help at the store itself. (See Figure 8.11.)

That's exactly what branding should do: make potential customers feel that the real thing is even better.

Include great customer service tweets in your timeline—tweets that address problems and tell people exactly where they can find solutions—and you'll add one important characteristic to your branding story.

FEEDBACK

Feedback tweets are similar to customer service tweets but with an important difference. Customer service tweets are likely to be initiated by the customer. Instead of sitting on a phone line for half an hour wondering whether they should press 1, enter the hash key, or hurl the phone at the wall, customers can send a quick direct message to a company rep on Twitter and receive a response.

The customer gets the answer he needs almost right away. The company gets to help one customer and show lots of other customers that it's helpful, friendly, and keen to lend a hand.

But not all customer service comments are sent as direct messages or even as replies to tweets on the company's own timeline. Often they're just comments—usually rants—on their own timeline.

A company looking to use Twitter for branding can spot those tweets through alerts and react to them in the hope that it can stop negative publicity from spreading.

That's not always possible, but again, it does show that the company cares and that even if it's not perfect it is trying to improve. That can be an important part of a brand image, too.

Feedback though isn't just about listening to what people are saying about your company. It can also mean inviting people to say something about your company.

Starbucks has a second Twitter account at @mystarbucksidea that supports its My Starbuck Idea web site (mystarbucksidea.force .com). The site lets customers send in their proposals to improve the company and see how they're implemented. (See Figure 8.12.)

The Twitter timeline allows the company to thank the customers for their ideas and explain what's happening to them.

It's a great way for the company to show that it sees itself as just one part of the Starbucks community—even if it doesn't produce immediate, direct sales.

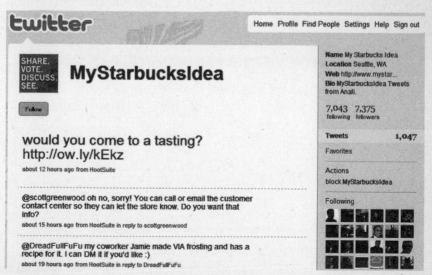

Figure 8.12 MyStarbucksIdea gives customers feedback and shows that the coffee chain is listening.

SPECIAL OFFERS

Special offers are standard marketing practice and as we've seen they can work on Twitter as much as anywhere else. Reward followers for reading your tweets by giving them exclusive deals that they feel they can't get anywhere else and you'll give them an incentive to keep reading. (See Figure 8.13.)

You'll also give yourself some extra sales.

Even an online publisher could do this by mentioning a great deal being offered by one of its affiliates. Include either your affiliate link in the code or link back to your Web page and you could well generate some useful commissions.

Companies using Twitter for branding though have to be a little careful with the way they use special offers.

While discounts can be a very powerful way to drive customers to take immediate action, branding doesn't demand action. It simply requires the follower to keep reading and to think about the company in a certain way.

Make lots of special offers and instead of thinking about the company as a trusted friend that always delivers quality goods and services, they'll see it as a corporation keen to push its products.

Those special offers start to look like a hard sale and hard selling doesn't work on Twitter.

> Our Funtennial celebration is still going strong. Find out this week's offer here: http://tinyurl.com /yozqgq
>
> *05:11 PM March 17, 2008 from web*
>
> CarnivalCruise

Figure 8.13 Carnival Cruises (@carnivalcruise) uses a range of social media strategies to promote its business and was a Twitter early adopter. It makes occasional special offers in its timeline.

If you want to make immediate, direct sales through Twitter, then regular special offers could be very effective. If you want to use the site to build a brand and create a community around your firm, then special offers should be scattered throughout your timeline just to reward your followers and keep them interested.

There's no golden rule about how many promotions is too many. It all depends on what else you're saying and who's following you. If you're making offers more frequently than one in five tweets, though, then you're probably doing it too often.

Reinforce the Core Message

All of these tweets should look fairly familiar. There's a good chance that you're writing them anyway as you use Twitter to drive customers to take action.

But there's one type of tweet I haven't mentioned.

It's the one that the site was really created for and one that I use frequently on my timeline: random thoughts.

People write all sorts of strange things on Twitter. It's one of the service's attractions. It's as though people have put a window on the side of their head and are letting the rest of us peek in every now and then to see what thoughts are passing through. (See Figure 8.14.)

Yes, it's a bit nosey, and it really shouldn't be very interesting.

But it really is!

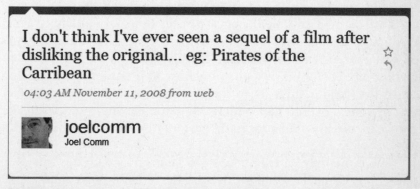

Figure 8.14 One of my random thoughts. They help with my brand image but would they help a company? I doubt it.

Tweets like these might be fun but they aren't actionable. Tell your followers that one of your affiliates is running a special offer and include the link to your site, and you can expect people to click through.

Break news about a blog post that you've just put up, and you can expect people to come and read it.

Write a tweet that tells people that you're thinking of eating a donut and to blazes with the calories, and the best you can hope is that they'll smile—and feel closer to you.

That's the benefit of these sorts of tweets: They create a better relationship with your followers, your customers, and your community.

You're not just the owner of a web site or some blogger on the Internet a million miles away. You're a real human being who thinks, works, and feels guilty about eating donuts.

That sort of feeling can do wonders for the connection you have with your customers and with your readers.

But I'm not sure that it will help with corporate branding.

A company's tweets should appear human, but they're not about the Twitterer; they're about the company. Adding what the Twitterer thinks about a piece of news he's broadcasting or an answer to a customer's question shows that the company really does care. Mention that it fancies pizza, and the firm starts to look a little strange.

That isn't to say that random thoughts can play no part in branding on Twitter.

They do play a role *but only in personal branding*.

I use them in my timeline because they help to brand me as a regular guy. That's important because I don't want other entrepreneurs to feel that Internet marketing is only for people with tons of marketing experience or who know how to program or who understand everything there is to know about the Internet. The fact that anyone—even a family-focused, game-playing, non-coder like me—can do it is an important part of the story I want to put across.

The same may be true when the Twitterer embodies the company. Tony Hsieh, for example, is the CEO of Zappos, an online retail store. He tweets on behalf of his company at @zappos. Because this is his personal Twitter timeline, there's nothing wrong with Tony including random thoughts in his tweets—his tweets are first about him, not his company. (See Figure 8.15.)

But because he's also the CEO of Zappos, something his background image makes clear, what he says also reflects the company.

This isn't exactly the same as branding though. Tony Hsieh's tweets provide publicity for his company and build a community out of his customers. But beyond indicating that his company is open and approachable, they say little else about the firm.

By personalizing his tweets in this way, Tony turns his timeline into a branding tool that reinforces his image as the CEO of Zappos. That can be effective, too. British tycoon Richard Branson has made a fortune by portraying himself as the face of Virgin. He's become a celebrity, and every time he appears in the press he's promoting his business. Twitter is doing the same thing in a smaller way for Tony Hsieh: It's allowing him to build a personal brand that promotes his firm.

This is all about sticking to the core message. Once you know what you want your brand to look like and what you want it to say, it's important to make sure that your tweets only say that and don't confuse the message.

Figure 8.15   Tony Hsieh, CEO of Zappos, builds himself a brand and promotes his company at the same time.

If you're tweeting on behalf of a company, keep it human but not too personal.

If you're tweeting on behalf of a personal brand, include the random thoughts but reduce the offers.

Those simple guidelines should help to keep your tweets on message.

Repetition, Repetition, Repetition

To keep your tweets on message, though, you will also have to repeat them.

One of the challenges of any branding campaign is that the effect is never long-lasting. That's why even companies like Coca-Cola have to keep spending millions of dollars every year to keep their products in the public eye.

When you're using Twitter for branding, you don't have to spend millions of dollars to keep your market's attention.

You just have to keep sending out tweets.

There are companies that make the mistake of starting a Twitter campaign to promote a particular product, drop Twitter when the campaign ends, and then try to pick it up again months later. It's a strategy that can work—if you're not sending out tweets, you're not bothering anyone, so few followers will block your tweets. But you will lose momentum and your community can disappear.

When you're using Twitter as a branding tool, you need to be tweeting at least once a day, and ideally far more often than that.

That doesn't have to be as hard as it sounds.

Writing the Tweets

I admit, it does sound hard. I like tweeting. It's fun, it's interesting, it's enjoyable. I've had some great virtual conversations with some wonderful people, learned all sorts of fascinating things, and picked up information that I couldn't have learned any other way than on Twitter.

But it takes time, and when you're a busy executive using Twitter to promote your business rather than just tell the world what you had for breakfast, that time is an investment.

This is where the difference between a corporate Twitter account and a private Twitter account is important.

Zappo's CEO might be writing his own tweets, but not everyone does that. The tweets of big companies like Delta and Carnival Cruises aren't written by the corporations' CEOs. They're written by employees or public relations firms who have been given the job of promoting the company's brand on the Web.

You can do the exact same thing.

If you don't want to write your tweets yourself, hand over the job of creating your business's tweets to someone in your office. Let them be your company's Twitter presence. Give them the freedom to be human and include their opinions as well as your company's. Be sure to put their name in the bio so that readers know who's writing them.

And tell them to mix up each of the different kinds of tweets, too.

You'll still get the familiarity with your followers that only Twitter can bring. But you'll do it without any effort, and your helper will probably enjoy it, too.

Win Retweets

The best people to write your tweets for you though, are other Twitterers. When it comes to viral marketing and the ability to spread a brand, nothing beats posting a tweet that flies around the Twitterverse. Instead of just showing your name to your followers, people who already know you, you get to be seen by their followers, by those followers' followers, and so on.

Being retweeted is like hitting the marketing jackpot.

But it's a jackpot that you can rig. With a little care, you can increase the chances that a tweet you post will be shared across Twitter.

Clearly, the more followers you have the greater the chances that some of those followers will want to share your posts. But there's a lot more to winning retweets than just building a big follower list. According to Dan Zarrella, a "viral marketing scientist" who has conducted some in-depth analyses of the way retweeted posts spread on Twitter, some types of tweets are more likely to be shared than others.

Content that's timely, such as news items, tend to be shared often, as do tweets about Twitter itself. Around 70 percent of retweeted posts contain links, says Dan, with list posts particularly popular. The most popular subjects to win retweets are news, instructional content, entertainment, opinion, products, and small talk, in that order.

Of course, links to giveaways also do well. One of the most successful retweet campaigns took place in July 2009. Moonfruit (@moontweet), a Web design company, decided to celebrate its tenth year in business by giving away one Macbook Pro every day for 10 days. To be eligible, Twitterers needed to do nothing more than write the hashtag "#moonfruit" in their posts. The more posts they wrote with that hashtag, the greater the chances they would win. Additional prizes of iPods were given to the most creative entries.

The results were phenomenal. At one point, Twitterers were writing 300 tweets per minute about the company, tweets with the hashtag made up 2.85 percent of all tweets posted, and it was the most popular trending term. The company's web site traffic also increased by a factor of eight. In fact, the campaign was so successful that the company chose to end it three days early, giving away the remaining computers in one big giveaway.

In general then, give away valuable items (especially Apple products) or post links to exclusive, timely information related to your industry and there's a good chance that people will pass it on—especially if you're polite. One of the most reassuring aspects of Dan Zarrella's research is that the most popular words in retweeted posts are "you," "twitter," "please," and "retweet." Asking politely for a retweet really does work.

And the best news of all is that the clickthroughs work, too. Dan's day job is with Hubspot, a company that sells inbound marketing software. Leads that reach Hubspot through Twitter, Dan says, are among the prospects most likely to buy.

Create Hashtags and Run Hashtag Chats

Retweets help to spread your brand. But if you want to deepen your brand as well, show that you are knowledgeable about your industry, and demonstrate that your company is the leading source of information about your topic on Twitter, then hashtags can be particularly helpful.

A hashtag is simply a keyword marked with a # symbol. By placing hashtags in tweets that cover a particular topic, people interested in following discussions about that subject on Twitter can easily find all the posts without wondering which keywords to search for.

That's particularly useful for breaking news stories. When wildfires threatened the California town of Santa Barbara, for example, residents were able to keep up to date with evacuation warnings by reading tweets with the hashtag "#jesusitafire." After the Iranian elections in 2009, demonstrators let the world know what was happening by adding "#iranelection" to their tweets. On applications like Tweetdeck, on which tweets are updated automatically, users were able to see an ongoing stream of news updates, staying in touch with events as they unfolded.

Most hashtags don't work in this way though. Instead, they usually act as a kind of label allowing people to find a particular type of content. Aspiring novelists, for example, can search for "#pubtips" to read tips posted by literary agents about writing queries and getting published. Any agent who wants to share a tip only has to add the hashtag to a tweet to get his or her name in front of thousands of wannabe authors. It's a great way to become part of a community on Twitter, and contributing regularly to your industry's hashtags allows you to demonstrate your expertise to a select audience.

And if there aren't any active hashtags for your industry, there's nothing wrong with creating one. Simply tell your followers that you're creating a hashtag for a particular theme and start adding it to tweets on that subject. So the owner of a garden center, for example, could create a hashtag for gardening advice. Contribute plenty of tips and that business owner will come to be seen as a leader on his subject.

Hashtags really become powerful though when they're updated at set times in a kind of public, real-time chat session. In addition to reading the "#pubtips" hashtag, for example, authors of children's books can also take part in "#kidlitchat." Agents representing authors of children's books make themselves available to answer questions from writers and talk about the publishing industry. It's not as touchy-feely as a conference, but it does allow writers and agents to get together, trade information, and get to know each other.

Some chats are very organized. Tim Beyers' chats for journalists and editors, for example, can be found by searching for "#editorchat". They take place every Wednesday at 8.30 P.M. EST. The chat has a web site at www.editorchat.net that announces the issues to be discussed during the next chat and posts transcripts of previous talks. Participants have included the editor of *BusinessWeek*.

Other chats though happen spontaneously. A group of experts who happen to be on Twitter at the same time sometimes decide to take questions for the next hour or so, and invite people who want to take part to add a hashtag to the end of their tweets. Those are likely to bring in fewer people, but they can be fun and engage other Twitterers who also happen to be online.

Most important of all though, when you're among the people taking the questions, you position your brand as a leader that's reliable, knowledgeable, trustworthy, and prepared to give back to the community. That's powerful branding.

Like any effective marketing channel, Twitter can be a valuable branding tool. It can work as a personal branding tool, giving any individual an image that's memorable and recognizable, and it can function as a corporate branding tool helping companies to stand out, win trust, and turn their customers into a community.

Even some of the world's biggest companies have recognized the power of Twitter to drive home their message, and while not all of them are doing it correctly, a number have come up with some valuable models that anyone can copy.

Branding brings long-term results. You can also use Twitter to create instant results. In the next chapter, I'm going to discuss some of the ways that you can drive behavior in your followers.

9

Leveraging the Power of Twitter to Drive Behavior in Your Followers

We've seen that there are all sorts of different ways of writing tweets on Twitter. And we've seen, too, that there all sorts of different uses to which you can put Twitter.

Probably the most common way marketers want to use Twitter, though, is to achieve immediate results. They see their followers as a pool of people who will one day give them money—either directly or with the help of advertising—and they want to write tweets that create those effects.

There's nothing wrong with that. It's a little short-sighted, but there's really nothing wrong with it.

You can certainly create tweets that drive your followers to take the steps that you want them to take. But you do have to be a little careful.

Your Twitter timeline is not a sales page. Gripping headlines and hard calls-to-action on Twitter are more likely to drive people away than drive them to buy. Your tweets need to be subtle. They have to build interest and trust. Only then will your followers feel that doing what you want them to do will be worth their while.

In this chapter, which may be the most important chapter in the book, I'm going to explain how to drive traffic to a web site, how to use surveys to gain data and build responses, and how to mine your customers for valuable feedback.

I'll then discuss how to build effective, action-oriented tweet strategies and, perhaps most important of all, how to keep track of the results.

Let's start by looking at the ways that you can drive followers to a web site.

Driving Followers to a Web Site

We've already seen that it's possible on Twitter to include a URL in tweets. We've also seen that there are even systems available that can create these kinds of tweets automatically.

But that doesn't mean that anyone will click those links. Nor is it particularly useful if you want to send your followers to a site that isn't a blog.

Although driving traffic towards other content pages has to be one of the most common uses of Twitter, you might also want to send them to a purchase page, to a registration page, or to a page on which you hope they'll click an ad.

All of those are possible on Twitter.

Promoting a Blog on Twitter

When publishers first started writing blogs, they were meant to be nothing more than online diaries, a place for people to write their thoughts and feelings and let anyone read them who wanted to.

They've become much more than that.

Today, blogs are a very effective publishing system. They've evolved to become online magazines rather than personal pages.

The benefit is that publishers can now write about anything they want—and get paid for it too.

The disadvantage is that they're no longer personal.

If readers used to come to blogs to find out what the writer was doing or thinking, today's blogs are often not even written by the bloggers themselves. Good, professional blogs tend to be filled with guest posts, paid writers, and ghostwriters. And there's nothing wrong with that.

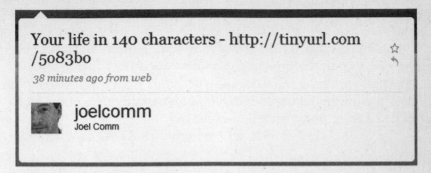

Figure 9.1   Headline and blog post URL make for an easy tweet and some helpful extra traffic. But is a headline enough to turn a follower into a reader?

The first thing that Twitter can do for a blog then is to bring back the personality of the publisher.

Bloggers can use Twitter to give readers a peek behind the scenes of their business, provide quick notices about their plans and the posts they're working on, and answer direct questions put to them by readers.

Sure, you can also do all of this on your blog—and ideally, you should. (See Figure 9.1.)

But when your blog really takes off, it's unlikely that you'll have time to respond to every comment your posts receive. Articles about your blog are also likely to be less interesting to your readers than posts about cars, photography or whatever it is that users are visiting your site to see.

Twitter can give publishers of blogs an alternative space to get closer to their readers, even when they're using content written by professional writers.

But what if you want to bring in new readers or increase the views of occasional visitors?

Twitter can help there, too.

The principle is very simple. If you were to put an ad on AdWords to promote every blog post you publish, you'd have to pay a lot of money. Assuming you got the arbitrage right by weighing the cost of the ads against the revenue from the Web pages, you might make a small profit. But you'd need a lot of visitors to make it worthwhile.

Placing an announcement of a new blog post on Twitter is a very easy way to let lots of people know about it.

We've seen how Darren Rowse does this with his photography blog—a fantastic example of a highly successful blog that's much more of a magazine than a personal diary.

That's one very simple way to drive traffic from Twitter to a blog.

But that works because Darren Rowse's site is already well-known. He doesn't have to do anything but remind his regular readers that a new post is online for those readers to stop by and take a look.

Darren's personal timeline is much more complex. His tweets contain a mixture of news announcements about his blogs as well as personal comments and answers to readers' questions.

That combination is important. Blog post headlines by themselves look very weak on Twitter. Even the sort of hard-hitting headline that social media types love (something like "20 Ways To Gain More Followers") can look desperate when it appears in a tweet.

Instead of saying something *about* you, they tell the reader that you really want them to be doing something *for* you: You want them to be reading your blog post.

That's exactly the wrong way to go about Twitter, and it's certainly the wrong way to go about driving followers to a blog post and to become regular readers.

Twitter works best by creating curiosity. People read your tweets, become a part of your life, and want to see what you're up to next. When you announce that you've just written a new blog post, they'll stop by to read it not just because the content is interesting, but because they're interested in what you wrote, or in what you published if you didn't write it yourself.

Curiosity though doesn't come as a result of one tweet. It happens through publishing good tweets regularly.

When you first join Twitter then, don't rush to fill your timeline with links that lead to your blog. Tweet about yourself, about what you're doing, thinking, and would like to be doing.

Reply to other people's tweets, especially those people who appear to have an interest in your topic, and in particular Twitterers with large followings so that their reply to you will turn up in their timeline for everyone else to see.

Offer advice and solutions to Twitterers who have posed questions or are struggling with something in your field of expertise.

All of that will start to give you a core group of followers who are interested in who you are and what you can do for them. And so far, all you've done is help them. In effect, you will have been priming your market by handing out freebies in the form of free advice—a tested marketing strategy.

Now when you introduce your blog posts, you should find that many of your followers will click through to read them. They'll know that you deliver good advice, and they'll be hungry for more.

You can then continue this strategy of providing regular updates of informative and entertaining tweets dotted with links to your blog.

And if you've already started Twittering, then it's never too late to begin this strategy!

Just make sure that you've added plenty of good tweets before you next post a link to your blog.

Priming your followers in this way should help to maximize your clickthroughs, but usually blogs, like Twitter, are a means to an end.

The end result that most publishers want is for their readers to click an ad or make a purchase. With a little thought, you can use Twitter to increase the chances that that will happen, too.

This takes a little skill and some planning. You have to know what sort of ads are likely to appear on your blog page, and you have to prepare your followers for them on Twitter.

That's unlikely to happen with your AdSense units. I'm a big fan of AdSense and you should definitely be using it on your web site, but because the ads can change so unexpectedly, you can't create interest in a particular product so that your readers are more likely to click an ad for it. You can only create top-quality content and optimize the units so that readers click the ads to find out more.

Curiosity is a powerful driving factor on blogs, too.

But AdSense isn't the only way you can put ads on a blog, and therefore it's not the only way you can monetize your Twitter followers.

You should certainly be including some cost-per-mille ads that pay for every view you receive. That will give you some money for every follower who clicks through, even if the individual amounts are small.

More important though is that you load up on affiliate ads. These are predictable—you choose the products—and unlike the products promoted in AdSense units, you can recommend these yourself.

Do you see how this creates a golden opportunity on Twitter?

Imagine that you ran a blog about video games. You could create a series of tweets about the game.

The first tweet could say that you're going to buy it.

The second tweet could say that the graphics have blown you away and that it looks like a killer game.

The third tweet could say that you've discovered a bunch of fantastic strategies and that the game is even better than you expected.

And the fourth tweet would include the URL of a blog post that offered a complete review of the game or tips to complete it. Included on the Web page would be an affiliate ad from Amazon that led directly to the game.

You can add these affiliate links very easily by signing up as an Amazon Associate (the site's term for affiliates). You'll be able to choose the product you want to promote and paste the code onto your Web page. Every time someone clicks on that ad, you get a share of the revenue. (Just be sure to embed the link into your text. Most professional bloggers find that that's the best way to earn through Amazon's affiliate program.)

You'd need to run a tweet series like this fairly quickly. You want people to buy from your site; you don't want them to get excited and buy directly from Amazon, cutting you out of the loop. To keep your keenest followers waiting for you—and for everyone else to catch up—you could point out that your blog will soon be running a review. That should give them a reason to put off their decision to buy until they've read what you have to say—and seen your ad.

The result should be that Twitter gives you the chance to create a kind of teaser campaign that can give you affiliate earnings when you launch your blog post.

Twitter as a Resource for Post Ideas

So with the right combination of tweets, you can use Twitter to drive followers to a page with a targeted ad. But you can also use your followers for a second purpose, and one that's no less valuable.

You can use them as a resource for blog post ideas.

Ask your followers what sort of posts they'd like to see on your blog and you're likely to get swamped with ideas.

That makes life very easy for you.

At the beginning of every month, you could just ask your followers what issues they'd like to see covered on your blog in the next few weeks.

No more beating your head against the wall trying to think up new content. And no more wondering if people are going to like the concept either.

Before you write about a particular subject, you could just ask your followers what they think. If everyone says it sounds a bit dull or asks how you're going to deal with this aspect or approach to that problem you haven't even considered, you can start thinking again.

You won't have to wait until you've been sweating over the post for a couple of hours to discover it isn't going to work.

And of course once you've written it, you can be sure that when you announce that it's online you'll have an audience for it.

This can be fascinating stuff. Mine your followers for information and you'll be amazed at the responses you get. More importantly, asking a crowd for ideas will help to keep your blog fresh and ticking over, an important consideration when you've been doing it for a while and you've already covered all the information that you think important several times.

Fatigue is one of the biggest dangers for a mature blog, but by giving you a giant bank of editorial advisors to call on, Twitter can help your blog stay young and fresh.

There are a couple of ways you can mine this kind of information.

The first is to ask a straightforward, open-ended question. A tweet that says, "What would you like to see covered on the blog this month?" could get you a ton of interesting answers.

A tweet that said, "Want to guest post on my blog? Send me a DM" would land you a ton of interesting content.

But you do have to be careful here. Your blog is successful because *you* create it. You came up with the subject, you set the topics for the posts and for the most part, you're likely to be writing it. Hand over too much influence to your readers—or followers—and there's a risk that you'll dilute the characteristics that have made your site so interesting.

While readers might say they want posts about this subject or content about that topic, they're often the worst judges of what they really need, and they certainly want to be surprised by excellent content that they hadn't thought of themselves.

That's why a good alternative option is to give your followers a choice. Instead of asking them what content they'd like to see, offer them three subjects and ask which they'd like to see most. That will give you a good idea of your followers' preferences, and if you get a close call, you can still write about all of them.

Announcing your new blog posts on Twitter can help to create a few more views and win you some extra revenue. Using your followers as a resource for post ideas can help to keep your blog focused and informative. And of course, the people who see tweets about your blog posts won't be restricted to your followers. Although your followers are likely to give you the highest number of click-throughs, plenty of people will also click through your timeline without following you. They'll see your blog links and your supporting tweets, too, and many of them will visit your blog as a result.

Those extra clicks, both from dedicated followers interested in you and your topic and from curious passers-by, are important reasons for marketing a blog on Twitter. It's why blog promotion is one of the main uses of Twitter, even if that use is often restricted to automated Twitterfeeds.

But Twitter can do a lot more than drive followers to a blog page.

It can also drive them to buy.

Driving Followers to the Mall

Look through my timeline and you'll see lots of different kinds of tweets. You'll see links to my blog posts. You'll see replies to my followers. You'll see my opinions on politics, gaming, and social media. You'll even see the odd quote that I've thrown in for fun and to spark some comments.

What you won't see are tweets that tell people they should be buying my products. (See Figure 9.2.)

That's not what I use Twitter for. I prefer to use it to build a brand and a community. In time, that will bring me more loyal customers and more sales overall. I can already see it happening in the number of visitors to my blog and the type of comments those visitors leave.

But that doesn't mean you can't use Twitter to drive direct sales. You can, but you have to follow a number of simple rules:

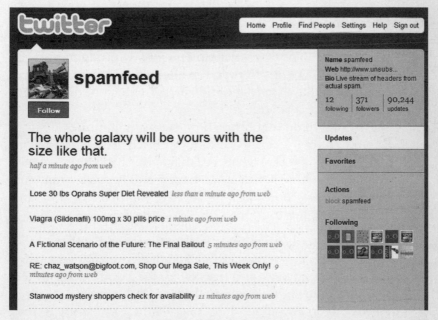

Figure 9.2   Spamfeed (@spamfeed) tweets real spam headers—and has plenty of followers. Incredible. When you're looking to drive sales through Twitter, don't be Spamfeed.

♦ **Don't do it too often.**

A special offer once a week is plenty. More than that and you'll start to look like a commercial Twitter timeline rather than a personal one. That will reduce the number of your users.

♦ **Make the offers really special.**

Time-limited offers and discount coupons make followers feel that they're being rewarded for reading your tweets. Being part of an exclusive club is a powerful motivator to keep reading.

♦ **Keep the offers targeted.**

People will follow you for all sorts of reasons. They might have seen your Twitter URL on your blog. They might have seen a reply to you in someone else's timeline. Or they could have read one of your re-tweeted messages to name just three.

And they'll stick around because they find your tweets interesting and entertaining.

With a group of followers that could be quite varied, the temptation might be to make offers for any products you can think of. If someone offers you an interesting-looking joint venture, you might want to mention it on Twitter, offer a discount code, and see if anyone bites.

You could do that. And some people might bite.

But if your keep your offers closely targeted to your specialized subject—whatever that subject might be—you'll continue to come across as an expert and because your trust levels on that topic will be higher, your conversion rates should be higher too.

♦ **Don't link to a sales page without a special offer.**

Although Twitterers understand that companies are using the site for branding and marketing, they don't want to feel that they're being pushed into buying. If the tweets are interesting and entertaining, then followers will be happy to read them.

In fact, they'll enjoy them and they'll see the company as having its finger on the pulse, as a firm that feels that it's part of their community and that knows how to follow the community's rules.

Companies that are seen to view followers as nothing more than walking moneybags though aren't going to pick up followers. They're actually more likely to lose followers who were once customers.

Link directly to a sales page without making the follower feel that they're receiving special treatment and you create the impression that you really want to sell, not tweet.

Usually, the best way to drive followers to buying pages then is to use the strategies we've seen already: Create entertaining tweets, and throw in occasional special offers that appear to reward followers while avoiding the appearance of a hard sale—or even that you're marketing.

There is one exception though. A number of timelines have turned up on Twitter that take exactly the opposite approach. They're a bit like Darren Rowse's Twitterfeed account: They provide just one type of tweet and followers know exactly what they're getting.

In this case, they're getting nothing but special offers.

Figure 9.3   Once in a while MomsWhoSave (@momswhosave) will toss in a personal tweet. But it's mostly discounts and coupon codes for its 8,375 followers.

Timelines like these have the potential to be good revenue generators. Building up followers will be a challenge, though. Because a Twitter running a timeline like this is rarely going to be interacting with other Twitterers, it will be harder than usual to pick up momentum and build a big follower list.

You could tap the users of your web site, which will turn the timeline into a kind of RSS feed that reminds your regular readers that you have new content.

Or you could set up a separate timeline with a mixture of different kinds of tweets, like Darren Rowse has done, and re-tweet occasionally from your sales timeline to share the followers.

And of course, each time you send out an email burst of coupons, you could make sure that it includes your Twitter URL to turn your list into followers.

Above all though, you're going to need a regular supply of great offers!

Can You Put Affiliate Links on Twitter?

It's just so tempting. You've spotted a great product, you've got an affiliate code that could land you piles of cash if you can persuade people to buy, and you've got a long follower list made up of people who could really benefit from the product.

So all you have to do is toss a short version of the link into one of your tweets, and—presto—piles of cash. Right?

Actually, yes.

Well, okay, there's a little more to it than that.

Just like any item you're hoping to sell through Twitter, affiliate products have to be well-targeted to suit your followers. The people who read your tweets should be able to see that you're genuinely interested in benefiting them rather than in benefiting yourself. (See Figure 9.4.)

Like affiliate links anywhere, you'll always do better when you recommend the products you're linking to rather than just throwing them at your readers cold.

And like any marketing push on Twitter, try not to do it too often and make sure that you include plenty of other kinds of tweets to soften the marketing effect and increase the feeling that you're recommending a chance find.

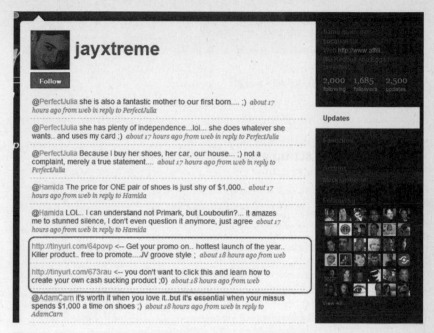

Figure 9.4   Internet entrepreneur Jamie Holt (@jayxtreme) scatters some affiliate links throughout his timeline.

If you're in any doubt—or if you find that start to lose followers after including affiliate links in your timeline—you can always place the link on a Web page and promote that page instead.

Driving Followers to Register

So you can use Twitter to build a brand, and you can use Twitter to drive followers to buy right away, too.

But there are even more things that you can do with Twitter and, with the right tweets, persuade your followers to do.

One action that's become very popular with bloggers, for example, is persuading readers to sign up for their RSS feeds. By itself, that doesn't generate revenue. But it does mean that readers are more likely to return, less likely to miss posts, and more likely to click ads or make a purchase one day.

On the one hand, persuading followers to do this is very simple. If your followers enjoy your tweets and if they're clicking through

Figure 9.5   Alaia Williams (@cogentdiversion) makes a not very subtle request for subscribers. Notice how she adds a comment to it as well, though, so that it doesn't look like spam.

the links to your blog post, then they're likely to be keen to read more. Sending a tweet pointing out that they can sign up for your RSS feed should be enough to persuade many of them to click through and hand over their email addresses.

That's particularly true when you make those invitation tweets look like opportunities for the follower rather than a benefit for you.

When Alaia Williams, a professional organizer and blogger, suggested that her followers should sign up for her mailing list, she softened the request by adding that she should get some sleep. (See Figure 9.5.)

That was a nice way of signing off for the night, which also told her followers how they can continue reading even while she's not available.

Any Twitterer could follow that example by tweeting something like:

"That's all for now, I'm off to watch telly. You can read more at http://tinyurl.com/afsfbi and don't forget to join the mailing list"

Do you see how a tweet like that doesn't just recommend that your followers sign up, but leaves them somewhere to go to continue reading your content?

If you can frame your recommendations in a way that looks like you're helping your followers, rather than trying to get them to help you, you'll always get better results.

Tracking Results and Testing Strategies

The success that I've enjoyed at Internet marketing didn't come about through good luck.

I'd like to say that it happened because I'm incredibly talented and interesting, but no, I can't say that either. Not honestly anyway.

In fact, my Web pages started bringing in revenue because I'm incredibly boring.

Sure, the content I was putting up on my sites was good. It had to be good otherwise no one would read it, no matter how well I marketed the site. Reading my site was interesting—at least my users thought so. The boring stuff came after the content went up.

I would keep a diary that described exactly what each ad unit looked like, where it was located on the page, and what kind of ads it was offering. Next to that description, I would write exactly how many views those ads received, how many clickthroughs, and how much money the page generated.

Then I would change the color or the placement or a few keywords and track the result of the change for a week.

It was painstaking stuff and strangely a lot more interesting than it sounds. But within a few months I understood what kind of ad formats generated the most clickthroughs, in which locations, and with what sort of content. I also knew which subjects gave me the highest-earning keywords.

It was a huge breakthrough, and it meant that I could target my content and my ad space to bring in the maximum revenues. Every time I made a change or put up a new Web page, I knew what the result would be.

It didn't give me complete control over all the money-making aspects of my web site because traffic flows and Google, like the weather, can be unpredictable. But I think I got as close as it's possible to get, and I certainly got to enjoy the rewards.

I was able to collect that data because AdSense supplies some pretty detailed stats. What Google wasn't telling me I could pick up from my server logs. With some quick calculations, it became pretty easy to test, track, and record.

It's no surprise then that I'm a huge fan of testing on Internet marketing. It's the only way keep control of your site and avoid wasting time and money on experiments that don't pay off. If you're not earning all the income you think you should be, you can spot the problem quickly and correct it. It takes a little while, but once you understand exactly what makes your site tick—and the money flow through—you should have no problem at all keeping it profitable.

The same principle is true on Twitter, but there *is* a problem: Twitter doesn't provide detailed stats—at least not yet.

According to an announcement made at the end of August 2009, Twitter does plan to roll out stats to commercial users at some point. Biz Stone wasn't saying when, but it's possible that by this book is released those stats will be available.

In the meantime—and for people who don't want to pay for a commercial Twitter account—the only figures that Twitter will tell you are how many people you're following, how many people are following you, and how many updates you've posted.

In addition, URL shorteners will tell you how many views a link received and how many clicks—that's going be vital.

That's useful as far as it goes, but it really doesn't go very far.

Testing and tracking on Twitter will involve looking at your Twitter stats, your timeline, and your alerts. And it will also involve looking at your server logs.

Twitter alone will be able to tell you:

♦ Which kinds of tweets generate the most replies;

♦ Which kinds of tweets get the most retweets; and

♦ Which replies from which other Twitterers bring you the most followers.

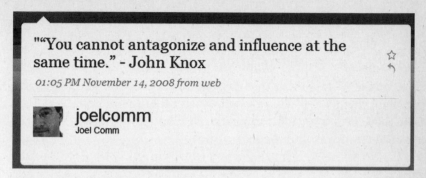

Figure 9.6   What does this quote do, I wonder...

To gather this data, you would need to test different versions of each kind of tweet. Let's say, for example, that you had tweeted something that had little to do with your business but which you thought your followers might find interesting, such as an inspiring quote. (See Figure 9.6.)

You post the tweet, record it in your Twitter Journal and you wait a day to see how many replies and retweets that tweet receives.

Now, a day on Twitter can be a long time. On a blog, it usually takes a week to see how a different ad placement or a post on a particular topic affects your revenue, but on Twitter you have to move much faster than that. A day is plenty of time to deliver the data you need.

It *is* possible to post other tweets in the meantime, but when you're testing, I don't recommend it. Followers are more likely to comment on the newer posts than the older ones so you'd skew the results. You might want to set aside one day each week for testing but change the day regularly so that your followers feel that they should be looking out for your tweets every single day.

Let's say then that out of 200 followers, your inspirational quote generates 12 replies, and you can see by searching for your username that it also picked up four retweets. The following week, you might want to try it again with a different quote to see if you get a different result. But let's say you see similar figures.

You also find that while your follower list has been growing at an average of, say, 10 followers per week, the weeks in which you include an inspiration quote give you 13 followers.

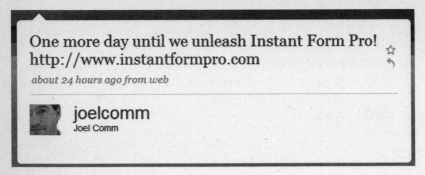

Figure 9.7   And what does this tweet do . . . ?

So now you can say that tweeting inspiration quotes gives you around 12 replies, four retweets, and three additional followers.

That's valuable information. Now you can compare it to a different kind of tweet. This time you post a tweet that alerts your followers to a new product you're launching: (See Figure 9.7.)

Again, you'll want to:

♦ Record the tweet in your journal;

♦ Count the number of replies you receive;

♦ Note who replied so that you know which of your followers are most likely to respond to your tweets;

♦ Track how often the post is mentioned and retweeted based on your username alerts; and

♦ Add up the number of new followers you receive in the hours following the post.

That will tell you the effect the tweet has had on your Twitter account. But when you're including a link, you'll also want to know how many people are clicking through. You can discover this from your server logs and from your URL-shortening service depending on the service you're using.

You might find then that a tweet with a link to a product gives you six replies, including four from regulars, three retweets, and three new followers.

You might also find that according to your server log you got eight clickthroughs from Twitter and made two sales.

Now you know that a tweet like that is worth three new followers, a 4 percent clickthrough rate, *and* $60 if the product costs $30.

So all you have to do is keep sending out tweets like this and you'll make $60 each time, right?

It's not that easy.

Tracking Multiple Tweets

If you remember just one piece of information from this book, make it this:

TWEETING IS A PROCESS

Write a blog post and you can see the results right away. You'll be able to count the views, check the clickthroughs, and calculate the value of a post on that topic.

Most important, those figures are relatively consistent.

Although there's no such thing as complete predictability on the Internet, each time you put up a blog post that covers the topic and is optimized in the same way, you should see roughly similar results.

The same isn't true on Twitter.

Discover that a certain kind of tweet gets your followers clicking through to your web site and persuades a few of them to buy or click ads, and you might be tempted to do it again a few hours later.

This time, though, instead of picking up three new followers and earning $60 in sales, you get no new followers, one clickthrough, and no sales.

What went wrong?

It's not the tweet with the link; you've already seen that tweets like these can work.

It was the tweets that came before the link tweet.

Followers don't want to receive the same content all the time on Twitter. And they're not going to click every link you offer them.

If you want to increase the odds that your followers click a link that you offer them on Twitter, make the sure that the previous tweets *don't* contain links.

They won't be suffering from click fatigue, and because linking isn't something you do too often, the link will appear to be more valuable.

So if you wanted to post a tweet that drove your followers to a web site where you were selling a new ebook or which included a valuable affiliate link, you'd want to prepare the ground with five or six tweets that offer interesting content or that let people know the product is in preparation.

How will you know which kind of content to include?

By looking back at your timeline.

Looking at your timeline will tell you which tweet sequences you've used in the past in the build up to the link tweet. By comparing those sequences with differences in the clickthroughs and conversions from those link tweets, you should be able to see which sequence of tweets is likely to be the most effective.

Let's see how this might work in practice.

Imagine that you're the publisher of a blog about gardening. You use Twitter to build a community of readers, answer questions about gardening issues, mine your followers for knowledge about sourcing seeds and cuttings, and of course, to send them to your blog posts.

You then make an agreement with the author of an ebook on managing a small garden, but before you put up a tweet containing a link to the sales page and urging people to check out a great book, you want to make sure that you get as many clickthroughs as possible.

So you look back over your Twitter Journal to see which of the tweets you've posted in the past that contain links generated the largest number of clickthroughs.

You find that tweet in your timeline, and as well as checking what you wrote in that tweet, you also examine what you wrote in the five or six tweets that came before it.

Let's say that those tweets were:

"First daffodil of the spring bloomed yesterday. What a sight!"

"Thinking of replanting my bonsai. Anyone know which store has the best selection of pots?"

"Putting down a new layer of mulch. Whiffy stuff."

"Spraying the bougainvillea. I wish it wasn't so big and thorny."

"A beautiful spring day—warm, sunny and with just a few clouds. Let's keep the rain off for a few days."

You could then categorize those tweets as:

1. Random thought.

2. Question.

3. Action.

4. Action.

5. Random thought.

And to increase the chances that your link to the ebook affiliate link would generate at least an equal number of clickthroughs, you could repeat the sequence before you posted that tweet:

"I love walking around my garden in the evening. It's so quiet and colorful!"

"Apple tree is starting to blossom. Anyone know whether the bee population recovered this year?"

"Looking at designs for small gardens. So many wonderful new possibilities."

"Thinking about laying a new garden path."

"Small gardens can look so beautiful . . . when they're well planned."

"John Smith has written a wonderful book about miniature gardening. Check it out at http://tinyurl.com/hihiyi."

Is it possible that a different sequence of tweets would have produced more clickthroughs? Of course, but when you're Twittering for money, it's a good idea to play it safe—and besides, unless you're tracking the results of your tweets, you won't know which sequence!

One of the most enjoyable aspects of using Twitter is that you can do it spontaneously. Maintaining a blog requires thought and planning. The posts themselves take time to research and write, but Twitter is something you can use whenever you feel like it.

That ease of use is part of what makes Twitter so much fun.

Even when you're testing and tracking in the way I've described in this chapter, you can still tweet spontaneously. There's nothing wrong with continuing to post individual tweets as well as tweet sequences.

Nor do you have to record the results of all your tweets. A representative sample should be enough let you understand what different tweets and sequences do.

Tracking can take time and it demands a little attention. But it can churn up some fascinating information, and it means that you can maximize the chances that a tweet will have exactly the effect you want.

And as you're recording your tweets, there's another factor you have to bear in mind too: when you post your tweets.

Unlike blogs, tweeting happens in real time, and it's most effective when your followers are online. There are all sorts of theories about when exactly is the best time to post a tweet. In general, midday and midweek tend to produce the best results, but there is a foolproof method to identify the best time for *your* community: When you find that you're seeing the greatest number of new tweets appearing on your Twitter page, that's always going to be the best time to post tweets that you want your followers to act on.

That's not always easy to assess, especially when you're following lots of people. So focus on a few. Look at when your most important evangelists are online and tweet then. (And the same is true when you're looking to catch the eye of someone else on Twitter: The best time is always when they're online and tweeting.)

Making the Most of Twitter's Trends

So far I've been talking about the statistics you can pick up about your own tweets. But there's another kind of data that you can pick up on Twitter.

You can see what topics other people are discussing.

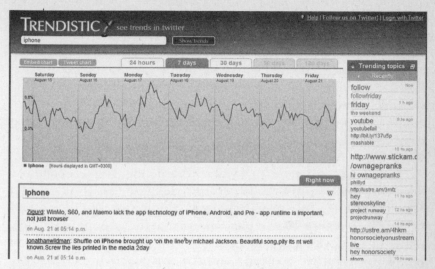

Figure 9.8 Trendistic tells you exactly what's hot on Twitter and when!

Twitter provides some information about trends. You can find a list of trending topics on your Twitter page, and you can also see them on the search page. Much more detailed—and far more interesting—is the information provided by search company Flaptor's Trendistic program (www.trendistic.com). (See Figure 9.8.)

The service, which used to be called Twist, looks a little like Alexa and offers a graph showing the number of times a chosen topic has turned up in tweets over a period of time. You can enter more than one topic to compare the most popular terms, and you can zoom in to see the stats for a chosen time.

You can even see sample tweets containing the terms you're looking at.

The right of the screen shows the current 10 most popular topics and another 10 topics that were recently popular.

It's all fascinating stuff and you can have a lot of fun tossing in keywords to find out whether "Mac" is more popular than "PC," "trees" more popular than "flowers," and so on.

But the information you find on Trendistic can be valuable too. *It lets you attract lots of followers by tweeting about popular topics, and it means you can tap a known market.*

There are limitations here, of course. Stray too far from the usual subject of your tweets and you'll struggle to turn readers into followers and you'll struggle even harder to keep them as followers.

And if you simply add a popular hashtag to the end of a tweet that has nothing to do with the topic—as spammers do—you'll do nothing but irritate other users. That's no way to succeed on Twitter.

But if you can combine your usual topic with a popular subject—and offer good, unique content—you'll have a passport to the largest discussions currently taking place on Twitter.

Let's say, for example, that you're a gardening Twitterer and you wanted to build up your follower list quickly so that you could get as many people as possible clicking your link.

A glance at your Twitter page shows that the most popular topic currently being discussed on the site is "Gmail" and the second most popular is "themes." You can't find any reasonable way to link gardening with Gmail, but you could enter a discussion about themes by asking what kind of flower themes people might like to see. (See Figure 9.9.)

A search for the term on Twitter's search engine shows that the themes that people are discussing are, not surprisingly, Gmail's themes. It also shows who's discussing them.

What it won't show, unfortunately, is how many followers those people have. You'll only be able to tell that by clicking through to their tweets until you find someone with a good number of readers and, ideally, a few tweets about gardening, too.

You follow them, then reply to their tweet about themes with a tweet of your own:

"These themes are cool. Do you know if it's possible to edit them? I'd love to use a pic of my garden."

When that Twitterer replies, it should bring a few of their followers clicking through to your Twitter page. And because it's a hot topic, *if your tweet is a genuinely valuable contribution*, there's also a good chance that the discussion will spread to other Twitter pages, too, giving you even more followers.

Make this follower-building strategy part of your preparation for an important link tweet and you'll be able to make the most of a Twitter campaign.

Figure 9.9 So who's talking about themes then?

Twitter works in all sorts of wonderful ways. Usually, it works as a fun way for people to keep in touch with others, make new friends, and join discussions. That's how most people use it.

It also works as a tool for mining information and finding expert advice.

And plenty of smart companies are using it to build a brand, turn their customers into a community, and cement the name of their products in the minds of their market.

But it's also possible to use Twitter to prompt people to take a particular course of action.

In this chapter, we've seen how it's possible to use tweets to send people to a blog, to persuade them to buy, and to add them to your email list.

And we've seen to how tracking your results and your tweets—and trends too—can help you to get the most out of the actions you want your followers to take.

In the next chapter, I'm going to introduce a few strategies that have been known to deliver *instant* results.

10

Quick Ways to Make Money on Twitter

When Twitter took off, a lot of people saw its business potential right away. They recognized that when a site has millions of members—both individuals and companies—talking and making connections, big deals wouldn't be far off.

But a lot of people got the wrong idea, too. They saw Twitter as a kind of get-rich-quick scheme, a place where they could come and immediately make giant piles of cash.

Twitter just doesn't work that way. The power of Twitter lies in the connections you forge and the relationships you build on the site.

Those take time to create. A large following doesn't happen overnight. Tweet well and tweet regularly, and it will happen, but don't expect to have 10,000 followers a week after opening your Twitter account.

And don't expect to close your first deal the day after posting your first tweet.

What Twitter supplies isn't a tool for making money online immediately and with little effort. You're not going to be able to create a bunch of Twitter timelines that will allow you to soak up the sun in Waikiki while the revenue continues to flow in all by itself.

Twitter delivers something much more valuable. It provides the basis on which all successful businesses are built.

It delivers trust.

I don't know of any other service that can take entrepreneurs so easily through the process of "Know me. Like me. Trust me. Pay me." and with so many people.

A business built on that foundation and strengthened by a web of good feeling and friendship will always be much more stable than one that relies on quick deal after quick deal.

But that doesn't mean that earning quick money on Twitter is impossible. It *is* possible. We've already seen that it's possible to drive followers through an affiliate link on the site, but there are a number of other methods that Twitterers have come up with to turn their Twitter presence into instant cash.

In this chapter, I'm going to explain how the most effective of those strategies work. You can use some or all of them if you want to. They're already making decent amounts of money for some people, and there's no reason they can't make a little extra cash for you, too.

But if you are going to use these methods, make sure they form just part of your Twitter strategy, and not your entire Twitter presence. If all you do is use Twitter to try to make a quick buck, then you'll be missing out on a giant marketing opportunity.

Earn with Advertising on Twitter

Advertising has always looked the most obvious way to make money out of a Twitter timeline. If you can generate income by placing ads in front of blog readers—and you can certainly do that!—then surely you can also make money by placing ads in front of your Twitter followers.

Or maybe not. A blog page has all sorts of elements. You can place ads in a range of different places and in a number of different ways. But the idea is always to make them unobtrusive. The better you can blend your ads into a Web page, the more people will click on them and the more money you'll make.

On Twitter though, there's no way to make the ads unobtrusive. Worse, there's always the fear that readers would be put off by an ad. It's as though you were holding a conversation with someone, then broke off suddenly to recommend that they buy a can of Coca-Cola or use a particular credit card.

Figure 10.1   Sponsored Tweets insert ads into your timeline. You set the price and write the copy. Sign up at twitpwr.com/earn.

It's not the kind of thing that makes for a smooth conversation, and the concern has always been that users won't accept ads in timelines. They'll stop following.

In practice, those fears have turned out to be largely unfounded. A number of services have turned up that deliver ads from advertisers to Twitterers, and provided it's done carefully, their services can provide positive results. SponsoredTweets.com is the one that I like the best, and it has a number of advantages, each of which I think is important on Twitter. (See Figure 10.1.)

First, it requires 100 percent disclosure. For this kind of advertising, that's vital.

When I place an affiliate link on a web site, it always points to a product that I've used, tested, and feel comfortable recommending. If I'm not certain that my readers would benefit from using that product, I wouldn't advertise it.

But I haven't used the products advertised in my timeline, and I don't want people to think that I'm recommending it. It's important to me then—as it's important to my followers—that they can see that that tweet is an ad and not a comment from me. (See Figure 10.2.)

Every ad posted by SponsoredTweets is clearly marked as an ad. That might make it less effective, but it does make it more honest. I'd rather lose a few bucks than lose the trust that my followers have in me. That's worth a lot more.

Secondly, I retain control. Some Twitter advertising systems require you to hand over your password so that they can insert ads automatically and with hardly any restrictions into your timeline. I don't want a company placing sales messages in my Twitter timeline unless I've had a chance to review them first. With SponsoredTweets, not only do I get a chance to review them, I also have the opportunity to write them.

When you sign up, you'll be asked to choose between posting ads that you write, ads that the advertiser writes, or either of those options. Initially at least, you should be choosing to write the ads yourself. They'll still be marked as ads but you'll be in control. If you manage to build a relationship with an advertiser, then at some point you might trust them enough to let them write the ads. But at the beginning, write them yourself. They'll have your voice, so they'll be less obtrusive and your clickthroughs will be higher, too.

You also get to set the price. That's vital, too.

SponsoredTweets pay in two ways. They pay on a cost-per-mille basis for each ad tweet that you show, and they also pay on a cost-per-click basis that delivers a flat fee for every follower who reaches the advertiser's web site.

You get to set those rates. That means you're never earning less than you think your timeline is worth.

Calculating those figures though isn't easy. Internet marketer and blogger John Chow (@johnchow) has been known to charge $250 per tweet on a timeline with almost 60,000 followers. That might not sound like much per follower, but it can still deliver a sizeable sum simply for writing a tweet. But the amount will vary depending on the subject you tweet about, the number of followers, and the value of your brand too. If you're tweeting legal or financial advice, and you're well-known and trusted with a name in your field, you should find that advertisers are prepared to pay a great deal more.

Figure 10.2   A SponsoredTweet ad as it appeared in my timeline. If it looks like an ad, it can't be my comment.

The same is true of the amount you want to charge on a per-click basis. The best way to figure out this amount is to open a Google AdWords account first. Use the keyword tool to generate keyword tags for your SponsoredTweets account, and use the "estimated average cost-per-click" for each of those keywords to produce a quote that lies in the middle of the range. Google will be one of your competitors so those are the prices you're competing against.

You'll need at least 200 followers to qualify for a SponsoredTweet ad, and the account needs to be at least four months old. Once you start receiving the ads, do pay attention to the number of your followers. If you find that the number falls significantly after an ad appears, then ask your followers what happened.

That's what's great about Twitter. On a web site, it's very difficult to get feedback from your readers about their reactions to an ad. You're largely restricted to looking at stats and trying to figure out what's happening. On Twitter, you can ask your readers what they think and see whether they found the ad helpful or obtrusive. You might find that it's the advertiser or the copy, not the ad itself that was causing the problem.

I think that SponsoredTweets is very promising, and there's a whole range of different strategies that you can use to maximize earnings. The first step though is to reach 200 followers, be online for at least four months, and sign up.

There are other ways of accepting ads in your timeline, of course; Ad.ly (www.ad.ly.com) offers a similar service, placing one preapproved ad in your timeline at a price that you've set. With Twitterers as well known as Dr. Drew (@drdrew) and Nicole Richie (@nicolerichie) already signed up, the service is helping to make in-stream advertising mainstream. Robert Scoble has also posted tweets from Seagate, his long-term sponsor. Again, these were clearly marked as ads, but it's important that he was recommending a company that he was already associated with. No one was surprised, and while the tweets were marked "ADVERTISEMENT," they also looked like personal recommendations. That's an ideal combination, but finding a corporate sponsor is always going to be difficult—unless you're as well known in your field as Robert Scoble is among technology readers.

Picking up a couple of hundred followers and waiting a few months will always be easier. You can sign up for SponsoredTweets at http://twitpwr.com/earn.

Offer Specialized Services

Inserting ads into your timeline was always going to be an obvious way to make money out of a large following. Justin Rockwell, who calls himself a "CSS freak," has come up with a much more creative method. (See Figure 10.3.)

Using his timeline, @ThatCssGuy, Justin scans Twitter looking for people who need help with their CSS problems and offers them quick solutions. He also throws in little CSS tips that allow him to build up his follower list. (See Figure 10.4.)

That activity is the free stuff that helps Justin to build his brand. Web developers with more complex problems can click through the link above Justin's bio to his web site, www.thatcssguy.com. Here, they can complete a form that describes their problem, then choose how much they want to pay for a solution.

That's right, they get to choose the rate. Justin has created a neat slider in which the more someone pays, the faster they get a response. The prices start at $35 for a wait of up to three days and rise to $135 for an almost-instant two-hour service.

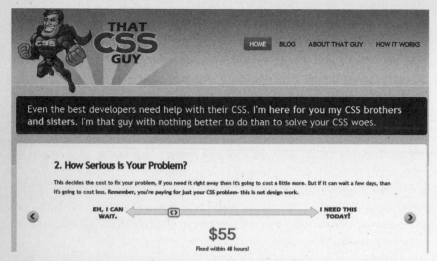

Figure 10.3   ThatCSSGuy.com is where "CSS freak" Justin Rockwell accepts orders for his advice from Twitterers who need his help. Buyers choose the price they want to pay.

@mharis w/ visibility:hidden the browser creates the right size space in the page for the information when it loads. (Think transparency)
9:51 PM Jul 29th from Tweetie in reply to mharis

@crazybilly 'hidden' hides the element, but keeps it's space in the layout. 'none' removes it from the document completely.
9:36 PM Jul 29th from Tweetie in reply to crazybilly

@pashaps I would suggest for temporarily elements- depends on what you're doing. Sounds like a new blog post if you ask me!
9:28 PM Jul 29th from Tweetie in reply to pashaps

Remember kids: Always use {visibility:hidden} over {display:none} for your unseen elements
9:13 PM Jul 29th from Tweetie

Figure 10.4   Justin Rockwell's timeline throws in valuable tips to attract targeted followers. Note home those tips take a set format, spark conversations, and show off his expertise.

Cleverly, the slider is set to a default of $55, which then looks like a recommended price. According to one report, Justin has been earning about $1,400 a month offering advice in this way. That won't allow him to give up his day job, but it is a nice supplement to a regular income.

It's also a model that anyone with expertise to share—in just about any area—can copy. There's no reason why a gardening enthusiast can't offer paid tips to people battling weeds. A mechanic could offer advice about fixing cars. A tutor could offer advice about the subjects she teaches.

But the way you do it is important. Justin Rockwell keeps his timeline and his web site very relaxed. He always creates the impression that he's not giving advice to make money but because he enjoys helping people. On Twitter, that kind of informality is important.

Offer your help for free, suggest that people pay if they want to—and help them out by suggesting a reasonable fee—and you should find that people who really do need your help will reach for their wallets.

Barter, Buy, and Sell Your Way to Profit

Twitter is full of opportunities, and just as people have managed to make livings out of buying and selling on eBay so it's possible to be make money out of the arbitrage opportunities that have now cropped up on Twitter.

This is all very straightforward. You're going to be looking for products that you can buy for a price lower than you know you can sell it for elsewhere.

The best places to browse are the many Twitter timelines that act as classifieds. You can find a list of these at Twellow, the Twitter directory. OLX_English (@OLX_English), for example, is the Twitter stream of OLX.com, a kind of free online classifieds service that regularly posts announcements of important new items for sale. Bear in mind too that a number of other classified sites and even newspaper services stream additions to their listings directly to Twitter, giving you a huge choice of items to browse from your home page.

In effect, by looking for and then following a range of different classified timelines, you'll have created one central place to view items listed for sale.

As always, the key to success with this kind of arbitrage is to know the prices in one small niche. Try to spot a bargain in a field about which you know little and it's likely that you'll be paying the market rate. Specialize in one type of product, whether that's DC comics, Mustang cars, or Barbie dolls, and you should find it easier to spot the underpriced goods and generate a profit when you sell it elsewhere.

With such a huge number of products flowing through Twitter, you might even want to create a timeline specifically for trading. That will prevent your main home page from being swamped with sale offers, drowning out your other messages. But because it won't always be possible to filter the types of classifieds you're seeing, you might struggle to find the items you really want.

One option then is to use iList Micro's (@ilistmicro) hashtags. This is a very neat service that allows Twitterers to make each other offers. You won't be accessing all of the classified ads posted on other sites in the way that following a range of classified timelines will allow you to do, but you will be able to focus on a particular type of product and let other people know you're in the market.

The web site itself, micro.ilist.com, allows buyers and sellers to search for items. To add an item to the listing, Twitterers only have to include the hashtags "#ihave" or "#iwant" to their tweet. So someone selling a telescope, for example, would tweet the telescope's details then add the hashtag "#ihave" at the end. (See Figure 10.5.) A trader specializing in telescopes could find that listing by searching for telescopes on iList Micro's web site. Alternatively, they can tweet the keyword "telescope" together with the hashtag "iwant." Whenever someone posts a tweet with those keywords, iList Micro would then send the trader a tweet with a link leading to the post. You can even restrict your searches by location or include those with pictures.

For eBay-traders in particular, Twitter can massively broaden the sources of the goods they buy and sell.

And if you don't want to pay for those goods, there's always the option of barter. As well as straightforward classifieds on Twitter,

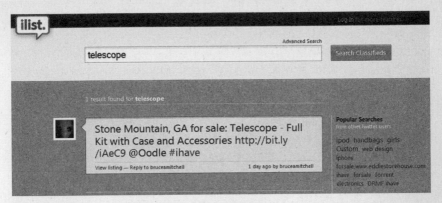

Figure 10.5 Want to buy a telescope?

you can also find plenty of people offering services and goods in return for things they need. You're not going to get rich this way, but you might find that you're able to trade something of little value to you for something that you value far more. That's a profitable trade.

Twitter is not a get-rich-quick scheme at all, and thinking about it that way is only going to lead to disappointment. It's a place to get to know people and build the relationships that lead to long-term deals. These simple examples may help you to make a little extra money on Twitter, but they're not what make Twitter useful for entrepreneurs.

In the next chapter, we'll look at some of the tools that make Twitter even more useful.

11

Beyond Twitter.com: Third-Party Tools You Will Want to Know About

One of the things that really makes Twitter fun is that it comes with lots of optional add-ons. Twitter allows programmers to write applications that anyone can use and that extend the power of the service.

Some of them are a little odd. (I've yet to find a good use for Twitter in Second Life.) But some of them are extremely helpful. (There are all sorts of applications that let you send and follow tweets without opening your browser, for example.)

That makes for hours of exciting experimentation—just the sort of thing that tech-minded people love to do.

On the other hand, if you want to skip straight to the most useful apps, here are some that I recommend.

SocialOomph

Follow someone on Twitter and there's a good chance that they'll follow you in return. It's not guaranteed, but it does happen a lot, and it's why one strategy to pick up followers is to do a lot of following.

The reason it happens a lot is that reciprocal following looks like good manners. If someone's following you, then it only seems right you should follow them back. As we've seen that might not

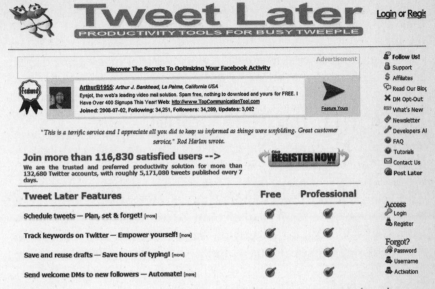

Figure 11.1   SocialOomph lets you schedule your tweets in advance.

be the smartest move—it can make you look like a spammer and you can't possibly follow everyone on a long list closely—but many people do it anyway.

And one reason they do it is that it's easy. SocialOomph (www.SocialOomph.com) lets you set up auto-follows. Whenever someone follows you, you'll automatically follow them in return. (See Figure 11.1.)

That can be a pretty neat trick, but it's not the service's main function.

The biggest reason for using SocialOomph is that it lets you set up tweets in advance—a bit like an autoresponder.

Now that really can be valuable.

It means that you can keep your timeline ticking over even while you're sleeping, working your day job, or spending the weekend with the kids. You wouldn't want to create a false impression on your timeline by preparing tweets that say you're hard at work on a blog post while in fact you're relaxing at a spa, but you can prepare some random thoughts and other tweets to keep your timeline active.

Best of all, you can use SocialOomph to prepare a series of tweets that lead up to a link you want your followers to click through.

SocialOomph also provides keyword alerts, which can be useful, and automatic "thank yous" to followers, which you need to use carefully. Fill your timeline with personal thank yous and your tweets look dull for everyone else. SocialOomph recommends sending your welcome messages by direct message, but I don't think that's a good idea either. You can save the reward of a mention for people who reply to your tweets or say something nice about your product. The biggest comes when you make your gratitude public.

SocialOomph is free and available at www.SocialOomph.com, but you might also want to check out Twittertise (www.twittertise.com). This does almost exactly the same thing but also lets you see the number of clickthroughs on links that you insert into the tweet.

Twitterrific

Twitter might have been designed with mobiles in mind, but it was never very mobile-friendly. Dialing a number every time you wanted

Figure 11.2　Twitterrific puts Twitter in your pocket.

to send a tweet was a bit of a nuisance, and what if you wanted to send a direct message or reply to a friend's tweet, let alone see them all?

Fortunately, developers have come up with some pretty neat alternatives.

Twitterrific is a Twitter client that sits on a Mac's desktop. It shows tweets from your followers and lets you tweet back in return. The interface is attractive and fun, and the program means you don't have to work with your Twitter page open in your browser. (See Figure 11.2.)

Best of all, Twitterrific is also available for the iPhone. It even comes with a mini-browser so that you don't lose your timeline every time you click a link, and it lets followers see where you are.

It's a very neat solution for Twitterers on the move. Twitterrific is available for download from Icon Factory at http://iconfactory .com/software/twitterrific. The free version is funded by ads but you can get an ad-free version for just a few bucks.

Twhirl

Twitterrific might be very cool and a neat solution for iPhone users (and Tweetie, available from the iPhone app store is

Figure 11.3   Twhirl lets even PC users tweet off-site.

great, too.) Owners of other kinds of mobile phones can try TwitterMail (www.twittermail.com) for email-enabled phones; Cellity (www.cellity.com) for Java-enabled phones; and Blackbird (http://dossy.org/twitter/blackbird/) for BlackBerry phones.

For desktop Twitterers, Twitterrific is also limited; it only works on the Mac. PC users have to look elsewhere for a Twitter client. Many of them look to Seesmic's Twhirl. (See Figure 11.3.)

Like Twitterrific, Twhirl frees Twitterers from Twitter's Web page, letting them send and receive tweets from an attractive, instant message-style client. It's packed with all sorts of other useful goodies too, such as automatic short URLs, search, and image posting to TwitPic. It's built on Adobe AIR, so you'll have to download that first, but both are free and available from www.twhirl.org.

Twitterfeed

I've mentioned Twitterfeed a few times in this book. Spend any time at all reading tweets and you're going to come across plenty of examples of its use.

As a way of adding one particular type of content to your timeline, Twitterfeed can be very useful. But do bear in mind that the price you're paying for the ease of providing blog updates through Twitter is a loss of the personal touch. If your blog is hugely popular, you can get away with a Twitterfeed timeline dedicated solely to informing followers of your latest posts.

For most people though, Twitterfeed's updates become just one kind of tweet, but one that they can set up and leave.

Sign up for free at www.twitterfeed.com.

Trendistic

There are a number of different services that allow Twitterers to keep track of the popularity of various topics and keywords on Twitter. Some use a frequently updated tag cloud to show relative popularity, but I like the graphs on Trendistic. It's accurate and detailed, and you can make comparisons between different terms and even see samples of the tweets you're examining. (See Figure 11.4.)

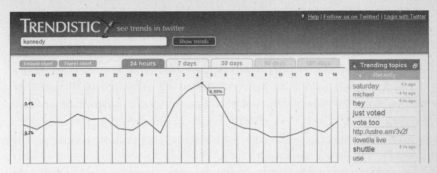

Figure 11.4   Trendistics makes looking at graphs fun.

It can be a very useful way to make sure that you're targeting the most popular terms and look for other people Twittering about your topic.

And it looks very neat, too.

Use it at trendistics.com.

Twellow

Trendistics can help you find people with similar interests to your own, but Twellow makes it all much, much easier. Run by

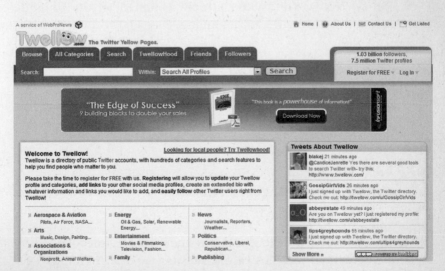

Figure 11.5   Twellow: Twitter's Yellow Pages.

WebProNews, it's supposed to be a kind of Yellow Pages of social media, but it operates more like a Twitter Yahoo!. (See Figure 11.5.)

The site tracks conversations on Twitter and places the Twitterers behind them into various categories. Click one of those categories and you'll be able to see a list of suitable Twitterers, complete with sample tweet, bio, image, and the number of their followers.

For Twitterers looking for interesting and useful people to follow, it's a fantastic resource.

And clearly, for Twitterers who want to be followed, it's hugely valuable, too.

Once you start sending tweets, you should find that you're added automatically, but if you can't find your name on the site, you can add it yourself. In any case, it's certainly worth checking the categories that you've been listed under and self-editing them if necessary.

Keep Twellow close by at www.twellow.com.

TweetBeep

Twellow tells you who tends to talk about what, but you'll also want to know who's talking about your topics now.

TweetBeep, which as we've seen sends out regular alerts whenever a keyword is used on Twitter, is really a must for anyone thinking about marketing through microblogging. (See Figure 11.6.)

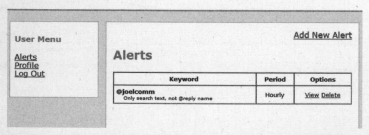

Figure 11.6 TweetBeep lets you know when someone's talking behind your company's back.

Remember that tracking your username or your company name and diving right into a conversation can look a little creepy. If you see someone has mentioned you, it's often a good idea to follow them before replying.

You can set up your alerts at www.tweetbeep.com.

TwitterCounter

There's one more useful matrix you might want to know when you're looking for people to follow though—and when you want to know how you're doing too—and that's the rate of follower growth.

When you're tracking your own tweets and their results, you should have those figures handy, but when you look at someone else's profile, there's no way of knowing whether they picked up all of their followers a year ago or whether their tweets are still generating interest.

Figure 11.7 Numbers aren't everything on Twitter, but TwitterCounter's growth charts can provide some interesting stats.

TwitterCounter lets you see anyone's follower numbers over time. (See Figure 11.7.)

Just toss a name into the site and you'll receive a graph showing how their follower numbers have risen and fallen over the last week.

It's interesting and, when you're looking for people on the up to follow and be followed by, useful too.

Have fun at www.twittercounter.com.

TweetDeck

Twitter's strength is its simplicity. Short posts, short replies, and quick conversations make for a service that's simple to use. But it's also very limited. It's not easy to keep track of conversations, for example. You'll be holding multiple chats with multiple followers all at the same time and often on different topics. As one tweet comes in, the last one will pushed down the list making it difficult to follow the course of an exchange. (See Figure 11.8.)

Nor does Twitter allow you to group tweets according to subject. TweetDeck lets you do that.

This service really is a must-have for anyone with a large list of followers. You can create multiple columns and group them according to topics. It's the closest you're likely to get to Facebook's groups.

Figure 11.8   TweetDeck supplies a control panel for multi-tasking Twitterers.

It's also very useful for following hashtag chats and current events. Because the tweets are updated in real time, you'll be able to keep up with conversations and updates without refreshing the page.

You'll need to download Adobe AIR again, but it's still free and available at www.tweetdeck.com.

As of this writing, I've begun beta-testing another desktop-based Twitter client that may one-up TweetDeck. It's called TweetGlide.com, and it may well be worth a look.

TwitThis

TwitThis isn't exactly a Twitter application, but it's certainly useful nonetheless and should be a basic tool for any Twitter-based marketer. (See Figure 11.9.)

You've probably seen all the buttons at the bottom of blog posts urging people to Digg the article or send it to StumbleUpon. With TwitThis, you can also ask them to send a URL of the page together with a brief description to their Twitter followers.

It's a simple and effective way to help your blog or web site make the most of Twitter's viral power.

Load up on your buttons at www.twitthis.com.

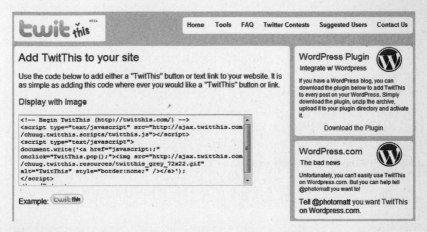

Figure 11.9 Pick up some instant viral marketing with TwitThis.

TweetAways

One of the most powerful marketing uses of Twitter has been contest and giveaways. Companies have managed to drum up huge amounts of publicity and exposure by giving away everything from books and show tickets to cameras and computers. The usual method is to ask people to follow you, retweet a message, often with a link, and include a hashtag to make it easy to identify. One tweet is then picked at random at a set time and the winner notified by direct message.

It's very straightforward and the viral power is clear. It only takes a few people to tell their followers that they're hoping to win whatever it is you're giving away for the message to spread right across Twitter. And the more valuable the item you're offering, the faster and further you'll find it spreads.

The tricky bit though is choosing a winner, and that's where services like TweetAways come in so useful. They'll do all the hard work for you. They'll keep track of all of the tweets that qualify then choose one at random at the time you select. All you have to do is collect the name and address and arrange the shipping.

You can find it at www.tweetaways.com, and you can also take a look at www.twiveaway.com, which does the same thing.

HootSuite

HootSuite is a comprehensive Twitter client for serious business Twitterers. It allows multiple Twitterers to operate the same account, keep track of more than one timeline, follow statistics, and monitor their brands—and do it all in one place. (See Figure 11.10.)

Once you're using Twitter seriously for marketing, there's a good chance that you'll find yourself using HootSuite—especially as it's free. It just makes doing all of those essential elements that are a part of using Twitter for business so much easier.

Download it from www.hootsuite.com.

TwitPic

And finally, TwitPic is probably the most used extension to Twitter. (See Figure 11.11.) It lets Twitterers post pictures along with their

Figure 11.10   HootSuite calls itself the "professional Twitter client."

tweets. Or rather it lets them include a link with their tweets to an image at TwitPic.com.

You can upload your pictures from a number of Twitter clients, including many that work on mobile phones with cameras. It's just a matter then of shooting, opening the Twitter client, and

Figure 11.11   Probably Twitter's most popular extension, TwitPic adds images to your tweets.

choosing your image. Your followers will also be able to add comments beneath the pictures, continuing the discussion in a whole new way.

As for the sorts of pictures you might want to upload, anything goes. If it makes your tweets more interesting, adds a personal touch to your timeline, and illustrates what you're discussing, it can only bring you benefits.

You can find it at www.twitpic.com, and on your Twitter client.

This is just a number of the most useful tools that I've found for Twitter. There are plenty of others, and new ones are coming out every day with better interfaces, more features, and neater designs.

You can have hours of fun just downloading them and trying them out until you create the toolkit that works best for you. Because many of them are fairly similar, much comes down to personal taste.

On the whole though, your toolkit should contain applications that let you find people to follow, track keywords, organize your followers, and tweet and reply easily. Those are the basics.

12

Building Powerful Solutions on Top of the Twitter Platform

So we've seen that there are a number of extensions and tools that make Twitter use so much easier. Many of Twitter's users, in fact, never return to Twitter's Web page once they've set up their account. All of their interaction with the site—and with other Twitterers—is done through clients such as Twhirl and Twitterrific.

But these tools weren't all created by professional software companies looking to make a pile of cash. Many were designed by Twitter enthusiasts who knew something about coding and wanted to make life better for other Twitterers. TwitPic, for example, is the work of lone developer Noah Everett (@noaheverett). Other extensions, of course, were created by companies with at least one eye on the profits that can come from meeting a need with a smart product. Twitterrific, for example, is produced by The Icon Factory, a company made up of designers and programmers that has been around since the mid-1990s.

Whether they're produced by individuals or by companies though, the reason that anyone is able to build applications on Twitter is because one of the smartest decisions that the Twitter's founders made was to make its API available.

In this chapter, I'm going to explain what an API is, what Twitter's API can do, and what it might be able to do for you.

This is fairly advanced stuff, and it's not an essential part of achieving success with Twitter. You can still dominate your market with Twitter without knowing a line of code or understanding the difference between an API and an apple. There's nothing wrong with benefitting from the API work that other developers have completed for Twitter's users.

But understanding APIs can deliver opportunities that can benefit both individuals and companies, and it's worth at least knowing about them.

So What Is an API Anyway?

API stands for Application Programming Interface. It's a language that enables one program to talk to another. There's nothing to stop you, for example, from creating a program that sorted all of the tweets that mention your company's name into different categories and forwarding them to selected employees to answer. But to operate, the program would need to be able to access Twitter, ask for the data it needs, and be able to download it.

The way that program would interact with Twitter is by using an API.

Twitter actually has two different APIs. The REST API enables programs to contact Twitter's servers and access timelines, post tweets, send direct messages, follow users, and do all of the other things that users can do from Twitter's Web page.

The Search API lets a program search Twitter's databases and draw down selected information that it finds.

That division isn't ideal, and there are plans to unite them, but at the moment these are two separate APIs and any application that wants to use both functions have to use both APIs. Many do.

And there's a third way that Twitter allows developers to access its servers. Data feeds simply access Twitter's databases and download data. They don't allow the program to interact with Twitter or issue commands such as sending a tweet or following a Twitterer.

So there's a range of different ways that developers can interact with Twitter. However they do it though, it's not the API (or the data feed) itself that's particularly clever. It's what developers do with it.

What Can You Do with Twitter's API? Automating Your Twitter Experience

In the previous chapter, I listed some of the most useful applications that were built using Twitter's APIs. You can see just by looking at that short list how even Twitter's simple syntax can deliver a huge range of benefits from alerts and automated tweets to comprehensive clients that allow teams of Twitterers to access the same accounts, run multiple accounts, and monitor Twitter in real time.

One of the most obvious uses for a Twitter application will be *automation*. Instead of logging in to Twitter each day and checking to see who replied to your tweets or mentioned your company, you could create a program that will do much of this work for you. Every time someone mentioned "bug" and the name of your software product in the same tweet, for example, your application could automatically send a tweet asking if they need any help or inviting them to open a service ticket.

But I wouldn't recommend it. Unless you're picking up dozens of complaints every day—in which case, you've got a problem that Twitter can't solve—you'll always be better off responding to mentions in person. It doesn't take long, and it shows you care.

But you could set up a program that posted a random quote at regular intervals to keep your timeline ticking over or that offered valuable tips related to your product. That could help to reduce your workload while still keeping your timeline interesting.

You could also create an application that preserved all of the tweets mentioning your company, your product, or even your industry. Twitter's search engine is notoriously unreliable. Old tweets have a habit of not turning up in results, and while you can search for specific tweets on Google (use the format "[keyword] site:twitter.com/[username]" to search a Twitterer's timeline), automatically downloading tweets might be better if you want to be absolutely certain that you're not losing valuable information.

Another use to which you could put an app is to republish tweets. We've seen that Twitter does supply widgets that you can put on Web pages, but creating your own application would allow you to choose exactly which kinds of tweets you republished. So you could show tweets that mention your product, your industry news, or which were sent within a set radius of a particular location. You could even allow your users to interact with those Twitterers.

Imagine, for example, that you had a web site about Asian antiques. You could create an application that searched Twitter for anyone mentioning different kinds of Asian antiques and reposted them in a module in your site. Collectors would be able to come to your site, read your content, and interact with other enthusiasts in real time without ever going to their own accounts at Twitter. What uses can you think of that would benefit your online business?

And, of course, you can create an application that *earns money* itself.

That's not easy to do. There are thousands of applications already available and most are free. But that doesn't mean that some aren't making money. While figures aren't readily available, Twitterific's free application is a great promotional tool for its ad-free premium service. HootSuite is planning to start charging—once enough people have realized what a valuable tool it can be.

If you can come up with an idea for an application that delivers a truly valuable service, you can certainly try charging for it or supporting it with ads.

Creating Your Twitter App

If you know how to write code, then you'll know exactly what to do to create an application that does what you want. But I'm not a coder, and this isn't a manual for application programming. The application that my company created, TwitPwr.com, was created by our in-house programmers, as was my iFart iPhone app. I didn't write a line of code in either of them.

Even if you're not a coder then, you can still benefit hugely from APIs by hiring developers to do the number-crunching for you.

At the bottom of Twitter's Web pages, you'll find a link marked "API." Click that link and you'll be taken to Twitter's API Wiki. (See Figure 12.1.)

This contains a ton of information about Twitter's API and what it can do, but more importantly for non-coders it's also a good place

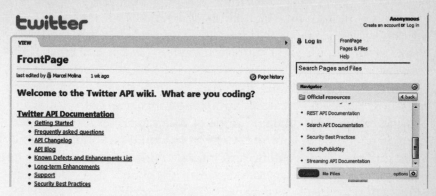

Figure 12.1   Twitter's API Wiki is a rich resource and a good place to pick up coders.

to find developers. At the bottom of the page, under "Community Resources," you'll find a link marked "Developers for Hire." That will take you to a page full of programmers ready to do your bidding—for a fee, of course.

Be sure to check out their web sites and read their tweets, too, before you hire someone. That should give you a good idea of their personalities and how easy they'll be to work with.

Above all, though, make sure that you know exactly what you want your application to do. The developer should be able to give you ideas and suggestions, but the clearer your instructions, the better the results should be.

Creating an application can be a lot of work. But it can also save you a lot of work and earn some real cash. If you've got an idea for an app that can work on Twitter, it's worth looking into.

13

Putting It All Together

So Twitter is both incredibly basic and incredibly powerful. Twitterers are using the service to network and have fun, but many corporations also have found that microblogging can have a huge impact on the closeness of their communities, on the traffic they pick up at their web sites, on their relationships with their customers, and on the reach of their brands.

It's simple to use, enjoyable, and effective.

But I want to make it even simpler for you. Whenever you pick up a new tool, there's always a period of playing, time in which you get a feel for the way the system works and figure out how to make it work best.

That can be a useful period, but it's also a dangerous one.

Because this isn't a time when they get results, commercial users can start to wonder what all the fuss is about. They don't see their traffic increasing, they don't see their sales rising, and they don't see their follower lists growing at a rate that will have enough of an effect on their brand.

So they stop doing it.

That's a huge waste.

The benefits—and the fun—of Twitter aren't at the beginning when you're building your follower list. They happen once you're up and running, when you have a community of people to chat with, and when you can see people clicking through from your web site to your Twitter timeline and vice versa.

In this chapter, I'm going to try to get you to that stage as quickly as possible by providing you with 30-Day Plan for Dominating Twitter.

I'm not going to promise that at the end of the 30 days if you do everything I suggest here you'll have a thousand followers or anything of the sort. The degree of success that you have depends too much on the subject of your tweets—and, of course, on their quality.

And once your timeline has been set up, you'll also need to continue tweeting, replying, and adding new followers every day. The daily goals are in addition to those basic actions.

Clearly, this isn't the only way to build a foundation of success on Twitter or the only schedule you should follow. It is however one way in which you can get up, running, and delivering results quickly and easily.

A 30-Day Plan for Dominating Twitter

DAY 1. SIGN UP AND SETTLE IN

Begin by completing the registration form. Decide whether your first Twitter timeline will promote your personal brand, your web site, or your company, choose a username that's suitable and easy to remember, and write a short, snappy bio. Using one of the templates in this book should make that easy for you. Remember, you can always change it later.

For a first-time user, Twitter can look like a strange place in which strange people post odd messages about what they're doing while answering questions from complete strangers.

This is what Twitter's all about so spend a little time today clicking through followers and reading tweets. You should find that you have to tear yourself away.

You can also sign up for TweetBeep today and create alerts for your company name and products. You might well be surprised to find that people are already talking about you.

DAY 2. CREATE YOUR BACKGROUND IMAGE

A day for creativity. Your background image is important so it's worth doing it right. Using a free template will get you moving quickly, but you might want to contact a designer to produce something unique or play around with designs yourself.

Take a look at the images used by leading Twitterers at Twitterank for ideas.

DAY 3. READ AROUND

You'll soon be building up a bank of tweets for your new followers to read so spend today preparing with some dedicated reading of your own. This should be fun but do read critically. Focus on the sorts of topics you'll be tweeting about, pay attention to the sorts of tweets that generate replies, and note who takes part in the discussions.

You'll probably find that while there are plenty of followers willing to read tweets about a certain subject, it will be the same handful that are the most active in the conversations.

But don't start following yet. You first want to have some tweets to show when those Twitterers visit your timeline.

DAY 4. WRITING YOUR FIRST TWEETS

This is going to be a day of tweeting. Download a Twitter client such as Twhirl or Twitterific so that you don't have to leave the browser open, and every couple of hours or so, post a quick sentence about what you're doing or thinking.

Don't worry about writing something silly—remember, tweets can be deleted—but focus on making them entertaining, interesting, and fun. Enjoy yourself, but remember from now on you're going to be tweeting every day!

DAY 5. START FOLLOWING

And now things can really get moving. By now you're probably itching to start adding followers. Your reading should have alerted you to the main Twitterers in your field and with a bank of tweets that show you have something to offer in return, you're ready to start following them.

Hit the "follow" button and see which of them follow you in return. By the end of the day, you should find that you've picked up your first followers—and they might well be important ones.

Don't forget to keep tweeting!

Day 6. Add Friends and Acquaintances—and Start Replying

Start expanding your follower list by looking for your friends, acquaintances, and contacts on Twitter. You might not find many, but you should find some. Once you've added them, don't be afraid to send a reply to one of their tweets. While you can direct message them, replying will give you extra content in your timeline, and when they reply back, you'll appear in their timeline, exposing your name to their followers—an easy way to gain additional users.

Day 7. Start Catching Big Followers

By now you'll have a few followers. Some will be the main Twitterers on your topic that you'll have identified during your reading. Others will be people you know who you've found on the site.

Spend today making a real effort to add as followers Twitterers with large follower lists. Use Twellow to identify the main movers in different fields, follow them, and reply to their tweets with interesting, valuable information.

Day 8. Add More Followers

The main Twitterers—the people who post regularly and have long follower lists—are like nodes in a network. That makes them good places to start: Every time they reply to you, your name spreads out along their network. But you can travel along their networks, too.

Spend today checking the followers in their lists. Follow them, reply to their tweets, and see how many of them follow you in return.

Day 9. Ask a Question

By now, you should have a long enough follower list to start making use of it.

Tap the information that your followers possess.

Ask a question that you'd like answered and see if you can pick up a response.

The question itself won't matter too much today—I just want you to see one thing that Twitter can do for you. You'll be amazed at how much your followers know.

DAY 10. ANSWER A QUESTION

So you've discovered how useful Twitter can be. Now it's time to recognize that you have to pay your dues by answering a question.

If one of your followers has asked something you can answer, you'll have an easy opportunity. If they haven't though, try using the search page to find someone who posed a query. Follow them, then reply with your answer. They might be surprised, but these sorts of random encounters are part of what makes Twitter so exciting.

DAY 11. HAVE FUN!

Twitter might be a valuable marketing tool but it's also very enjoyable, and enjoying it is a great sign that you're doing it right and will keep doing it, too.

Just relax today and have fun. Write tweets that make you laugh and think, reply to tweets you find interesting, and don't think too much about adding to your followers or keeping them entertained.

If you're entertained, they will be too.

DAY 12. LOOK FOR YOUR EVANGELISTS

Now for a change of tack. Some of your followers will be far more active in your timeline than others, replying to your tweets and sending you direct messages. They're among the people you want to encourage and keep entertained.

It's possible that there are others out there, though, people who mention your web site or discuss your products on Twitter. Use Twitter's search to draw up a list of your main evangelists and potential promoters.

DAY 13. REEL IN YOUR EVANGELISTS

Once you've drawn up your list, you can start putting it to use. Follow your evangelists and reply to them as usual, but show that you value their opinion by asking them questions about your product, addressing any issues they've raised, and offering them sneak peeks at projects in the works.

These are the people who will be promoting your name for nothing on Twitter, so it pays to keep them happy!

DAY 14. DO SOME CUSTOMER SERVICE

While evangelists can bring plenty of benefits, you might well find that there's no shortage of people on Twitter not entirely happy with your service. Today, you can squash those negative comments.

Search for the name of your product or your company and reply to any complaints with an apology and a request for more information.

DAY 15. POST A LINK TWEET

You should be tweeting every day and doing it several times a day, too, so you've probably posted at least one link tweet already, complete with short URL.

Today you're going to do it deliberately and measure the results.

Choose a page on your web site and review the stats for the last week. Post a tweet recommending the page and add a link. The difference in page views might be minimal, but pay attention to the number of ad clicks and the comments left on the page after the tweet. You might well find that your Twitter traffic is small in number but large in influence.

DAY 16. POST A DISCUSSION TWEET

And today we're going to do the same thing with a discussion tweet on Twitter. State an opinion and ask your followers what they think.

Although this won't have any effect on your web site, it will show you how active your followers are and how willing they are to contribute to your timeline.

DAY 17. POST AN ACTION TWEET

A link tweet is one type of action tweet; it encourages your followers to click through to a Web page you recommend. But Twitter can deliver much more powerful results than that.

Today, you can see the results.

Encourage your followers to take an action that will deliver something of value. You could recommend an affiliate product and include a link or ask people to join your mailing list, for example.

Don't expect too much at this stage—these are early days still—but few things are more encouraging than seeing your followers earn you money.

DAY 18. START PUTTING YOUR TWEETS TOGETHER

Over the last few days, you'll have been experimenting with different kinds of tweets. You should have been enjoying the results, too. Today you can try creating a sequence of tweets that leads to a call to action.

Start by deciding what action you want your followers to take at the end of the sequence. Then, use TweetLater to create a series of tweets, spaced throughout the day, that guide your followers to that action.

DAY 19. TRY A DIFFERENT SEQUENCE

Today you can do the same thing but with a different sequence of tweets and a different action at the end. That will let you compare two different tweet sequences to see which delivers the best results.

You'll be spending a lot of time testing tweets and tweet sequences so this is a good chance to practice!

DAY 20. HAVE FUN!

You've been driving your followers fairly hard during the last two days, so pull back today. Tweet, join discussions, and read other people's timelines while looking for new people to follow.

It will be a break for your followers and for you too!

DAY 21. DO SOME OFF-TWITTER MARKETING

By now, your timeline should be moving along nicely. You should have a reasonable-sized number of active followers (remember, you only need to have 100 followers to be doing better than 96 percent of all Twitterers!), and you've already felt the benefits of driving those followers to take action.

Today, you can extend your follower list even further by doing some off-Twitter marketing. Register at TwitThis to add their icon to your blog posts. Post a Twitter badge on your web site, and make sure that your email and forum signatures include your Twitter URL.

And don't forget to keep track of the results so that you can measure the effect.

DAY 22. COMBINE YOUR SOCIAL MEDIA TOOLS

Some more off-Twitter marketing today, but this time we're going to use the power of your other social media tools.

If you're using Facebook, add the Twitter application to your account so that your tweets turn up on your Facebook page. Mention your timeline on your other social media accounts to make sure that people know what you're doing and come to see what you're up to.

And if you're not yet using other social media tools, this is a good time to start!

DAY 23. DRIVE FOLLOWERS TO PURCHASE A SPECIAL OFFER

Now we're going to start moving up a level. You've already done the basics and seen the results, so let's make things a little more complex. Over the next few days, you're going to be driving your followers to take actions that are more valuable and tougher to carry out than you've done in the past.

Start by driving your followers to purchase something with a special offer. You could use one of your own products with a special discount code or set up an affiliate relationship with a retailer that lets you offer a cut price.

You can then either create a tweet sequence that primes your followers before dropping in the call to action or just throw it in and see what happens. Whichever you choose, be sure to record the results.

DAY 24. DRIVE FOLLOWERS TO A BLOG

Persuading people to purchase is always going to be a little tricky so now do something easier: link to your blog.

Don't just put up a Twitterfeed-style headline though; announce that a new post has gone up and invite people to comment. Find out what happens to your discussions when you really push your followers onto your blog.

DAY 25. DRIVE FOLLOWERS TO SUBSCRIBE

Follow up yesterday's Twitter goal by turning those followers into RSS subscribers.

You could try doing that by bringing the discussion on your blog back onto Twitter. Ask your followers what they thought about the post, talk about it during the day, and at the end of the day urge them to become subscribers.

DAY 26. DRIVE FOLLOWERS TO PURCHASE WITHOUT A SPECIAL OFFER

Now for the big one. Persuading followers to buy with a special offer is relatively easy. You've made them feel part of an exclusive club and rewarded them for following your tweets. Just invite them to buy and you'll have to work a little harder.

Create a series of tweets that discuss the product you want to sell—an affiliate product will do. End with the call to action and track the results. Whether you generate sales or not, you'll have a baseline to which you can compare your future promotions.

DAY 27. HAVE FUN!

After all that effort, it's time for another fun day to show your followers that you value them and not just their wallets.

DAY 28. CREATE A SECOND TIMELINE

With your timeline moving along nicely, you're ready to set up a second account. Not everyone needs to do this but having more than one timeline can be a useful way to create separate brands for different products.

You can even use this second timeline just for automated tweets.

DAY 29. FIND FOLLOWERS FOR YOUR NEW TIMELINE

Spend today building followers for your new timeline. You might not have to work too hard for this depending on what you want your timeline to do. For an automated timeline powered by Twitterfeed, just telling the followers on your first list about it could be enough.

DAY 30. HAVE FUN!

And finally, end your 30-day crash course the way you mean to go on: by enjoying yourself with tweets, replies, and chats with your growing list of followers.

14

Power Twitterers

In a way, Twitter can be classified as a broadcast channel. And like other channels, Twitter has its own celebrities. While @barackobama has more followers than anyone else, his political campaign used Twitter only for one-way communication. I'm sorry to say that he didn't actually tweet while on the campaign trail.

But there are other Twitter users with tens of thousands of followers who use the site to truly build relationships and interact with other members. They run the gamut from actors and sports figures to CEOs and industry pundits. This chapter spotlights just a few of these "Power Twitterers."

Robert Scoble (@scobleizer)

Self-described "tech-geek blogger," Scoble is a tech enthusiast and video podcast evangelist. His contributions to *Fast Company* magazine spotlight the ways in which new technology is changing the Internet. The majority of Scoble's tweets are replies to his followers. With plenty to say about social media, he can frequently be found tweeting about FriendFeed, Facebook, Google, Qik, and Flickr. Scoble averages 24 tweets/day and is likely to interact if your tweet is engaging and on topic. Follow Robert Scoble at twitter.com/scobleizer or visit his site at Scobleizer.com.

Gary Vaynerchuk (@garyvee)

Entering the Twitter scene in 2007 and becoming a Twitter "rock star" in 2008, Gary Vaynerchuk is a poster child for social media and the way in which the Web is launching people to celebrity status. Simply put, Vaynerchuk is passionate about wine. To be more specific, he believes that the wine-tasting culture has become too exclusive for the average Joe. And that's a shame, because there is no reason everyone of legal age shouldn't be able to enjoy the experience. His Web-based broadcast of WineLibrary.tv reaches "the everyman" with down-to-Earth wine analysis and a healthy helping of good-natured fun. With his irreverent approach and valuable insights, Vaynerchuk has caught the attention of the mainstream media with appearances on *Conan, Ellen, Nightline*, and a number of other shows. He averages 10 tweets/day, and you can follow him at twitter.com/garyvee or visit his site at WineLibrary.tv.

Peter Shankman (@skydiver)

There's more to publicity than sending a press release, and no one knows this better than Peter Shankman. CEO of The Geek Factory, a boutique marketing and PR strategy firm in New York City, Shankman is notorious for helping clients create events that get media attention. Along with working with some of the biggest corporations in the world, Shankman is frequently invited as a pundit on major national and international news channels. The accomplishment that is getting him more recent attention is his three-times-daily email newsletter, "Help a Reporter Online." This free publication connects journalists with the sources they require. With more than 36,000 members as of this writing, Shankman's grassroots endeavor is providing PR opportunities in the unlikeliest of places. He averages six tweets/day; you'll want to watch him for potential media opportunities that may come your way. He is a self-confessed ADHD thrill seeker, and you can keep up with Peter's latest stunts at twitter.com/skydiver or visit his site at Shankman.com.

Kevin Rose (@kevinrose)

Digg.com has become one of the world's most popular and influential social bookmarking sites. As founder and site architect of Digg, Kevin Rose has become a social media celebrity who wholeheartedly embraces the spotlight. Along with his flamboyant co-host Alex Albrecht, Rose broadcasts his weekly Web show, *Diggnation*, to scores of loyal viewers. Kevin has tens of thousands of followers on Twitter, yet he does not follow as many in return. Nevertheless, he tweets an average of seven times/day via his iPhone. You'll frequently find him discussing technology and rock climbing. Follow Kevin at twitter.com/kevinrose or visit his site at KevinRose.com.

Guy Kawasaki (@guykawasaki)

A technology evangelist and managing director of an early-stage venture capital firm, Guy Kawasaki is well-known throughout the technology and business sectors. A Stanford and UCLA graduate, Kawasaki is a high-profile public figure known for his time at Apple Computer, Inc., as well as for his numerous books. Extremely active on Twitter, he is known to tweet an average of 30 times/day. Frequently promoting his latest venture, AllTop.com, an online magazine rack of popular topics, Kawasaki tweets a mix of AllTop articles and replies to his followers. You can follow him at twitter.com/guykawasaki or visit his site at GuyKawasaki.com.

Michael Arrington (@techcrunch)

Founder of TechCrunch.com, a weblog dedicated to "obsessively profiling and reviewing new Internet products and companies," Michael Arrington is an active Twitter user known for tweeting tech news. Discussing everything from Microsoft and Google to Mobile and MySpace, Arrington tweets an average of 13 times/day. This is a great follow if you want to keep up with the latest tech news. You can follow Arrington at twitter.com/techcrunch or visit his site at TechCrunch.com.

Wil Wheaton (@wilw)

Best known for starring in the hit film *Stand by* Me and his recurring role as Ensign Wesley Crusher on *Star Trek: The Next Generation*, Wil Wheaton's Twitter bio states, "I'm just this guy, you know?" Not one to follow others at random, Wheaton is a self-professed geek and libertarian who has embraced Twitter as a platform for sharing his views. Tweeting an average of seven times/day, Wheaton's entries are more of a "life-cast" than promotion of any particular projects or reporting of current events. True to Twitter's original intent, he uses the site to state what he is doing right now. You can follow Wheaton at twitter.com/wilw or visit his site at wilwheaton.typepad.com.

Chris Brogan (@chrisbrogan)

Chris Brogan is a social media advisor who helps businesses and individuals leverage technology to accomplish their goals. A very active Twitter member, Brogan is engaged and interacts with his followers on a regular basis. With an average of 35 tweets/day, he mixes his technology commentary with plenty of real-life dialogue. To expert Twitterers like Chris, it's all part of the same thing. The discussion doesn't begin and end—it just is. You can follow Brogan at twitter.com/chrisbrogan or visit his site at ChrisBrogan.com.

Shaquille O'Neal (@The_Real_Shaq)

Hoops superstar O'Neal signed up for Twitter in November 2008 and immediately began tweeting an average of nine times/day. In just 30 days, word spread that this basketball legend had joined the Twitter ranks and nearly 20,000 people became followers. The first to admit that his typing is subpar, O'Neal clearly enjoys sharing his current thoughts and happenings. From commenting on the Phoenix Suns' recent performance to letting us know he has just seen *The Punisher* on DVD, Shaq appears excited to have this new technology in his life. He shoots, he scores! You can follow O'Neal at twitter.com/The_Real_Shaq.

Justine Ezarik (@ijustine)

Hailing from Los Angeles, Justine Ezarik brings her own sense of femininity and Internet savvy to social media. Her videos and tweets are meant to entertain and, well, entertain. Self-described Mac user, blogger, and Internet user, the online persona of iJustine is a what-you-see-is-what-you-get experience. Averaging eight tweets/day, Justine is a breath of fresh air in a world that often takes itself way too seriously. You can follow Justine at twitter.com/ijustine or visit her blog at TastyBlogSnack.com.

Rick Warren (@rickwarren)

Rick Warren is the pastor of Saddleback Church in Lake Forest, California, a mega-church with weekly attendances of more than 15,000. He is also the author of the best-selling book *The Purpose-Driven Life* and mentor to millions. Rick's timeline reinforces his personal brand—he looks relaxed, approachable, and at ease in his background image—but more importantly, his tweets extend the reach of the wisdom in his books. He quotes from the Bible, describes his beliefs, talks to his followers, and uses Twitter to inspire. For followers, those tweets always welcome additions to their Twitter page. You can find them at twitter.com/RickWarren, and his site is at www.purposedriven.com.

Carrie Wilkerson (@barefoot_exec)

Carrie Wilkerson is a consultant and strategist for work-at-home professionals, especially moms and women. She guides rising entrepreneurs through all of the difficulties of building their businesses, from dealing with the nitty-gritty of organization and paperwork to spotting opportunities and turning them into revenue. Her tweets are packed with solid information, great ideas, and plenty of the buzzing energy we all need to build success! You can read her tweets at twitter.com/barefoot_exec and her blog at blogbarefoot.com/

Pete Cashmore (@mashable)

Pete Cashmore is the founder of Mashable, a social media site that is ranked as one of the top 20 blogs on the Internet. Pete himself is a great example of how a successful business can benefit from personal branding, and his timeline shows one particular way of issuing tweets. You won't find many personal tweets in his timeline. Instead, he posts links to articles that have gone up on his site and to others related to social media on the Web. Some of those tweets are headlines, but others are personalized. It's enough to give him followers that run into seven figures. Pete Cashmore is at twitter.com/mashable, and his blog is at www.mashable .com.

Ashton Kutcher (@aplusk)

Celebrities use Twitter in all sorts of different ways. Some use it as a PR stream for their products and events. The smart ones use it to connect directly with their fans. They get to skip past the tabloids and keep their fan base engaged and informed without having to give interviews or pose for pictures. Some have even been known to use their followers to force gossip columnists to apologize for unpleasant allegations. Ashton Kutcher, actor, star, and Demi Moore's husband, uses Twitter for the best reason of all: because he likes it. He tweets about the causes he supports, his interests, and his life. He also engages with his followers and replies to their tweets. And he's a Twitter evangelist, too. His race to a million followers with CNN brought the site a huge amount of publicity and showed the mainstream media just what they're doing wrong. Become one of his millions of followers at twitter.com/aplusk.

Tony Hsieh (@Zappos)

Tony Hsieh is the CEO of Zappos, an online store that was bought by Amazon in 2009 for just under a billion dollars. When someone that successful is sharing his thoughts, entrepreneurs and business owners should be paying close attention. Tony has been on Twitter for a long time, and he knows what it takes to create an engaging timeline. He throws in quotes, writes about his company, and, most of all brings people into his life. You can read the tweets of a billion-dollar executive at twitter.com/zappos.

Conclusion

Twitter is surprising. The idea is ridiculously simple. But the benefits and the enjoyment are both incredible. It's addictive, it's fun, and it's very, very effective.

For Web users it's a great way to keep in touch. For online publishers, nothing makes readers and customers feel closer. And for commercial users it's a hugely powerful branding tool.

In this book, I've introduced some of the ways in which Twitter can help with online marketing.

I began by putting Twitter in context. The site is just one—although by far the most successful—of the microblogging services available on the Web, and it's a part of the social media phenomenon that has revolutionized the Internet and the world of publishing.

Understanding that anyone with a computer and a connection to the Internet now has the power to speak to millions of people around the world is vital to recognizing what Twitter and other social media services can do.

The power to broadcast is in your hands—as well as the power to earn from those broadcasts.

That's especially true of Twitter, many of whose users are high-earning, highly educated professionals. When you send out tweets to your followers, you can be sure that they're being read by a valuable market, one which can also supply all sorts of useful information and connections.

So it's important to start right, with a username that's easy to remember, a bio that explains who you are, and a background image that builds your brand and guides curious new followers to your commercial web sites. I explained how to do that.

And I talked too about building a following on Twitter and how to create a follower list that balances high-quality, key followers with large numbers of readers.

Keeping that list growing though will depend on producing the right tweets: short posts that are entertaining, informative, and fun, which follow tweet etiquette and drive follower behavior.

But persuading followers to take action isn't the only thing you can do with them. Twitter's users are a valuable source of ideas and feedback, and the site itself can function as a very useful communication tool. I explained how to make the most of both of those methods.

I then talked about how major companies are using Twitter to build a brand, and reviewed some of the most important strategies for communicating your brand's message.

I also talked in detail about using tweet sequences to drive followers to take specific actions, introduced some of the most important tools that extend the use of Twitter, and revealed how to build powerful solutions on top of Twitter's basic platform.

Finally, I provided you with one 30-day schedule to get up and running quickly with Twitter.

All of the methods in this book can help anyone to build a long follower list and market their products, their business, or their web sites with Twitter.

The results can certainly be impressive, but perhaps the most surprising thing about Twitter is just how much fun reading and writing 140-character posts can be. There are few marketing tools that both deliver a powerful punch and are such a blast to use.

So if you decide to use only one strategy on Twitter as a result of reading this book, make it this: Have fun.

On Twitter, that's a pretty good indication you're doing it right.

Directory of Twitterers

I've mentioned a lot of Twitterers in this book, and there are plenty of other Twitterers who I think do great work that I didn't mention. Take a look at their timelines and see what you can learn from the way they use Twitter.

Companies

Whole Foods Market (@wholefoods)

SmartyPig (@smartypig)

Direct2Dell (@direct2dell)

Dell Cloud Computing (@dellintheclouds)

Dell Small Business (@DellSmallBiz)

Dell Your Blog (@dellyourblog)

ClearTrip (@cleartrip)

Carnival Cruise Lines (@CarnivalCruise)

Delta Airlines (@deltaairlines)

JetBlue (@JetBlue)

Amazon (@amazondeals)

Forrester (@forrester)

GM (@GMblogs)

M&Ms (@msgreen) (@mmsracing)

Comcast (@comcastcares)

BestBuy (@bestbuy)

Starbucks (@starbucks) (@mystarbucksidea)

The Home Depot (@thehomedepot)

Zappos (@zappos)

SpringLeap (@springleap)

Institutions

The American Red Cross (@redcross)

British Parliament (@UKParliament)

Individuals

Barack Obama (@barackobama)

Bill Gates (@billgates)

Steve Jobs (@stevejobs)

Stephen Fry (@stephenfry)

Betty Draper (@betty_draper)

Don Draper (@don_draper)

Chris Pirillo (@chrispirillo)

Darren Rowse (@problogger)

Wayne Sutton (@waynesutton)

Natalie Jost (@natalie)

Angie Jones (@fitbizwoman)

Robert Scoble (@scobleizer)

Christina Hills (@christinahills)

Dan Perry (@danperry)

Trudy Valencia (@estediava)

Yanick Silver (@yanicksilver)

Jayxtreme (@jayxtreme)

Alaia Williams (@cogentdiversion)

Pastor Carlos Whittaker (@loswhit)

James Buck (@jamesbuck)

Jason Cormier (@jasoncormier)

Dave Baldwin (@highonbeingdave)

Bas (@spartz)

Andrew Sims (@sims)

Jonathan Fields (@jonathanfields)

Brian Williams (@brianwillms)

Cyruseftos (@cyruseftos)

Hephail (@hephail)

Web Sites

Spamfeed (@spamfeed)

MomsWhoSave.com (@momswhosave)

Digital Photography School (@digitalps)

MoonFruit (@moontweet)

Other books by Joel Comm

KaChing: How to Run an Online Business that Pays and Pays

www.KaChingBook.com

Starting your own online business is easier than you think. In this detailed and comprehensive book, Joel lays out the only road map you'll ever need to achieve whatever level of online success you desire. KaChing demystifies Internet marketing cornerstones such as affiliate marketing, content creation and management, AdSense and other contextual advertising methods, and much, much more. Whether you are a total newcomer or already have an online business and want to see it do better, Joel Comm can show you exactly how to use the power of the Internet to achieve your dreams. (ISBN 9780470597675)

The AdSense Code

www.TheAdSenseCode.com

The definitive guide to making money with Google's AdSense program for site publishers, this 230-page book provides the strategies and techniques used to generate passive income with any content-based web site. A *New York Times* bestseller, Comm's easy-to-read and -apply instructions have been applauded by thousands of readers. The hands-on solutions address the concerns and challenges faced by content publishers in their quest to attract targeted traffic, improve content relevance, and increase revenue streams. The world's recognized expert on Google AdSense, Joel Comm provides you with the keys you need to "crack" the AdSense Code and unlock the secrets to making money online. (ISBN 1933596708)

Click Here to Order: Stories of the World's Most Successful Internet Marketing Entrepreneurs

www.ClickHereToOrderBook.com

Most people associate being an Internet millionaire with the dotcom craze of the late 1990s. But a small band of Internet marketing pioneers were quietly making their fortune before anyone Googled the term "making money online." *Click Here to Order* shows how ordinary people became Internet millionaires by applying their skills, talent, and passion to the Internet. Learn the history of the Internet from the 1960s to the present day, and be inspired by the stories of those who paved the way for the rest of us. Features stories of legendary Internet marketing figures, such as Mark Joyner, Armand Morin, John Reese, Yanik Silver, Jeff Walker, and many more! (ISBN 1600371736)

Index